Object Relations and the Developing Ego in Therapy

Object Relations and the Developing Ego in Therapy

Althea J. Horner

Jason Aronson Inc.
Northvale, New Jersey
London

THE MASTER WORK SERIES

First softcover edition 1995

Copyright © 1984 by Althea J. Horner

Library of Congress Cataloging-in-Publication Data

Horner, Althea.
    Object relations and the developing ego.

    Bibliography: p. 371
    Includes index.
    1. Psychotherapy. 2. Ego (Psychology) 3. Self.
4. Psychotherapist and patient. I. Title. [DNLM:
1. Ego 2. Object attachment. WM 460.5.02 H8160]
RC480.5.H66 1984   616.89'14   83-22315
ISBN: 1-56821-708-0

Manufactured in the United States of America. Jason Aronson Inc. offers books and cassettes. For information and catalog write to Jason Aronson Inc., 230 Livingston Street, Northvale, New Jersey 07647.

To my children
Martha, Anne, David, and Kenneth

Contents

Preface

The validity and hence the usefulness of any scientific theory derives first from its correspondence with the data (clinical observations, in the case of psychoanalysis) and, second, from its own internal consistency. The predictive validity of psychoanalytic theory is put to the test when we base a system of treatment upon it.

As clinical observations and explanatory concepts regarding the nature and development of object relations continue to proliferate, the construction of an integrated and comprehensive theoretical system becomes increasingly important. A useful theoretical system should provide the clinician a logical framework within which he can order his own day-to-day observations—to make sense of them and to act upon them in the service of the therapeutic process.

This book presents such a framework. It should enable the clinician to better understand his patient and to formulate therapeutic goals based on a character diagnosis in developmental terms. Moment-to-moment interventions can be made more confidently when they derive from such a formulation.

In this book attachment theory, cognitive theory dealing with mental structures, and object relations theory are brought together, with the major focus on the evolution of a cohesive, reality-related, object-related self. This self develops within the context of the maternal matrix, and the primary mothering person is viewed as the mediator of organization. Analogously, psychotherapy (or psychoanalysis) is conceptualized as a therapeutic matrix within which the therapist is the mediator of organization.

This presentation may also be understood as a theory of the self. The shift from drive theory to object relations or self theory is completed with the position that instinctual drive is only one aspect of experience and must be integrated, along with other aspects of experience, within the self-representation. Concepts of the structuring of drive, like the structuring of affect, relate to their integration within a cohesive, reality-related, object-related self.

This book should also allow for the integration of new data and, in so doing, lay the groundwork for future theory building. The theoretician interested in developing a mathematical model of the human psyche, which would make possible the application of sophisticated computer technology to clinical observation, is likely to find the concepts of self as presented here compatible with the concepts of set theory. The development of rating scales along the three axes of cohesion, reality relatedness, and object relatedness would permit the application of research techniques to the clinical situation. And remaining within the purview of psychoanalysis, old concepts can usefully be reconceptualized within this framework, leading to further development within psychoanalysis rather than to a fragmentation of points of view. Those who view instinctual drive as the prime motivator and those who place affect in that role might well be reunited under the umbrella of the concept of an integrated self.

It is hoped that this book will provide its readers both the impetus and the means to pursue their chosen ends—whether the pragmatic concerns of the clinician who needs to understand his patient and to formulate an appropriate treatment plan, or the more esoteric concerns of the theoretician.

Introduction
to the Second Edition

I am pleased to have the opportunity, with this second edition, to spell out the developmental issues of the transition from the pre-oedipal stage to the oedipal and to clarify the structural and psychodynamic issues relevant to both.

In my view, an object relations theory fits squarely within psychoanalysis proper and is not an alternative to classical analytic theory— a direction in which Kohutian self-psychology appears to be moving. Rather, it is an extension downward that allows us to understand and treat a variety of developmental disorders that originate in the first or second year of life. In a well-evolved, differentiated, and integrated patient, we take the self for granted and focus on the dynamics of conflict and defense in the context of the classical psychoneurosis.

More and more I see the borderline diagnosis inexactly and carelessly applied. The distinction between developmental deficit and regression as a defense, sometimes difficult to make, is often not even attempted. Certain catchwords or phrases, such as "I think I have an identity problem," used by both naive and sophisticated patients, become the basis for the diagnosis and treatment plan, with no attempt to clarify the meaning of the phrase for the specific patient. The identity issues of a well-evolved, albeit passive and compliant, individual, bear no resemblance to those of the patient who truly lacks a cohesive self-representation, even though they use the same words.

The fashions and trends we see in both theory and clinical practice are part of the psychoanalytic zeitgeist. They are exciting, and often we think we detect them in all our patients, much like medical students who believe they suffer from each of the diseases they encounter in their studies.

In my experience, I find the resistances to oedipal issues—sexual striving as well as the aggression inherent in competition—to be far more intransigent than those of the character-disordered patient, inasmuch as they are highly elaborated and rationalized. For example, the oedipal woman's hostility to her mother is "justified" by the mother's actual limitations, whereas the patient refuses to admit and thus come to terms with her own wishes and her need to make the mother bad in the service of the illusory oedipal triumph. Many patients prefer to be seen as "sicker" than to deal with the anxiety and guilt of the Oedipus complex.

In this book I have reemphasized the importance of the structural diagnosis, lest I make one of two possible errors: to approach developmental, structural pathology with interpretations based on inaccurate assumptions about the integrity of the self, interpretations that may traumatize the ego of the patient or intensify character defenses, or to treat well-differentiated patients who use regression as a defense or who regress under certain psychological pressures as being sicker than they actually are, thereby reinforcing the regression as a resistance.

Since the initial publication of this book, I have been gratified by the many communications from students and practitioners at all levels, from this country and abroad, echoing the comments of Samuel L. Bradshaw, Jr., M.D., in the *Bulletin of the Menninger Clinic*: "Perhaps the acid test for any book on psychoanalytic theory is the light it sheds on the complex problems that a therapist faces. This book passes that test with flying colors. I now see my patients in a different light and I have changed my approach with beneficial results" (1982). Anyone dedicated to teaching can have no greater reward than the knowledge that one has made that kind of contribution.

Chapter 1

ORGANIZING PROCESSES AND THE GENESIS OF OBJECT RELATIONS

OBJECT RELATIONS DEFINED

The term *object relations* refers to specific intrapsychic structures, to an aspect of ego organization, and not to external interpersonal relationships. However, these intrapsychic structures, the mental representations of self and other (the object), do become manifest in the interpersonal situation. That is, "the inner world of object relations determines in a fundamental way the individual's relations with people in the external world. This world . . . is basically the residue of the individual's relations with people upon whom he was dependent for the satisfaction of primitive needs in infancy and during the early stages of maturation" (Phillipson 1955, p. 7). The concept is not new to psychoanalytic thinking, and the precursors of modern object relations theory are present in Freud's work. As early as 1923 he spoke of the ego as the repository of abandoned objects. Nevertheless, early psychoanalytic focus on the object was in terms of object choice in libidinally invested relationships rather than as a structure of the personality. What is new is the change of focus and emphasis in which object relations thinking has become central rather than peripheral to the understanding and psychoanalytic treatment of the person.

Also changing is the view of the role of instinct in the development of the individual. The relationship between instinct theory
and object relations theory varies from writer to writer. The role of
instinctual aggression is central to Kernberg's thinking (1976). He
stresses the importance of the aggressive drive per se and its own
vicissitudes in the genesis of pathological narcissism.

At the other end of the spectrum is the view, put forth in the
present work, that instinctual drive is only one aspect of experience, which must be integrated within the self along with other
aspects of experience. Ego controls are an outcome of this integration. Failure to achieve control of the instinctual drives suggests a
failure of the organizing processes which lead to a structuring of the
ego and of the self in particular. The structuring of drive, or the
structuring of affect, relates to their integration within a cohesive,
object-related self-representation.

For us to understand the concept of object relations and its complex ramifications, it is helpful to consider how these psychic
structures come into being, to think in terms of the early mental
processes by means of which the newborn infant organizes its world
into meaningful patterns. One basic pattern is that of the self—the
self-representation—while another is that of the object—the object-
representation. The object refers to the primary mothering person
or persons in the environment of the infant and the very young
child. The structural and dynamic relationships between the self-
representations and the object-representations constitute what we
refer to as *object relations*.

These patterns evolve over the first three to four years of life and
are the basis for enduring mental configurations. In healthy
development these intrapsychic structures continue throughout life
to be modified by experience. But in pathological development they
are organized early on in a rigid and distorting manner that results
in fixation at a pathological, infantile level of development in certain aspects of feeling, thinking, and behaving. The nature of this
evolution, its stages and processes (Horner 1975) constitute a
developmental framework that enables us to understand both normal and pathological development, their consequences for the character of the adult, and their implications for the psychoanalytic

treatment of the adult patient. That is, we can expect to find certain kinds of disturbances to be associated with maternal failure and/or the inability of the child to respond to normal mothering at any of these developmental stages or during the transitional processes that lead from one stage to the next.

Blanck and Blanck (1974) observe that concepts of internalization and of object relations are basic to psychoanalytic developmental psychology and that these concepts are central to considerations of both theory and technique. The structuralization of the personality entails internalization of object-representations—that is, the process of making that which was once external a part of the self. "Psychoanalytic psychology is developmental psychology in that it accounts for the structuralization of the personality from birth onward" (p. 4).

Blanck and Blanck equate the pathology of borderline and psychotic structures with pathology of object relations, inasmuch as the development of the human being proceeds within the mother-child dyad. It is their view (p. 338)—and that of the present work—that therapy must address itself to this feature of development. That is, what the therapist says and does in the treatment situation should be predicated upon the developmental formulation and character diagnosis.

The early processes of organization lead to the structuring of the ego in general and of object relations in particular. Ego psychologists conceive of object relations as one of the functions of the ego. According to Beres (1956) these functions are:

1. relation to reality
2. regulation and control of instinctual drives
3. object relations
4. thought processes
5. defense functions
6. autonomous functions
7. synthetic function

Hartmann (1964) first described the developing levels of object relations as part of his ego psychology. The present work shares this developmental perspective but relates all the other aspects of ego development to object relations development, which is viewed as central. This shift from an ego psychology to an object relations theory reflects the emphasis on the central role of object relations development in the overall structuring of the ego.

Of the functioning of the ego as defined by Beres, the synthetic function appears to be fundamental, representing as it does the innate tendency and capability of the organism itself to assimilate, organize, and integrate its experiences from the very beginning. Although this tendency is innate in the organism, even in an organically competent infant these capabilities can be overwhelmed by excessively chaotic or disruptive environmental conditions.

So far as the remaining functions are concerned, the quality of object relations as they themselves develop, provides the matrix within which the other functions unfold. These include functions that are essentially autonomous insofar as they are the manifestation of the biological maturation of the child—walking, talking, thinking, sensing, etc. The autonomy of these functions may be taken for granted until we see deviations in their development in consequence of disturbed object relations. And when they develop completely outside the orbit of object relatedness, in an *apparently* conflict-free manner, there are serious repercussions with respect to the development of healthy self-esteem (see chapter 10). In this instance, exercise of the autonomous functions is associated with object loss, and they may be assimilated into a pathological grandiose self-structure.

Hilde Bruch's work (1973) on hunger awareness illustrates how "seemingly innate functions, specifically hunger, require early learning experiences in order to become organized into distinct and useful behavior patterns" (p. 54). She recognizes as crucial in many patients with serious eating disorders "the basic delusion of not having an identity of their own, of not even owning their body and its sensations" (p. 50). In short, Bruch relates eating disorders to deviant object relations development. For instance, in anorexia nervosa the relationship to food is a manifestation of the relationship with the object. The need to ward off the engulfing, impinging mother (a need manifested in the rejection of food and the

mobilization of the grandiose self as defense against object loss)
alternates with "object hunger" (manifested in bulimia and readiness for merger).

In a study of language and communication disorders in children,
Wyatt (1969) concludes that a continuous, undisrupted, and affectionate relationship between a mother and her young child provides
the optimum condition for learning a language successfully. This
optimum manner of relating is "manifested in frequent and appropriate communication, both verbal and non-verbal" (p. 19).

Wyatt also points out that both the meaning and the learning of
language are embedded in the total relationship with the mothering
person. Languages, for the young child, cannot be reduced to
abstract symbolic systems to be interchanged at will.

How the thought process in a highly intelligent adult can be compromised by object relations pathology is seen in the following
excerpt from an analytic session. This young woman struggles with
issues of differentiation of self from object.

> I'm conscious of weaving what the other person says into a
> unit, to get it to blend with the position I want to take. I get
> the idea that my thought *processes* should be the same as the
> other's. It never is. I'm not conscious of the paths. I'm trying
> to match his *path*. . . . Another ramification of trying to match
> the path of thinking—I not only abandon what I thought, but
> am fearful that he'll think I'm stupid. I try to come to the
> same conclusion *for the same reason.*

With respect to the reality function of the ego, the development
of the sense of reality also takes place within and through the relationship with the mother. "The most important transitory step in
the adaptation to reality," writes Mahler (1952), is the one "in
which the mother is gradually left outside the omnipotent orbit of
the self." She is referring here to individuation and separation out
of the symbiotic merger with the mother.

In his elaboration of the concept of the false self, Winnicott
(1965) points out that the mother serves as a bridge between the
child's experiences of self that originate within him and those that

originate in the external world of reality. As such, her interventions make possible the consolidation of a reality-related self-representation, that is, an identity based on a real self. When she fails in this function, the real self is cut off from reality and may be organized delusionally.

And so, if we view the self as developing within the context of the mother-child matrix—and this includes all facets of that self, including the way it controls its impulses, uses its potential intellect, or structures reality—then we can expect to find a correspondence between disturbances of that psychological self and the nature of the relationship with the primary mothering object. This will be manifest in the developmental history of the individual, in the nature of his inner psychological world, in the quality of present-day relationships and functioning, and, in particular, in the quality of his relationship with the therapist.

I repeat: while ego psychologists conceive of object relations as one of the functions of the ego, the object relations theorist stresses that all aspects of ego functioning become organized *within* the self-representation in healthy development and cannot really be separated from it. The failure of such organization is then viewed as a manifestation of pathology of the self (Kohut 1971, 1977).

Consideration of the basic processes of organization will clarify how these structures—the inner mental configurations of self and object and their interrelationships—come into being. What is the nature of the process? What is to be organized? What facilitates it? What interferes with it? What is the outcome of its failure?

The object relations paradigm, although powerful in its explanatory and clinical usefulness, can be an oversimplification. We need to look more closely—microscopically, as it were—at what goes into the buildup of the mental representations of self and object during each of the major developmental stages. Only then can we detect certain defects in the organization and integration of the self in the earliest stages of its evolution, defects that will reveal themselves later on when the thrust of development will be impeded by their existence. This is particularly true of the borderline patient. Because of a defective early organization the symbiotic partner continues to be needed, as a kind of prosthetic device, if the self is to be kept in any semblance of organization. The awareness of separateness kept in any semblance of organization. The awareness of separateness that is inevitable in the separation-individuation process evokes severe separation anxiety with restitutive efforts aimed at eliminating the psychic danger, the danger of dissolution of self.

Let us look first at the "how" of organization, as described by Piaget, and then at just what it is that is there to be organized.

EARLY ORGANIZATION AND THE EVOLUTION OF SELF AND OBJECT

The neonate begins life in a state of mental and psychological nonorganization and non-integration. With the mental equipment with which it is born, it must organize its entire universe of experience. There is a readiness, from the start, to perceive and respond to patterns in the environment (Fantz 1966). This process of organization is fundamental to the buildup of the character structure, to the structure of the ego, to the establishment of the self. Organizing tendencies and capabilities are intrinsic to the organism. These mental activities take place as a consequence of the synthesizing function of the central nervous system, which is the physiologic substrate of what ego psychologists call the synthetic function of the ego. This inborn and autonomous biological function can be interfered with by an inherent inadequacy of the organism, by failure of the environment, or by a combination of the two. This failure may be relative, occurring only in certain areas of functioning. For instance, schizoid defenses may enable the individual to organize the nonpersonal world of reality quite effectively, while failure of the schizoid detachment in an intense one-to-one situation may reveal the pathology in the organization of self- and object-representations.

A major approach to the understanding of the basic processes of organization is that of Jean Piaget (1936). His findings concerning cognitive development help demystify some of the metapsychological concepts of object relations theory, particularly the concepts of self- and object-representations.

Piaget describes the complementary processes of assimilation and accommodation, both of which contribute to overall organization and which entail the parallel processes of differentiation and integration. All of these go into the formation of schemas, or representations, of self and object.

Assimilation is the process through which new experiences are taken into and modified to fit with a preexisting mental organization. In our everyday life we interpret reality on the basis of what we already know and understand. This is the rationale of the projective test. The reported interpretation of the reality of the inkblot reveals the nature of the individual's existing mental organization.

Accommodation is the process basic to learning—the changing or adjusting of preexisting structures to accommodate reality. In analysis, transference is a manifestation of the process of assimilation, while the working-through process is a manifestation of accommodation.

The processes of assimilation and accommodation go hand in hand during the earliest stages of development, during which the infant organizes its experiences first into patterns and then into patterns of patterns. Eventually meaning is assigned to these patterns, which Piaget designates "schemas."

Flavell, in his exposition (1963) of Piaget's work, notes that a single schema is consolidated and stabilized by repetition. Through the process of generalization the schema comes to be the representation of a class of events or experiences. At the start, a schema tends to be global, but as the capacity to discriminate reality becomes sharper a global schema may be divided into several new ones. Thus the schema of person may be divided into big person and little person, or into male and female.

As individual schemas develop, they begin to form more complete and interlocking relationships with other schemas. "Two schemas may undergo separate development up to a point . . . and then unite to form a single, supra-ordinate schema" (p. 57). An example of this would be the gradual integration of good and bad object-representations into a single, ambivalently experienced representation.

A schema, then, is an enduring organization or structure within the mind and is the outcome of the processes of organization—assimilation, accommodation, generalization, differentiation, and integration. The various self- and object-representations (e.g., the self-object, the good self, the bad self, the good object, the bad object) can be understood as particular schemas that come about and undergo change in accordance with Flavell's narrative.

In the metapsychology of psychoanalysis this schema is referred to as the self-representation. Schafer (1976), in his concern for a more precise use of the terms *self* and *identity*, writes: "Self and identity serve as the superordinate terms for the self-representations that the child sorts out (separates, individuates) from its initially undifferentiated subjective experience of the mother-infant matrix" (p. 180).

In 1971 Guntrip expressed the view that problems of identity constitute the most important single issue of our time. He feels identity has always been an issue but that only now are we becoming explicitly conscious of it. He defines the issue as "the problem of having an unquestioned possession or else a lack of a sense of personal reality and selfhood" (p. 119).

The importance of understanding these very early mental events in their relevance to psychoanalysis and psychoanalytic psychotherapy is emphasized by Anne-Marie Sandler (1975), who writes of the important and infinitely varied feeling states that develop even in the first weeks of life. She notes that these feeling states can persist throughout the mental life of the individual: "In other words, a sensory-motor schema is formed which persists but is reorganized and absorbed in later phases" (p. 368). These very early experiences, she observes, become manifest in the course of analysis, "through action, through somatic channels or through some emotional experience which the patient cannot adequately put into words" (p. 368).

WHAT IS ORGANIZED

While Piaget writes of the *how* of early organization, Burnham (1969a) is concerned with *what* is organized. He refers specifically to the "subsystems" of drives, cravings, affects, and motor skills. What Kohut (1971, 1977) refers to as the "cohesive self" implies the successful integration of each of these separate facets of the organism's experience. Deficits in organization (patterning), integration, and differentiation have their parallel clinical manifestations.

If in the earliest months of life a deficit in organization leaves areas of experience unpatterned, the patient will under certain kinds of stress dis-organize. That is, the mobilization of any sensations, feelings, or impulses (as well as their derivative ideation) that lie outside whatever centers of organization might exist will have a disorganizing impact upon the individual. Disorganization is a manifestation of the failure of the basic schema of the self to hold together, resulting in a psychotic reaction. The autonomous functions may be seriously compromised under these circumstances.

If there is a deficit in the integration of organized sectors of the self- and object-representations, under certain circumstances the patient will dis-integrate. The precipitating factor is likely to be the simultaneous evocation of conflicting, split-off sectors of the self. Disintegration is a manifestation of failure in the knitting together of separate schemas, and is characteristic of the character disorders. In such cases the autonomous functions will remain intact.

If there is a deficit of differentiation between self- and object-representations, the patient will under certain circumstances de-differentiate. The precipitating event in this case is likely to be the experience of object loss and severe separation anxiety. The rigidity of defenses against the emergence of the unorganized or unintegrated, whose continued submersion may protect the individual from the experience of object loss, reflects the degree of structural pathology and its inherent danger to the integrity of the self.

At the very start of life the infant's world consists of a variety of sensorimotor, physiological, and somatic experiences. Feelings are global—either distress or non-distress. As they become more refined and specific to the stimulus in the form of pleasure, anger, or anxiety, these feelings become part of the world of experience to be organized and integrated. In this manner the predominant affect, whether the rage of frustration, the anxiety of uncertainty or overwhelming distress, or the positive feelings that go with basic trust, becomes an integral aspect of the self (Erikson 1950, p. 219). This includes rage when the environment fails in its need-fulfillment and tension-reducing functions. This rage may be organized, as it is within the bad self- and object-representations of the narcissistic personality (chapter 12), or unintegrated and disorganizing, as in some borderline personalities (chapter 12). That is, when there is a failure of integration of affect in this early phase of development, evocation of the same affect later on will have a disintegrating effect upon the self's organization. With integration, there is some degree of control.

Also to be organized and integrated are impulses, the felt precursors of motor activity. Of particular importance are self-initiated, assertive, and eventually goal-directed actions and their associated aggressive impulses. Looked at in this way, aggressive impulses are neither hostile nor destructive in themselves, but become so only when fused with negative affect. The infant reaching for its rattle is demonstrating nonhostile aggressive behavior.

Often in the clinical situation healthy aggression becomes available for goal-directed behavior only after it has been teased apart from infantile rage, which it became entangled with in the early stages of psychological development. I have in mind a thirty-five-year-old graduate student whose chronic complaint was his inability to make decisions and to carry through on a course of action. There was a marked passivity in his general attitude and behavior. He was cut off from both sexual and hostile impulses, which sometimes erupted as fragmented images of vaginas or knives. Oedipal factors were quite evident, but even more fundamental was the failure of both parents to mirror adequately, support, or even allow any self-initiated course of action. His frustration and anger were defended against with emotional detachment and passivity. As a consequence there was no healthy goal-directed aggression available to him when he needed it.

In addition to experiences generated within and by the organism itself, the presence and input of the mothering environment becomes organized and integrated into the mental pattern or schema that is referred to as the undifferentiated self-object representation characteristic of the stage of normal developmental symbiosis. In later stages of object relations development, this undifferentiated

mental representation will become differentiated into separate self-
and object-representations. Most important—and this is what I
mean by the need to look more closely at what goes into the buildup
of the mental representations of self and object—the adequacy of
integration of the differentiated self will reflect the adequacy of
integration of the earlier self-object representation. That is, what
was not integrated in the earlier stage will have to be kept split off
from awareness because of its potentially disorganizing impact.
The greater the extent of this kind of failure in development, the
more brittle the organization of the self and the greater the potential
for fragmentation. The defenses must be understood and respected
in the treatment process, with structuring and analysis of the
defenses going hand in hand.

Thus, the fragments of the child's own somatic, sensory, motor,
and affective and impulse experiences come into interaction with
that which is experienced vis-à-vis the mothering person. The
consistent and predictable presence of this individual throughout
the early months of life serves to tie the infant's experiences
together in a particular way. It is through her that the body, impulse, feeling, action, and eventually thought become integrated
not only with each other but also with the external reality of which
she is a representative. That is, she is a bridge between the child's
inner world and the outer world of reality.

Winnicott (1965) views the false-self identity as the consequence
of the failure of the mother to bridge these two worlds adequately.
In this instance a serious and consistent failure of empathy on her
part may lead to a situation in which her mothering efforts are
neither in harmony with the child's bodily needs and experiences
nor, later on, appropriately responsive to its feelings and goal-
directed actions.

When this happens, efforts at mothering become impingements
toward which the child can only react. There may be a defensive
withdrawal that will interfere with the attachment process itself
and with the establishment of object relatedness at the most fundamental level. Failure of attachment is a factor in autistic disorders
and in the evolution of the psychopathic personality (chapter 2). Or
there may be excessive rage that repeatedly disrupts the child's

budding ego organization and thereby interferes with the establishment of cohesion of the self, resulting in a more psychotic picture.
Or, in the instance of the false-self identity described by Winnicott,
the pseudoidentity is organized around reactions to the impinging
mother while the core self remains shut away from both reality and
human relatedness. This core self may become the nucleus for delusional thinking, as in the case of the woman who was hospitalized
with the delusion that she was pregnant with the Messiah. Only
several years later did the meaning of the delusion become apparent. At that time she began to talk about her "submarine self" and
commented on it: "She is really very strong. I have been feeding
her and making her strong." Then she added: "I am not just a
receiver. I am an acter too." The Messiah she was pregnant with
was her own delusional, grandiose self, which she considered the
most real part of her even though it had never actually become
related with the real, external world or anyone in it. At this point in
her treatment it became evident that the first major goal in therapy
would be to enhance the object relatedness of that core self and,
eventually, to bridge the gap between it and external reality, as
does the good-enough mother of early infancy.

Winnicott (1965) says of children with a false-self organization
that "a successful false self enables many children to seem to give
good promise, but eventually a breakdown reveals the fact of the
true self's absence from the scene" (p. 59). That is, in the context of
competent synthesizing capacities a false-self organization becomes
consolidated around the child's reaction to the nonempathic failures or
impingements rather than around what is intrinsic to the self; mean-
while the secret, real self attains its own delusional organization.

The mothering person does not simply mediate the process of
organization and reality relatedness; her image is actually part of
what is organized. The internalization of her image in all its aspects
eventually yields the object-representation, which emerges with
increasing integration and differentiation. When, for some reason,
this internalization does not occur, the child fails to develop the
capacity for object relatedness. This situation is described by
Bowlby (1946) in terms of the "affectionless character" which is the
outcome of the failure of the attachment process (chapter 3).

The disruption of developing object relatedness is described by Blanck and Blanck (1974) in their discussion of "premature ego development" (p. 56). With a superior child who is cut off from maternal support too early, the autonomous functions of the ego develop outside the sphere of object relatedness, resulting in an individual who seems to function well, who appears to have a cohesive self, but who complains of chronic depression and emptiness. This kind of character detachment, which has come about either in response to an emotional abandonment or as a defense against engulfment by the mother of symbiosis, also has serious repercussions with respect to the development of healthy self-esteem (chapter 10). The child eventually turns to its own ego in lieu of the lost object. This sidetracking of object relations development interferes with the achievement of object constancy (chapter 7).

In summary, then, the mother functions as the mediator of organization and of reality relatedness, and her internalized image becomes the cornerstone for the capacity for human object relatedness. This overall configuration of events sets the stage for the evolution of a cohesive, reality-related, object-related self.

Failure of cohesion, failure of reality relatedness, or failure of object relatedness each has its specific consequences in terms of character pathology, symptomatology, and implications for treatment. Cohesion, reality relatedness, and object relatedness develop side by side and influence one another in a reciprocal fashion, although we do not necessarily find one-to-one correlations between them. Furthermore, there may be an unevenness in any of the three domains, and it is important to construct as accurately as possible a structural diagnosis for any given patient. That is, the idiosyncratic patterns of a given individual's psychic organization constitute the structural basis for psychodynamic patterns. Just as a knowledge of anatomy aids us in our understanding of physiology, so a knowledge of an individual's intrapsychic structure enables us to understand his psychodynamics. For example, if we determine that a patient's obsessive-compulsive behavior acts as an external prosthesis to hold together a potentially fragmented self, we will not make the interpretation that this behavior serves as an ego defense against unacceptable id impulses. Rather, we will understand that this behavior serves as a defense against dissolution of the self, and we will therefore not interfere with it for the moment. Many such patients, wrongly diagnosed as neurotic obsessives, have done poorly with analytic treatment aimed at uncovering repressed feelings, thoughts, or impulses, as well as with some of the newer therapies which tend to override the defenses.

Another clinical situation that would require this kind of determination is that of the psychosomatic symptom. If we understand the symptom as a classical neurotic defense against the emergence of anger, for instance, or as an expression of repressed dependency needs in a differentiated, structured personality, our method and interpretations will be consistent with this kind of formulation. If, on the other hand, we view the symptom as a manifestation of the failure of the early mother to act as a bridge between external reality and the infant's bodily experiences, and of a consequent defect in the organization of the self, then our task is much more difficult. In this case the bodily response to anger has been cut off from both affect and cognition—a circumstance common to psychosomatic complaints—not because of later repression under the impact of id-superego conflict, but because of early failure of organization with respect to both reality relatedness and object relatedness. That is, the mother fails to adequately mediate organization and to function as a bridge between internal experience and outer reality. The "alexithymia" of the psychosomatic patient, the inability to put feelings into words, reflects the lack of integration of the subsystems of the personality. Our treatment plan will be consistent with our structural diagnosis and will take into consideration the quality and degree of cohesiveness, reality relatedness, and object relatedness. When we have determined that a failure or defect has occurred in the organization of the self in any of these major dimensions, we can view the most important function of the analyst or therapist as parallel to that of the primary mothering person or persons of early infancy: that is, as the mediator of organization.

CAUSES OF FAILURE OF ORGANIZATION

Failure or distortion of the overall process of organization may be the outcome of (a) biological inadequacy of the organism, (b) serious failure of the environment, or (c) a combination of the two.

One example of organizational failure due to biological inadequacy of the organism is a basic defect in the synthesizing capacity of the infant due to cerebral dysfunction. Ornitz and Ritvo (1977) describe the role of perceptual inconstancy in childhood psychosis, stating that this factor makes it impossible for the child to utilize external and internal stimuli to properly organize further development. Children suffering from a presenting problem of a learning disorder as a consequence of cerebral dysfunction are often also found to have a deviant ego organization as the result of the impaired synthesizing capacity of the central nervous system. An adequate differential diagnosis and treatment plan will take into account the contribution of such organic factors in psychological impairment. This is particularly important with respect to the attitude toward the mother and the approach to working with her.

Developmental failure may also occur when the synthesizing, organizing capabilities of a constitutionally competent infant are overwhelmed by the chaotic environment of a psychotic or alcoholic mother or by the excessive tensions resulting from the inadequate caretaking of a narcissistic, nonempathic, or depressed mother. The organizing capabilities of the infant may also be overtaxed by conflicting environmental input that it cannot assimilate, such as changing multiple caretakers, or the extreme ambivalence of the primary mothering person.

But still other factors may interfere. For example, if during the vulnerable early stages, severe and cumulative traumatization due to illness or to frequent changes of environment occurs with a constitutionally sturdy infant, organization may be impaired if the mothering person loses her capacity to function as a buffering and organizing agent for the infant.

A different problem is that of the constitutionally oversensitive or vulnerable infant when normal mothering may not be able to counteract the innate incapacity of the infant to utilize the mother in these important ways. The colicky infant or the infant with a defective "stimulus barrier" (Escalona 1968) are examples of this situation.

Whatever the etiology, ultimately the issue is one of impairment of the processes of organization, and pathology of structure is the outcome. That is, a variety of factors can result in an impairment of the synthesizing function with a consequent pathology of structure. Failure of the organization process can occur at any point along the developmental continuum. The earlier the failure, the more pervasive and malignant the pathology. In this instance, input from later stages of development must be assimilated into a more primitive and distorted self-representation, necessitating a greater distortion of external reality or defense against it. The achievement of later developmental tasks is inevitably compromised insofar as they are complicated by unresolved primitive fears and anger.

CLINICAL EXAMPLE

The following case discussion illustrates an example of partial failure of organization due to fragmented mothering. The result was the failure of object-relatedness of the cohesive self and failure of cohesion with the object-related self. Treatment goals were based upon the need to repair the early distortion of object relations development so that the patient might proceed along the normal path of this development.

Miss T., a highly intelligent businesswoman in her early thirties, experienced and expressed her rage in those intimate relationships in which the other person failed to validate her either by mirroring or by playing a role complementary to her own. She also reacted with feelings of abandonment and depression vis-à-vis the inconsistencies of their behavior toward her. When she compliantly mirrored or complemented the other in order to establish an emotional connection, she lost her sense of self. Under sufficient stress she would withdraw into a kind of solipsistic state that was short of autistic in that she was still in good contact with reality. She referred to this as depression and would often sleep excessively during these periods. Her highest functioning was in the use of her intellect. This involved a fair degree of emotional detachment, and inevitably an object relations hunger would draw her again into the conflict-ridden areas of her self.

For the first two years of her life, Miss T.'s father had separated from her mother and was out of the home. During this time she was tended by her narcissistic and depressed mother and a number of adult relatives, all of whom lived together. Because there was no single, primary attachment object, the multiple mothering interfered with the organization of a unified self-object representation. The image of a five-headed monster appeared regularly in her dreams and fantasies.

Deep depression, which was manifest in some of her early sessions, was at first interpreted as her attempt to be with her depressed mother through identification. The mother died when Miss T. was in her teens. However, it became evident that the depression was secondary to feelings of confusion and anxiety vis-à-vis conflicting demands of her interpersonal environment, demands with which she would try to comply in order to maintain the feeling of connection with the other. This would leave her feeling either unreal or fragmented, and she would withdraw in an attempt at restitution of the lost sense of a cohesive self, although this was a self that was not object related. The depression was the consequence of the defensive withdrawal and related object loss (Horner 1974).

This sequence was related genetically to her reaction as an infant to the confusing, organization-impeding impact of the multiple caretaker situation. At that time her reactive withdrawal from excess stimulation that she could neither organize nor integrate led to the experience of object loss and subsequent anaclitic depression. However, the withdrawal enabled the autonomous functions to unfold without conflict. This is the kind of small child whose development looks better than it is.

Her father returned to the home and the parents reunited when Miss T. was two years old; she turned eagerly to her father at this time. The attempt to form an attachment that might have enabled her to build a compensatory, cohesive, object-related self-structure (Kohut 1977) failed because of his many failures of empathy and because of excessive sexual stimulation and associated frustrations of their tickling games. Their close emotional relationship was abruptly terminated with the onset of puberty, at which time it became highly intellectualized instead. As a result, she could not integrate her adolescent sexuality, and it was subsequently repressed. The failure of this integration exacerbated the anxiety due to the earlier developmental problems.

Understanding the failure of the earliest organization of the self within the matrix of a satisfactory symbiotic relationship with the necessity for building a compensatory structure through the medium of the therapeutic relationship became evident and was a focus of her work. Her negative reactions to perceived changes in the appearance or demeanor of the therapist were felt as abandonments, as though the therapist had become someone else. These reactions were related to the traumatic multiple caretaker situation, and gradually the therapist's continuing identity (and through it, her own) could be perceived and felt. During this integrative phase of treatment, she observed that she had never before been able to share all aspects of her self with any one person. She commented, "You know more of me than any other person. As long as I have you, I don't feel fragmented in other relationships." Issues that appeared to be oedipal at one level were even more significantly related to her attempts at integration through her relationship with her father.

With the repair in therapy of the organization of the self-structure, Miss T. was able to move on toward greater differentiation and autonomy. A year later, although no longer complaining of experiences of fragmentation, she still struggled with issues of object-relatedness. "You're the only person with whom I have any continuity, with whom I can be myself." Gradually internalization of the therapist facilitated the separation-individuation process and the achievement of a modicum of object constancy.

Because she had been constitutionally robust as an infant and because the early caretaking environment had been satisfactory in other dimensions, Miss T. did not become psychotic. However, the deficit of organization set the stage for depression because of the failures of object-relatedness and for the emergence of borderline symptomatology because of the failures of cohesion under certain circumstances. A formulation based solely on the vicissitudes of the separation-individuation process was insufficient for the understanding and treatment of her problems. The specific and idiosyncratic nature of the symbiotic stage and its consequences for structure were a major factor in the quality of subsequent development.

Kohut (1977) points out the difference between the primary structures of the self, which develop out of the early process of organization within the symbiotic orbit, and later compensatory structures, which make up for defects in the primary structures. These are based upon later identifications, often with the father, and on the development of the autonomous functions of the ego and of ambitions and ideals. Miss T.'s superior cognitive development and good intellect formed the nucleus of the secondary structures that enabled her to function at a fairly high level. Unfortunately this necessitated emotional detachment, which led to feelings of object loss. The detachment interfered with the kinds of internalization of maternal functions that lead to the achievement of object constancy. The organizational pathology of the primary structures, that is, of self- and object-representations, continued to be manifest in her interpersonal relationships, in the transference, and in her symptoms.

Chapter 2

THE DEVELOPMENTAL PARADIGM

Psychological health and psychopathology can both be understood in terms of the vicissitudes of object relations development and its associated organizing and integrating impact. This developmental sequence begins with the stage of normal autism at birth and proceeds through the process of attachment to the stage of normal symbiosis, which is symbolized by the undifferentiated self-object representation. From this point the child faces the developmental tasks of the separation-individuation process. This process is subdivided into the subphases of hatching, the practicing period, and the rapprochement subphase (Mahler 1968), and it culminates in the achievement of identity and object constancy. At this point the child, and thus the adult he will become, has a firm sense of self and differentiated other, is able to relate to others as whole persons rather than just as need satisfiers, and can tolerate ambivalence without having to maintain a split between good and bad object-representations with its parallel split between good and bad self-representations. He also has the ability to sustain his or her own narcissistic equilibrium or good self-feeling from resources within the self, which are the outcome of the achievement of libidinal object constancy that comes about through the transmuting internalization (Tolpin 1971) of maternal functions into the self (Giovacchini 1979).

In brief, the stages and processes are (Horner 1975):

Stage I	*Normal autism*
Process A	*Attachment*
Stage II	*Normal symbiosis*
Process B	*Separation-individuation*
Stage III	*Identity, object constancy, and healthy self-esteem*

The work of Margaret Mahler (1968, Mahler, Pine, and Bergman 1975) on the separation-individuation process is particularly important to this formulation. I will review briefly the overall developmental paradigm and indicate a few of the relevant clinical issues of each stage. It should be readily apparent that the earlier the interference with the processes involved in object relations development, the more serious the psychopathology. The character structure of our adult patient as it is manifest in symptomatology, disturbances of interpersonal relationships, or in the transference, will be directly related to the relative successes or failures of this early development. Our developmental diagnosis (chapter 12) and treatment plans and strategies will be based upon our understanding of the character structure in this manner.

NORMAL AUTISM

At birth the child is in a state of what Mahler refers to as normal autism. Kohut (1971, 1977), who thinks in terms of the evolution of a cohesive self-structure, calls this same period the stage of the fragmented self. That is, while Mahler's term reflects her own object relations orientation, Kohut's term conveys his concern with the structure of the self. Freud referred to this same period as that of autoeroticism, which, of course, is consistent with a drive-theory point of view. Both object relatedness and the structure of the self are central to my discussion and, in general, I view them as interlocking concepts.

Clinical Issues

The most clearly stage-related pathology is that of early infantile autism, in which the child remains fixed at this earliest stage of life and makes no move toward attachment. Mahler (1952) sees constitutional factors operating in childhood autism and comments on the fact that there is no anticipatory posture at nursing, no reaching out gestures, and no specific smiling response. What is lacking is attachment-seeking behavior, and thus the mother-child matrix that fosters ego development is nonexistent. Rutter (1975) examines the basic cognitive defect in these children, which interferes with the basic organizational processes themselves. In situations in which the environment is grossly pathological, disrupting the organizing tendencies of the child, there may be a retreat into secondary autism (Mahler p. 259). Autistic withdrawal in response to environmental stress in the adult suggests that the point of environmental failure in early development may date back to these earliest months of life. Defensive or compensatory structures (Kohut 1977) or a false-self organization (Winnicott 1965) may allow for a higher level of functioning, but their failure would throw the individual back upon the core pathology.

FROM AUTISM TO SYMBIOSIS: ATTACHMENT

Over the earliest months of life we see the innate attachment-seeking behavior of the infant interacting with maternal behavior and response in such a way as, optimally, to bring about the stage of normal symbiosis. This is generally consolidated at around the age of five or six months. The earliest mental representations of self and object, the undifferentiated self-object representation or schema, is characteristic of this stage. There is neither physical nor psychic differentiation.

Important during this time is the mutual selection of cues by mother and infant. Mahler (1968) writes:

We observed that infants present a large variety of cues—to indicate needs, tension, and pleasure. In a complex manner, the mother responds selectively to only *certain* of these cues. [p. 18]

Mahler points out (p. 19) that this mutual cuing creates the complex pattern that becomes the leitmotif for what Lichtenstein (1961) refers to as *"the infant's becoming the child of his particular mother."*

Bowlby (1969) emphasizes the degree to which an infant himself plays a part in determining his own environment. Certain kinds of babies who tend to be overreactive or unpredictable make it difficult for the mother to provide good-enough mothering. But Bowlby concludes that the mother has a much larger role than the infant by the end of the first year in the determination of the quantity as well as the quality of the transactions that occur between them. When mothering is inadequate or unpredictable, the child may persist in his efforts to engage the mother with alternating reaching out, angry disappointment, and defensive detachment.

CLINICAL ISSUES: THE FAILURE OF ATTACHMENT

At the most primitive level, failure of attachment may carry with it severe deficits in the early organization of the self. The failure to develop attachment and to achieve a satisfactory symbiosis because of environmental factors, such as institutionalization, may lead to the development of characteristic disturbances such as the inability to keep rules, lack of capacity to experience guilt, and indiscriminate friendliness with an inordinate craving for affection with no ability to make lasting relationships (Rutter 1974). The "affectionless psychopath" is also characterized by the failure to develop the affectional bond that goes with attachment.

There may be a disruption of attachment due to separation and loss. Subsequent development depends upon the availability of a substitute attachment object. Such interruption may lead to a lifelong schizoid detachment. Rutter (1974) states that "many (but not all) young children show an immediate reaction of acute distress and crying (. . . the period of 'protest'), followed by misery and apathy (the phase of 'despair'). . . ." There may be "a stage when the child becomes apparently contented and seems to lose interest in his parents ('detachment') . . ." (p. 29). He concludes that this syndrome is probably due to the disruption or distortion of the bonding process itself.

We may also find a situation in which there are multiple, uninte-grated attachments that are paralleled by a failure of the integra-tion of the self-representation. This was the situation of Miss T., which was described in the first chapter. In this case, detachment was used as a defense against the frightening impact of object relatedness.

Another form of pathological attachment is attachment through the false-self organization. In this situation the real, core self has remained in a nonattached, non-object-related state. Since the self also lacks reality relatedness, the potential for psychotic decompen-sation is high. Because the false-self organization is a reactive self, its existence remains contingent upon the object. Differentiation cannot be achieved nor can there be any degree of autonomy. Thus there is an isolated, possibly psychotic true self alongside a symbiotically arranged false-self identity.

Defensive detachment, which is central to the character struc-ture, may occur at a number of places along the developmental continuum. The consequences of the disruption of object relations development will depend upon the point along that continuum at which the defense becomes operative. This can range from a schiz-oid character, to the "premature ego development" described by Blanck and Blanck (1974), to problems in self-esteem that go with the assimilation of the autonomous functions of the ego into a defensive grandiose self-structure (chapter 10).

The issues of attachment and detachment in the clinical situation will be central to the treatment of all patients for whom these have been developmental issues. In our reparative work, just as in early object relations development, the attachment vis-à-vis the analyst or therapist will provide the interpersonal matrix within which ego development as a whole proceeds (chapter 13).

HATCHING: THE BEGINNING OF SEPARATION

Mahler (1968) emphasizes the importance of the optimal symbiosis for subsequent differentiation of the self- from the object-representation:

> The more the symbiotic partner has helped the infant to become ready to "hatch" from the symbiotic orbit smoothly and gradually—that is, without undue strain upon his own resources—the better equipped has the child become to separate out and to differentiate his self representations from the hitherto fused symbiotic self-plus-object representations. [p. 18]

Mahler writes of the first shift of libidinal cathexis, the shift from inward- to outward-directed attention. Sensory and perceptual development are major factors in this shift.

> When pleasure in outer sensory perceptions as well as maturational pressures stimulate outward-directed attention cathexis—while inside there is an optimal level of pleasure and therefore *safe anchorage* within the symbiotic orbit—these two forms of attention cathexis can oscillate freely. . . . The result is an optimal symbiotic state from which smooth differentiation—and *expansion beyond the symbiotic orbit*—can take place. [p. 17]

During this process the mother functions as a frame of reference, a point of orientation for the individuating child. If this security is lacking, there will be a "disturbance in the primitive 'self feeling,' which would derive or originate from a pleasurable and safe state of symbiosis, from which he did not have to hatch prematurely and abruptly" (p. 19). That is, the self-representation is still intertwined with the object representation. Object loss evokes a sense of disorganization and dissolution of the self of which it is still a part.

CLINICAL ISSUES:
OBJECT LOSS AND SEPARATION ANXIETY

The experience of dissolution of the self associated with object loss in the borderline patient is analogous to this disturbance of primitive self-feeling of which Mahler writes. Anne-Marie Sandler (1977) relates eight-month anxiety to the child's growing awareness of the mother's separation from him. At this point the child faces the "loss of the heavily invested reciprocal dialogue between himself and his mother" (p. 197). This dialogue is the essential maternal matrix within which the organization of the self takes place, and this organization is still indistinguishable from the matrix itself. In the treatment of the borderline adult, the need for merger as a defense against that dissolution of self must be accurately assessed when we make our developmental diagnosis, as our treatment goals and strategies will be predicated upon that judgment. We will also be able to understand the patient's severe reactions to failures of empathy on the part of the therapist, which in effect deprive the patient of the therapeutic matrix, analogous to the maternal matrix and having the same organizing importance.

THE PRACTICING PERIOD: THE SECOND STEP IN SEPARATION AND INDIVIDUATION

From about ten months of age until approximately sixteen months, the child's focus shifts to the rapidly maturing autonomous functions, the autonomous apparatuses of the self—locomotion, perception, and learning. The child is increasingly confronted with the experience and awareness of separation from the mother. Her ready availability when he needs her and the pleasure he derives from the mastery of his new abilities make these small separations tolerable for the child. Mahler (1968) describes the child at this point of development. With the culmination of the practicing period around the middle of the second year, the toddler seems to be at the height of his mood of elation. This accompanies the experience of walking alone and upright. This peak point of the child's belief in his own magic omnipotence "is still to a considerable extent derived *from his sense of sharing in his mother's magic powers*" (p. 20).

Mahler adds that there is now a "complex affective representation of the symbiotic dual unity, with its inflated sense of omnipotence" and that this is "now augmented by the toddler's feeling of his own magic power . . . ." She sees this as the outcome of the spurt in the development of the autonomous functions (p. 23).

CLINICAL ISSUES: THE GRANDIOSE SELF

This inflated, omnipotent self-object representation is the nucleus of the grandiose self which obtains in cases of pathological narcissism, be it with the borderline patient or with the narcissistic personality disorder. Problems of subsequent development are related to the extent to which significant aspects of self are assimilated into the grandiose self structure and thus not available for conflict-free functioning or are otherwise kept out of the mainstream of normal maturation. Kernberg (1975) notes that because the forerunners of the ego ideal and the mature superego— the idealized object images—are thus taken into the self and made part of it in this manner, there is a failure to develop ideals and the superego as a mature structure. I discuss later (chapter 10) the concept of the grandiose superego.

When the autonomous functions are assimilated into a pathological grandiose self-structure, they are not available for achievements in reality that contribute to a healthy, reality-based self-esteem.

The secret grandiose self is often a significant factor with respect to resistance, and it must be identified and analyzed.

The grandiose self may be a manifestation of structural pathology from this point of early development, or it may be recalled as a defense mechanism against the dangers of loss of self-esteem in a more evolved character. Once again, a correct character diagnosis must take into consideration both structure and psychodynamics, with the structural issues requiring first attention.

RAPPROCHEMENT: THE THIRD STEP
IN INDIVIDUATION AND SEPARATION

At around the age of eighteen months, the toddler becomes increasingly aware of his separateness from mother and her separateness from him. His experiences with reality have counteracted his overestimation of omnipotence, his self-esteem has been deflated, and he is vulnerable to shame. Furthermore, his dependence upon the object who is now perceived as powerful confronts him with his relative helplessness. There is an upsurge of separation anxiety, and he may experience depression.

The mother is now perceived as the source of power and is called upon to support the toddler's dependency needs and, at the same time, to encourage and mirror his new achievements in reality. This balance can be difficult for the parent to manage, not only because of her own ambivalencies, but because the child's dependency needs and autonomy needs are themselves in conflict. The good-enough mother of this period will make it possible for the child to divest himself of his delusional power without undue anxiety or shame.

Mahler (1968) writes:

By the eighteenth month, the junior toddler seems to be at the height of the process of dealing with his continuously experienced physical separateness from the mother. This coincides with his cognitive and perceptual achievement of the permanence of objects, in Piaget's sense (1936). This is the time when his sensorimotor intelligence starts to develop into true representational intelligence, and when the important process of internalization, in Hartmann's sense (1939)—very gradually, through ego identifications—begins. [p. 21]

CLINICAL ISSUES:
THE IDEALIZATION OF THE OBJECT,
THE FEAR OF SELF-ASSERTION, AND ENVY

The major concern of the individual who struggles with issues associated primarily with this stage of development is the loss of support, love, and approval of the object with the assertion of will against the object. Still vulnerable to feelings of helplessness and shame, the individual idealizes the object and sees him or her as having the power to protect the self from those painful feelings. At the same time, the object may be envied and feared.

With more serious preexisting structural pathology, the increasing awareness of separateness from the object is in itself traumatic. In the absence of a cohesive self-organization, this awareness evokes the anxiety of potential disorganization or disintegration. The object is still the glue that holds the self-representation together. I disagree with Masterson's view of maternal failure (1976) *at this point in development* as the primary etiological factor in the genesis of the borderline syndrome. He writes of the borderline:

> The object relations theory suggests that the mother's withdrawal of her libidinal availability at the child's efforts to separate and individuate produces a development arrest at the phase of separation-individuation (rapprochement subphase). [p. x]

The "rapprochement crisis" (Mahler, Pine, and Bergman 1975) represents that point in development where the pathology of the borderline condition becomes apparent, not where it originates. We may observe the adult borderline patient use defenses of regression to the grandiose self-structure or to merger to protect himself from the anxiety of object loss and the consequent disorganization.

As with all earlier aspects of the separation-individuation process and its associated pathologies, what one does in the clinical setting will depend upon the structural, developmental diagnosis (chapter 12).

TO IDENTITY AND OBJECT CONSTANCY

Mahler views object constancy in terms of the internal good object, the maternal image that is now psychically available to the

child just as the actual mother was previously available for sustenance, comfort, and love. As Tolpin (1971) puts it, object constancy
constitutes a developmental leap that involves the gradual internalization of equilibrium-maintaining maternal functions that leads to
a separate, self-regulating self.

Burgner and Edgcumbe (1972) refer to "the capacity for constant relationships" and see this as a "crucial switch point in the
development of object relationships." They describe this capacity
functionally as "the capacity to recognize and tolerate loving and
hostile feelings toward the same object; the capacity to keep feelings centered on a specific object; and the capacity to value an
object for attributes other than its function of satisfying needs"
(p. 328).

Anna Freud (1968) wrote: "Object constancy means . . . to retain
attachment even when the person is unsatisfying."

Mahler (1968) writes of the time lag between attainment of
object permanence in Piaget's sense and object constancy in Hartmann's sense.

Attainment of *libidinal object constancy* is much more gradual
than the achievement of object permanency—and, at the
beginning at least, it is a faculty that is waxing and waning and
rather "impermanent." Up to about thirty months, it is very
much at the mercy of the toddler's own mood swings and "ego
states" and dependent on the actual mother-toddler situation
of the moment. [p. 24]

Mahler points out (p. 222) that in the earliest stages of the
separation-individuation process, there is a danger situation of
object loss, whereas the "specific danger situation toward the end
of the separation-individuation phase, as object constancy is
approached, is akin to the danger of *loss of the love of the libidinal
object,* although there may still remain some fear of object loss as
well." This is an important distinction, as the individual who has
achieved object constancy carries the internalized object with him
despite an interrupted relationship and can maintain a sense of
what Winnicott (1965) calls ego relatedness.

CLINICAL ISSUES:
DEPENDENCY AND DEPRESSION

The final shift to object constancy and a well-secured separate identity, with the capacity to regulate one's narcissistic equilibrium from the sources within the self, comes with the completion of the transmuting internalizations (Tolpin 1971), the assimilation of maternal functions (Giovacchini 1979) into the self-representation. Despite their failure to complete this process, we may find in these patients a cohesion, reality relatedness and object relatedness, an absence of splitting, and no significant degree of grandiosity. But there is a continuing dependency upon the object, who is still somewhat idealized, to provide a sense of well-being, be it security or self-esteem. I have found in these patients that there is a high level of ambivalence toward the mother and her functions. The refusal to identify is a recognition that "if I am like mother, I will hate myself as I hate her." This is the context of ambivalence—not splitting.

These patients are not borderline; they are not narcissistic personalities. Yet, they are preneurotic because of the failure to take this final step in the structuring of the ego and the superego.

When object constancy has not been well secured and still waxes and wanes, as in the case of the child in the final stage of the separation-individuation process, the individual may be subject to anxiety and depression associated with the threatened loss of the love of the object. The analysis and working through of impediments to this last step in object relations development become the focus of work, enabling the individual to meet the demands and stresses of his or her own life with greater equanimity and autonomy.

The following diagram, which summarizes the developmental paradigm, is reproduced with slight modification from an earlier paper (Horner 1975).

STAGES AND PROCESSES IN THE DEVELOPMENT OF EARLY OBJECT RELATIONS AND THEIR ASSOCIATED PATHOLOGIES (REVISED)

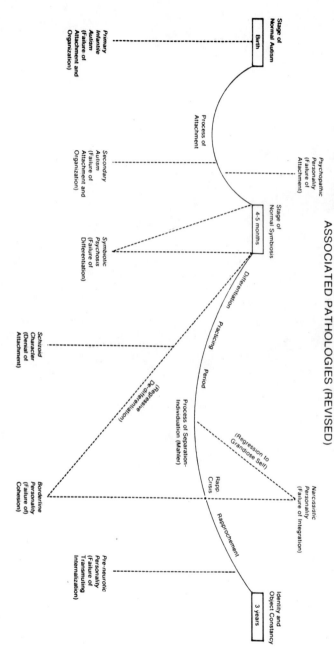

Chapter 3

ATTACHMENT AND DETACHMENT: DEVELOPMENTAL AND CLINICAL ISSUES

ATTACHMENT AND DEVELOPMENT

Interest in attachment behavior was stirred up in 1935 by the work of Konrad Lorenz on imprinting in ducks. *Imprinting* is currently defined as those processes that "lead a young bird or mammal to become preferentially and stably attached toward one (or more) figure or figures" (Szurek 1973, p. 200). John Bowlby (1969, 1973) has carried attachment theory further with his observations of attachment behavior in the human infant and with his observations of the reactions of the infant and young child to separation from the attachment figure. Bowlby defines attachment theory as a "way of conceptualizing the propensity of human beings to make strong affectional bonds to particular others . . . (1975, p. 292).

It is through the process of attachment that the mothering person becomes established as the partner of the symbiotic bond, the earliest stage of object relationship. That is, attachment behavior is fundamental to the buildup of the primitive mental structure of normal symbiosis, which is referred to as the self-object representation. At this stage self and object are not differentiated from one another. This mental representation is the springboard for the subsequent stages of object relations development, which entail the gradual differentiation of the self from the object as well as the firming up of the sense of relatedness with the other and of the sense of self. These changes come about through the separation-individuation process (Mahler 1968). Thus, early deviations or disruptions of the attachment process will have as their outcome deviations or disruptions of the nascent structure with relatively predictable sequelae in terms of psychopathology.

We see here the coming together of Bowlby's attachment theory, cognitive theory (which deals with mental structures), and object relations theory. A proper wedding of these three approaches will enhance our understanding of development as well as of associated clinical and treatment issues.

In the description of the basic processes of organization (chapter 1), the central role of the attachment figure—usually the mother—as mediator of organization was emphasized. *She functions as the mediator of cohesion, of reality relatedness, and of object relatedness.* And it follows that inadequacies of the attachment process will become manifest in deficiencies of cohesion, of reality relatedness, or of object relatedness. Each of these will have its own implications for adult psychopathology and for the treatment process. Bowlby is particularly concerned with the many forms of emotional distress such as anxiety, anger, or depression that are the result of unwilling separation and loss. His findings in this respect will be relevant to the patient whose early attachments were either tenuous or disrupted as a result of either physical or emotional separations and losses.

ATTACHMENT BEHAVIOR

Attachment behavior is innate to the normal organism. Bowlby speaks of it as "primary and autonomous." Attachment is not merely the outcome of the association of the mother with the feeding and caretaking activities, as was previously believed. Most important to the buildup of the attachment bond is the day-to-day social interaction between the infant and his primary caretaker. The importance of intense social interaction as compared with basic caretaking in the development of this bond is highlighted in the experiment of the kibbutz. Here the parents are found to be the principal attachment figures although contact is limited to a few hours each day and to the Sabbath, while routine, daily caretaking is given over to the nursery nurse.

The work of Harry Harlow (1958) with infant rhesus monkeys and a variety of mechanical surrogate mothers demonstrated the ascendancy of the comforting function of the mother over the feeding functions. It also demonstrated the fact that intense social interaction is a sine qua non for the development of normal emotional, social, and sexual behavior. With monkeys such interaction with peers was found to make up for the absence of interaction with a mother figure.

The human infant shows a readiness and capacity for social interaction from the first day of life. Recent research has shown that the newborn can see, focus, follow, and exhibit visual preference. Even in the first hour of life a baby will visually follow a facelike pattern in preference to others of similar brightness, complexity, and symmetry (Lozoff et al. 1977). The response of the caretaking adult to the child's eye contact behavior is one of the earliest manifestations of social interaction. The mother who returns her baby's gaze and talks to him during the feeding situation makes a significantly greater contribution to the attachment process than does a mother who reads or talks to someone else while feeding her infant. Breast feeding is no guarantee of an optimal mother-infant relationship. With such usually unmeasured, subtle attitudes of interest and disinterest, there will be a variation in the quality of mother-infant interaction from the start. The optimal attitude for the mother of the newborn was described by Winnicott (1956) as "primary maternal preoccupation." He sees this as a state of heightened sensitivity of the mother toward the infant, which brings her into smooth and harmonious interaction with her baby. Spitz (1965) speaks of their "dialogue" and of the importance of "mutual cuing" in their ongoing relationship.

Bowlby (1969) emphasizes that "although there is abundant evidence to show that the kind of care an infant receives from his mother plays a major part in determining the way in which his attachment behaviour develops, the extent to which an infant himself initiates interaction and influences the form it takes must never be forgotten" (p. 203). From two months on the infant is increasingly active in seeking interaction. This initiative has its impact upon the mother: she may experience it as demanding and unwelcome, or as inadequate and rejecting, or just right, responding favorably to it. Each member of the dyad influences the behavior of the other, maintaining and shaping responses by reinforcing some and not others.

Ainsworth and Bell (1969) point out that those mothers who can see things from the baby's point of view tended to adopt infant-care practices which led to harmonious interaction, and that their babies "tended to cry less, to learn modes of communication other than hard expressive crying, and to give more frustration tolerance than babies whose behavior made little or no difference in determining what happened to them" (p. 160). We might infer that a sense of mastery begins to develop very early when the infant's behavior does indeed play a part in determining what happens to him. This sense of mastery early on will at first be part of the infantile omnipotence and later on part of healthy narcissism, or self-esteem.

Although we cannot correctly speak of an attachment bond in the first two months of life, Sander et al. (1972) observed that even at the age of ten days an infant will show disturbance with a change of caretaker as a result of the loss of synchronicity. Lozoff et al. conclude that the neonate's organization of sleep-wake cycles is facilitated by continuous exposure to a single caretaker in the first ten days of life, highlighting the organizing impact of the maternal matrix.

Murphy and Moriarty (1976) write of individual differences in the infant that can be attributed to genetic tendencies, such as activity, sensory reactivity, functional stability, robustness, and cognitive activity. For instance, some infants have a greater tendency to react to a sensory stimulus with motor activity, others with cognitive activity. From the very start there is interaction with the child's genetic tendencies and the environment. These writers point out that "the sequelae of early interaction lead to further modifications of initial tendencies as mothers exploit, attempt to suppress, or tacitly encourage by their permissiveness whatever pattern is emerging, and also the baby repetitively enhances and generalizes behavior that is gratifying or inhibits or even abandons behavior that is frustrating." This statement is particularly relevant to Winnicott's concept of the false self (1965), which is the outcome of nonempathic, impinging mothering to which the child can only react. The identity that consolidates around these reactions constitutes the false-self identity. The good-enough mother, on the other hand, is reasonably responsive to the self-initiated behavior of the infant so as to encourage the emergence and organization of that which is inherent and intrinsic to the child—i.e., the true self.

Given a reasonably sensitive, responsive, and available attachment figure, there will be a predictable course of attachment behavior over the early months of life. The smiling response (Spitz and Wolf 1946), which appears around the age of three months, indicates recognition of that which is familiar. This response to the gestalt of the human facial configuration attests to the differential response to the human environment, although at this stage it is not yet specific to any given individual. Bowlby (1969) reports on the work of Ainsworth (1963), Schaffer and Emerson (1964), and Murphy (1962) with respect to the subsequent changes with age in attachment behavior.

He notes that, building upon the earlier ongoing interaction, the infant by the age of four months does respond differentially to the mother than to others: that is, he smiles and vocalizes more in response to her and follows her longer with his eyes (p. 199). Bowlby sees the emergence of proximity-maintaining behavior as evidence of true attachment behavior, as opposed to recognition. By proximity-maintaining behavior he means crying when the mother leaves the room or, when the child is able, crying and trying to follow her. The infant either brings his mother to him or tries to go to her. This is generally evident as early as fifteen to seventeen weeks in some infants. True attachment implies the achievement of the first stage of object relations, and it has its corresponding mental structure. In object-relational terms this is the point of normal developmental symbiosis. In cognitive terms it means the consolidation of the self-object representation. By six months the child also greets his mother with a smile when she returns, lifts his arms up to her, and crows with delight at her appearance. From six to nine months of age attachment behavior becomes more regular and more vigorous.

All the various forms of attachment behavior continue throughout the rest of the first and second year. Attachment behavior to other familiar figures appears shortly after the attachment to the primary mothering person, although that primary attachment is stronger and more consistent. The availability of the father at this point sets up the attachment that will facilitate separation and individuation vis-à-vis the primary mothering object (chapter 6).

Bowlby notes that by the eleventh or twelfth month the child becomes aware of an impending departure and begins to protest with this anticipation. Attachment behaviors are strong and regular until almost the end of the third year. Bowlby suggests that this shift indicates the passing of a maturational threshold. In object-relational terms, this is the point at which the child has fully differentiated self from object and is able to maintain the sense of relatedness with the mother as well as a firm sense of self. In cognitive terms there is a clear differentiation between the self-representation and the object-representation. Maternal functions have been assimilated into the self, leading to object constancy. With this shift the child attains a significantly higher level of psychological autonomy.

Attachment behavior is a major issue throughout life, although it changes in form and expression. The issue of attachment and its opposite, detachment, must inevitably be relevant to the treatment of the adult patient.

FAILURES OF ATTACHMENT

We cannot make the blanket statement that failure of the attachment process causes such and such a clinical picture. We must stipulate what kind of failure, what degree of failure, and under what circumstances it took place. Furthermore, there are differences in children—differences in activity or passivity, differences in persistence of object seeking, and differences in style of reactivity.

One may protest and become enraged. Another may give up with little protest and soothe himself with sucking his hand or rocking. The environmental context is also very significant with respect to the overall clinical picture. Was it overtly frustrating and/or hostile, or was it relatively benign? Was it an orderly environment, or was it chaotic and disruptive? Was it essentially an abandoning environment, or was it an impinging environment?

Despite the variety of clinical pictures that emerge as the results of these important differences, certain basic principles with respect to the development of object relations and the organization of the self will still pertain. And issues of failed attachment, disrupted attachment, or defensive detachment will still be foremost in the treatment, as will the overall goal of restructuring with respect to object relations and, in particular, the self.

I will not consider in this volume the failures of attachment that are due to a defect of the organism, such as the severe cognitive deficits associated with early infantile autism (Rutter 1975). These chapters are written with the assumption of a biologically competent organism.

A recent account (Kaufman 1976) of the recovery of an autistic child as the result of heroic measures on the part of his parents indicated (at least in this instance) that once the autistic shell was penetrated and attachment achieved, development proceeded normally, including language development. There seemed to be no indication of a cognitive disorder. Perhaps in this instances—and conceivably in others—the deficit may be in sensory reception rather than in the associational processes. We might view the pathology of the autistic child as the result of profound sensory deprivation due to the inability of the child to perceive that which comes in through intact sense organs. Breaking through the stimulus barrier (Escalona 1968) in the earliest months and years would then allow for the attachment process to take place and with it, ego organization. Postponement of treatment past the critical period for attachment and ego structuring would certainly be contraindicated.

Pathology of attachment can be thought of in the following ways, each having its own repercussions with respect to subsequent development.

1. failure to make an attachment ab initio
2. disruption of early attachment
3. unintegrated, multiple attachments
4. attachment through the false self
5. defensive detachment

SEPARATION AND LOSS: THE WORK OF BOWLBY AND SPITZ

The findings of both Bowlby and Spitz with respect to the child's loss of or separation from the primary attachment figure are basic to our considerations here. They are relevant from the point of view of their developmental implications as well as from a psychodynamic point of view in adult life in general and in the treatment situation in particular. The patient must deal with the loss of the analyst in a number of situations, ranging from momentary failures of empathy that are experienced as emotional abandonments to actual separations due to illness or vacations. The final stage of treatment, termination, must inevitably bring these issues to the fore for every patient.

Bowlby (1973) observes that "whether a child or adult is in a state of insecurity, anxiety or distress is determined in large part by the *accessibility and responsiveness* of his principal attachment figure" (p. 23, italics mine). Although his observations of the effect of separation and loss on the child were made in the context of actual physical separation from the primary attachment object, he believes as I do that the mother's emotional absence may have an analogous impact on the infant and young child. Although we are not likely to see many patients who had as part of their early experience the kinds of separations described by Bowlby and Spitz, we will see many people who experienced repeated emotional separations and absences in their formative years.

Bowlby noted a predictable sequence of reactions to separation in children between the ages of six months and three to four years. Children who had not yet consolidated the attachment bond prior to the age of six months did not show these typical reactions. The children observed had been placed in an institutional setting because of a family emergency of one kind or another. This sequence of reactions was first *protest*, secondly *despair*, and finally, *detachment*. The protesting child screams, cries, and cannot be comforted. He may resist caretaking efforts for as long as two weeks. The despairing child is preoccupied with his mother and is vigilant for her return. He will alternately cling to and then fling away his security blanket or teddy bear—his transitional object. And although he may permit himself to be tended by one preferred caretaker, his feelings toward this person will clearly be mixed.

The final stage, detachment, becomes evident as the child settles down and seems to be adjusting reasonably well. At this point, when the mother returns he behaves as though he does not recognize her, or he retreats tearfully from her. He may still respond with affection to the father, however. The longer the separation, the longer this period of detachment from mother. After the reunion and following the period of detachment, there is usually a phase of marked ambivalence toward the mother, who may have a great deal of difficulty herself in dealing with the child's difficult behavior.

Bowlby notes that the persistent longing of a young child for the lost love object is often suffused with intense generalized hostility. He says, "There is no experience to which a young child can be subjected that is more prone to elicit intense and violent hatred for mother than that of separation" (1960, p. 24). The detachment is not permanent if the separation is not too long, but Bowlby states that there is reason to believe that with prolonged and repeated separations during the first three years of life, detachment can persist indefinitely.

Bowlby also notes that the characteristic sequence of responses to separation does not become fully apparent before the age of twenty-eight weeks. Before this point he has observed a bewildered silence, which indicates the child's awareness of the change. These younger children tended to show little or no attachment behavior when they returned home, and their mothers experienced them as "strange." While separation distress per se reflects the consolidation of the attachment behavior toward a specific figure and the pain of the loss of this figure, the earlier reaction of bewilderment and the subsequent dropping out of attachment behavior suggest that the child's integrative potential is being stressed beyond its capacity to cope without residual structural deficit.

With the permanent loss of the attachment figure, as through death, the child will eventually make a new attachment if there is available to him one particular attachment figure to whom he can relate in an ongoing and uninterrupted manner. When there is no such person available and the child makes a series of brief attachments that are then aborted, he will become increasingly self-centered and prone to making transient and shallow, indiscriminate relationships. This is not unlike the behavior reported for institutional children who fail to make an attachment from the start. The implication of these findings with regard to policy making for child-care services are extremely important, although they are often neglected by courts and placement agencies.

In a study of working mothers, Rutter (1974, p. 101) found that the only group to suffer seriously were the children who went from "pillar to post" in a succession of unsatisfactory and unstable child-care situations. The behavior of these children in early childhood was characteristically clinging, dependent, and attention seeking, much like the behavior of those children who had no permanent replacement for the lost mother and like those children raised from the start in an institutional setting.

Spitz (1965) writes of two "emotional deficiency diseases," anaclitic depression and hospitalism. In his study he observed that the severe depression occurred with the child who was separated from the mother after a good relationship with her for the first six months of life. He described these children as weepy, withdrawn, and in general poor health. It was difficult to make contact with them, and there was a serious decrease in the developmental quotient, the index of general development. These cases of anaclitic depression recovered with the return of the love object. However, if the deprivation continued beyond five months, he noted an increasing deterioration with the sometimes fatal condition he referred to as hospitalism. According to Spitz, both anaclitic depression and hospitalism demonstrate that a gross deficiency in object relations leads to an arrest in the development of all sectors of the personality and that object relations plays a cardinal role in the infant's development.

Rutter (1973) points out that severe distress can be mitigated through the intense interaction between the child and *one* person throughout the separation experience. The general impairment observed by Spitz is now viewed as the result of the lack of social, physical, and verbal stimulation of that particular institutional situation. Nevertheless, Spitz's findings do alert us to the potentially disastrous effects of separation from the attachment figure in infancy and early childhood.

FAILURE OF ATTACHMENT AB INITIO: THE AFFECTIONLESS PSYCHOPATH

What of those children who are raised from the start in situations that do not allow for the development of the attachment bond? Attachments normally develop during the first eighteen months of life and, as Rutter points out, an institutional upbringing during the first two to three years of life is probably the single situation most likely to be associated with impaired bond formation. Failure to form bonds leads to the development of characteristic disturbance. These children are unable to keep rules, demonstrate a lack of capacity to experience guilt, and show indiscriminate friendliness with an inordinate craving for affection although they are unable to make lasting relationships. Stable institutionalized children generally have a history of having been with their mothers until after the first year (Pringle and Bossio 1960).

In his study of thieves (1946) Bowlby reported that the affectionless character was associated not with a prolonged separation but with many changes of home and of the primary caretaking figure. The result is not the same as in the case of bond disruption with the child who is admitted to an institution after the point at which an attachment has already been formed. As Rutter points out, it is less important with whom the bond is formed as long as it is formed. The child then seems to have the capacity, after the initial period of distress has passed, to make a new attachment. Rutter sees affectionless psychopathology as the end product of the failure to develop attachment bonds in the first three years of life.

Although as adults these children may come into a treatment situation through law enforcement agencies, they are not likely to present themselves for treatment. It has been my observation that the psychopathic individual who does seek treatment is more likely to have had an early attachment that was subsequently lost and not replaced. Rutter comments that if this condition is to be reversible, the child must have experienced normal relationships at one time in early childhood (p. 78). The deep despair that is reactivated periodically appears to be the motivating factor for treatment. This is not unlike the despair noted by Bowlby in the children who were in the throes of separation.

One such patient, a twenty-eight-year-old woman who was involved in drugs and prostitution, had a history of a relatively stable first two years with her mother, who then deserted the family. She was left with relatives in a chaotic household with a variety of caretakers. In spite of the pain of her despair she could not be engaged in the treatment process because of the characteristic defensive detachment and consequent resistance to any kind of ongoing relationship that carried the inevitable danger of new loss and thus heightened despair. Her detachment protected her from the pain as well as from the relationship that might be the key to ameliorating it. Lack of trust and a reservoir of hatred and rage were further impediments to the establishment of a treatment relationship.

The affectionless psychopath who is unable to form or maintain even a minimal therapeutic relationship should be differentiated from the narcissistic personality who may behave in an apparently psychopathic manner. Rather than being the result of an inability to follow rules or the absence of guilt, his antisocial behavior is more often a manifestation of his anger at having been "deprived" and his belief that he is entitled to reparation, even if he must seize it. Since he feels morally justified in his behavior, there is no guilt.

In the event that one is presented with the challenge of treating the affectionless psychopath with a history of lost attachment (rather than total failure to develop attachment in the first place), the characteristic detachment that protects the individual from the pain of despair would have to be addressed in the interest of forming a therapeutic relationship that would allow for treatment to be undertaken. Bowlby's observation that separation elicits in the child intense and violent hatred for the abandoning attachment figure alerts us to the kinds of feelings that are likely to emerge in the course of such a therapy. Developing an attachment where there is none would be the first goal and a sine qua non for further treatment. The young woman mentioned above could not be so engaged because she would return to the clinic only sporadically as her despair would reemerge and at which time her only interest was in being made to feel better.

Klopfer (1954), referring to the then emerging work of Bowlby and Spitz, wrote: "It seems that the gratification of the infant's security needs is a prerequisite for the development of constructive ego functions. On the other hand, the more the basic needs are frustrated, the more these ego functions tend to be become crippled" (p. 569).

In his study of the Rorschach records of psychopathic personalities Klopfer concluded that "the development of active mastery does not seem to be always dependent upon a high degree of emotional integration." He points out that children generally develop two different kinds of reality testing, one of which is emotional reality testing. This latter quality is absent in the psychopathic personality. He notes that the impostor type of psychopathic personality develops mastery to an extreme degree of skill, although this is "based on a limited kind of reality testing—with a conspicuous absence of long-range thinking—and on a fairly inadequate development of emotional integration" (p. 570). He adds that these Rorschach records also reveal a shallowness of affect and of capacity for object relations.

Klopfer's findings with respect to the Rorschach records of psychopathic personalities illustrate that although the maturing autonomous ego apparatuses (perception, intelligence) may enable the development of a kind of mastery of reality that makes it possible for the individual to negotiate the world in a nonpsychotic manner, something else is needed to produce a healthy personality. This something else is what he calls "basic security," the attachment bond that enables the development and integration of a full range of affect as well as the capacity for long-range thinking and for object relatedness. We can hypothesize that the capacity for long-range thinking depends upon the development of both self constancy and object constancy, in that these mental representations unite past, present, and future.

DISRUPTION OF EARLY ATTACHMENTS

Rutter (1974) states that "many (but not all) young children show an immediate reaction of acute distress and crying (. . . the period of 'protest'), followed by misery and apathy (the phase of 'despair'). . . ." Then there may be "a stage when the child becomes apparently contented and seems to lose interest in his parents ('detachment' . . .)" (p. 29). He concludes that this syndrome is probably due to the disruption or distortion of the bonding process itself. Such disruption or distortion, if not reversed, must be inevitably reflected in the quality of subsequent object relations development.

When we ask what the effect of the broken attachment bond may be, we must consider such factors as the age of the child, the quality of the preexisting mother-child relationship, the existence of other attachment bonds such as those with the father or siblings, and the availability of a substitute attachment figure and the quality of that relationship. For example, children who make poor relationships with adults and other children, who are socially inhibited, uncommunicative and aggressive are likely to be more distressed by the separation experience. Separation may be less stressful if the child remains in a familiar environment. Distress is much less if other attachment figures, such as a sibling, are still available, even if such a sibling is still too young to take on a caretaker role. Short-term distress is less if there was a good mother-child relationship before the separation. And stress is reduced if there is one substitute attachment figure available for the child throughout the separation. In this instance, the bonding process is protected.

In short, there are factors that will either mitigate or intensify the detrimental effects of separation from the attachment figure—usually the mother—during the vulnerable period between the ages of six months and four years. These factors must be considered when we attempt to understand and to treat the adult patient who has a history of broken attachment.

CLINICAL EXAMPLE

Mr. A. is a middle-aged man who presented with predominant schizoid defenses, chronic feelings of emptiness and depression, and a yearning for an idealized relationship with a woman who could meet his dependency needs. He had been married twice and seemed drawn to women whom he saw as crippled, whose needs quickly became a demand and a burden that enraged him. The quality of detachment permeated his behavior in all spheres, especially the treatment situation. This became the focus of the analytic work, which in turn promoted a degree of structural and behavioral change.

Mr. A. was the third of four children. His mother became seriously ill when he was two years old, at which time she was separated from the children for approximately six months. At that time their care was given over to nursemaids. Mr. A. reports that his bond with his mother was never reestablished, even after her return to the family. Because of her jealous and possessive attitude toward him in later life, we can surmise that she did not react well to whatever ties he had developed with the nursemaid in her absence. Furthermore, power struggles over toileting came to the fore during this critical year of his life. Anger at real or imagined demands with stubborn withholding were also prominent facets of his personality, and this would be acted out in treatment along with the characteristic detachment. Despite these issues there was an adequate therapeutic alliance and trust to proceed with treatment.

The early satisfactory bond with his mother and the experience of yearning for its rediscovery contributed to the alliance and trust.

Mr. A. never fully committed himself to any relationship, in his personal life or in his work. If he appeared to be moving in that direction, he quickly found someone to "be in the wings." Or he would simply "move on." He both anticipated and defended against the inevitable loss. His defending attitude, of course, brought about the very loss he dreaded. This stance was also evident in treatment. He first consulted me with his former therapist's approval to join my therapy group. At that time I became the figure in the wings. Five years later he finished with that therapist by their mutual decision and in a short time entered treatment with me. I saw him twice weekly in analytic therapy, using the couch. The detachment and negativism were immediately manifest in the transference.

I generally was able to identify those times when he was most detached by my own feelings of sleepiness. This is one of those situations in which the countertransference reaction gives information about the transference situation.

For some time the patient would repeatedly come to the edge of a frightening experience and then abort it. He would report feeling very frightened, gripping the edge of the couch, and then he would detach. He was able, finally, in one session to report the fantasy that went with the fear, the fear of being torn apart, his flesh torn from his ribs, of being torn limb from limb. He had the image of a harpylike creature emanating from me as I sat in my chair. He was silent for a few minutes, when I suddenly felt very sleepy. "Did you run away from fear?" I asked. "Yes," he replied. "I was thinking of how nice it was to play tennis last weekend." Analysis of the sequence of events that this fearful event fits into provided the following picture.

1. the experience of need
2. the feeling of being controlled by the powerful, needed object who could say yes or no
3. anger at the abrogation of autonomy and anticipated frustration of need

4. fear of retaliation with evocation of the archaic image of the harpy (the bad object of symbiosis) who will tear him limb from limb
5. detachment, which aborts the anger, prevents the anticipated retaliation, and eliminates the fear
6. resurgence of the emptiness and loneliness that is the consequence of the detachment and that stirs up the experience of need, starting the cycle once again

The character detachment of this cyclic pattern ultimately interfered with the achievement of the inner good object, which is referred to as object constancy and predisposed him to the feeling of emptiness and depression. But it protected him from the emergence of the frightening archaic images of the bad, abandoning object. Recalling Bowlby's comment, "There is no experience to which a young child can be subjected that is more prone to elicit intense and violent hatred for the mother than that of separation," we can reconstruct this aspect of his early development and its impact on subsequent object relations development. Compounding this was mother's anger at his turning to someone else in her absence, which can be derived from the following material.

I have a dream I can't remember. I don't want to talk. I guess I'm afraid to talk. I expect some disapproval from you. Partly I'm feeling closer to M, feeling affection for her. Letting you know this is difficult, like not letting my mother know I care for anyone else. You might make fun of her or attack her. I wonder whether . . . if I'm scared to talk to you about her is . . . is it . . . maybe it's on the level that becoming attached to her implies with me that I must necessarily leave you . . . on the archaic level . . . can only be either/or, can't be both.

I see my relationship with her in the way of working with you . . . admitting that I feel strongly about someone else, like the old feelings of putting you back in the role of monster and that you are going to attack me. (This sounds like the kind of anger your mother might have shown when she returned and you showed a preference for your nurse.) It feels on that level.

My decision to live with M feels like a reasonably healthy decision. I don't feel ashamed of it with you, more like being
disloyal to you. I think on some level you will hate me and
abandon me and hate the person I get involved with. I
wonder, I might be projecting. It may be that I am getting
involved with someone else because I hate you. (How would
that work?) Like I was angry at mother for abandoning me
and became attached to someone else. It would be against her,
and then I'd see her as angry at me. I don't see you abandoning me . . . not the vacation . . . it's not as if you were
terminating. . . . It's a reflex thing. If I get involved with
someone else, so I'd better not talk about it. . . . I feel like
crying.

The patient has reported that he has cried more in our sessions
than in his entire life. The tears often accompany the emergence of
good feelings and have been interpreted as the reemergence of the
grief experienced in association with the early loss. That is, as soon
as his detachment gives way and an affectional attachment is experienced, the old sadness returns.

I just need to accept it . . . sadness is definitely connected with
loving feelings. I've suppressed a lot of my feelings of love. I
don't know how to express it. I get extremely tearful. (Are you
ashamed of the tears?) Some, but not much. More afraid. I
don't know what would happen if I let myself go. It's more
that I'm afraid to show my feelings. It makes me vulnerable.
They used to tease me as a kid, they were mean. It's safer not
to show them; I learned to be a stoic. I could feel my throat
tighten up here. . . . I'm afraid I get so carried away I might
then be ashamed, I think I'm afraid to lose control. I think
sometimes I see a parallel in sexual behavior too. When I'm
feeling more comfortable I can really let go . . . sometimes I'm
quite controlled and wary. . . . [obsesses about women for a
bit] I think now I'm avoiding the sadness. I guess I don't want
to go back to it right now. I go blank. I don't want to think
about that. My legs ache, and my head feels full. I'm tired,

almost wish to go away and be alone . . . to be taken care of would stir up those feelings. I don't feel that intense sadness when I'm alone and isolated. It's related to my feelings about people when I'm with them, my protection is to withdraw. One thing I fear is to allow myself to be taken care of. This would stir up all those feelings. To let myself be loved and cared for is very threatening. Maybe I do want to be taken care of, but I'm very much afraid of it. (Instead you find others to take care of. You can gratify the need indirectly without having the painful feelings.) Yes. Then I get angry because they don't take care of themselves. I feel like I don't know what I do want.

Mr. A. sounds like the child described by Bowlby who, in his stage of despair, will not let himself be comforted or tended to.

In general, the goal of therapy was to explore the meaning and function of Mr. A.'s detachment, to enable him to relinquish it, and to reestablish attachment with the therapist, with the goal of his ultimately being able to make commitments in both his work and personal life and to enjoy the gratifications that they would engender. That this goal was in reach was reflected in the following session.

I'm feeling teary and don't know what it's about. I guess it's whenever I feel strong feelings of affection or love or even talk about it. It's almost as though I was realizing something possible of attainment, a glimpse of it. . . . I'm thinking now that I am a more loving person than I was a year or two ago . . . thinking of friends . . . feeling quite connected with several people.

The analytic work with Mr. A. revealed the core issues to be the disruption of the early attachment bond with the mother, the subsequent interference with the bond he established with the surrogate mother, the archaic rage at the abandoning object with its associated frightening fantasy figure, the power struggle around toilet training that further isolated him from good feelings toward the available caretakers, and the humiliating teasing of older siblings and playmates when he was overtly unhappy. The detachment, which was partly developmental as a consequence of the broken attachment and partly defensive against anxiety, grief, and helplessness, became central to his character structure, and concomitantly, its amelioration was central to the therapy. The achievement of a modicum of object constancy increased his emotional autonomy, reversing the vicious cycle described earlier.

UNINTEGRATED, MULTIPLE ATTACHMENTS

Bowlby (1969, pp. 303–304) asks (1) do children direct their attachment behavior toward more than one person? (2) if so, do these attachments develop simultaneously or does one always precede the others? and (3) when there is more than one attachment figure, does the child treat them all alike, or does he show a preference for one of them?

Bowlby answers that a majority of infants are directing their attachment behavior toward more than one figure during the second year of life. "Some infants elect more than one attachment-figure almost as soon as they begin to show discrimination; but probably most come to do so rather later" (p. 304). By the time a child reaches the age of twelve months, a plurality of attachment figures is probably the rule, although they are not treated as equivalents. Studies show that a child's attachment figures can be arranged in hierarchical order.

Since different figures elicit different patterns of social behavior, the child may turn to one when hungry or tired, and to another— possibly an older sibling—when in good spirits and wanting to play. The one individual, be it the mother or father or other persons in the household, who engages in lively social interaction with the child *and* who responds readily to his signals and approaches will probably become the principal attachment figure. Bowlby distinguishes "playmates" from "subsidiary figures." The father or sib may be a playmate, but will not necessarily be an attachment figure as well. The father who plays with his child when it is in good spirits but who does not respond more fully to its social and emotional needs is not as likely to become an attachment figure.

The child who develops a strong primary attachment is more likely—not less—to direct his social behavior to other discriminated figures as well, whereas an infant who is weakly attached is more likely to confine his social behavior to that one figure. One can hypothesize that the need for organization and to avoid the anxiety of disorganization is involved here. Once organization is secured within the symbiotic orbit, the child can move beyond it. Otherwise he must defensively cling to it.

Bowlby emphasizes that "it is a mistake to suppose that a young child diffuses his attachment over many figures in such a way that he gets along with no strong attachment to anyone, and consequently without missing any particular person when that person is away. . . . there is a strong bias for attachment behaviour to become directed mainly towards one particular person and for a child to become strongly possessive of that person" (1969, p. 308). Bowlby sees this bias as having far-reaching implications for psychopathology and refers to it as "monotropy." Rutter (1974) does not agree with Bowlby and states that "most children develop bonds with several people and it appears likely that these bonds are basically similar" (p. 125). The argument between Rutter and Bowlby seems to center around the issue of whether or not there is an innate tendency to monotropy, and whether or not it is, on this basis, biologically desirable. I'm not sure whether the answer to this question is important beyond its academic implications. More relevant to our concern are the developmental consequences of attachment behavior and its variations—particularly the impact on the organization process.

Since attachment leads to the object relations situation referred to as normal, developmental symbiosis (Mahler 1968), and since self- and object-representations are ultimately derived from this state of development, we must ask what the effect is of multiple attachment figures on this overall process. Undoubtedly the outcome will differ from one individual to another, and whether this outcome is healthy or pathological will depend upon the effect multiple figures have on the early organization of experience of self- and object-representations and ultimately the organization. Does the multiple-attachment-figure situation allow for adequate patterning of experience, or does it disrupt fragile, nascent patterns? Does the multiple-figure situation allow for the development of self-cohesion and self-constancy, or does it fragment experience in such a way as to impede this development? Most likely there can be no single answer to these questions because of the relatively idiosyncratic aspects of any single growing child's innate givens and experiences. Nevertheless, we can generalize in terms of the integral relationship between attachment and organization.

Confronted with a patient with problems of identity and with integration of the various aspects of the self, we must begin to formulate the relationship between these character deficiencies and the early attachment process. We must look into the specifics of this person's early experiences and relate them to the presenting picture. In some instances we may have reason to believe that the existence of multiple attachment figures in this individual's past did not serve to widen experience in a constructive and ego-enhancing manner as in the ideal situation, but instead had the effect of disrupting the developing self. Such was the situation with Miss T., the woman described in the previous chapter.

This woman was not psychotic because of her inherent competence with respect to the development of the autonomous apparatuses of perception and cognition. Nevertheless, these capacities had to be protected by withdrawal from the interpersonal environment, which disrupted and confused. Throughout life cohesion was maintained at the cost of object relatedness. The fragmented quality of her object-related experience was dramatically highlighted in her reactions to subtle changes in my mood, appearance, or demeanor. At such times she commented that it felt as though I had become another person, and she felt both abandoned by the me she knew and confused and anxious. Detachment through intellectuality became the primary defense against this vulnerability, but the detachment was not a central aspect of her character structure. The pull to object relationship continued to be strong. The reparative work of treatment was founded on the unifying impact of her developing attachment to me. The efficacy of this approach was confirmed by her comment in mid-treatment: "You know me more than any other person. As long as I have you, I don't feel fragmented in other relationships." And a bit later, "You're the only person with whom I have any continuity, with whom I can be myself."

ATTACHMENT THROUGH THE FALSE SELF: THE MAD SELF

Winnicott (1965) describes a continuum of false-self organizations. The earlier its place in the developmental continuum, the greater the pathology and the more grave its implications for treatment and treatment outcome. The first and earliest relates directly to a failure of the attachment process and is an outcome of gross and pervasive failure of empathy in the mothering person or persons. I will describe the five levels fully and then return to this most severe level of pathology, which originates in the attachment process.

1. At the earliest place on the continuum and the most serious disturbance of identity is the situation in which the false self is all that is seen or experienced. To all appearances, it *is* the real person. There may be a certain degree of competence or success. However, in relationships that require the presence or availability of a whole person, something essential is lacking. At this extreme the true self is hidden. The most severe pathology of the self can be traced back to the earliest stages of object relations development at which time, in this instance, spontaneity ceased to be a feature in the living experience of the child, and the self-as-reactor to a chronically impinging environment became central to the developing self-schema instead.

2. Less extreme is the case in which the false self protects and defends the true self. The individual is aware of a secret self that is allowed a secret life. In the treatment situation this patient may experience panic at the possibility of discovery of the true self by the therapist. It is as though this discovery will lead to the annihilation of the self. A correct interpretation may evoke a negative therapeutic reaction, being experienced as a violation of boundaries

and assault on the real self (Horner 1973). In chapter 13 I describe a therapeutic error that led to this kind of reaction of terror.

Winnicott views this situation as the outcome of the inconsistencies of mothering, whereby the child is first enticed into expression of the true self by the mother's apparent acceptance of and responsiveness to it. However, this experience is followed by rejection or assault upon the self by the mother because of her own ambivalence or shifting moods.

3. Toward greater health on the continuum of false-self organizations is the individual who uses the false self to search out conditions in which the true self can come into its own. The false self protects the true self from hurt or insult. Issues of basic trust or mistrust with fear not only of being hurt but also of being exploited or manipulated are relevant to this person. There will be a testing of the therapist just as there is a testing of others. If the therapist shows an overly positive response to the false self, this patient is likely to make the assumption that the true self would not be so welcomed. An example of this is the therapist who takes premature pleasure at how well the patient is functioning. The assumption is made that there would be a corresponding displeasure with this patient's dependent or frightened self. Analytic neutrality precludes the acting-out that goes with such assumptions.

The evolution of this false self takes place later in the process of object relations development, after differentiation and the establishment of the sense of "I am." The false self is not an integral part of the self-representation in this instance. It is a socially derived role identity developed in compliance with an environment that fails to support the spontaneously unfolding and elaborating self and its autonomy. As such, it develops after differentiation but before object constancy, in the rapprochement subphase of the separation-individuation process. This kind of patient is likely to be aware of being fraudulent with the conviction that the fraudulence is the price of love and acceptance.

4. Still further along the continuum, according to Winnicott, in the direction of greater health, is the false self that is built on identification. There is an established sense of "I am," but the elaboration of that self and its characteristics becomes channeled and

rigidified along the lines of the identifications rather than representing the unfolding patterns more intrinsic to the child himself. This process may be reinforced by the parent or parents, who take excessive narcissistic gratification from the child's normal imitative and identificatory behavior, while failing to reinforce and support the child's other spontaneous expressions of self.

I do not agree that the false self based on identification is as far along the continuum of health as Winnicott seems to indicate. Whatever the etiology of the persistence of identity based on identification, it would seem to involve the necessity for keeping split-off and repressed aspects of the self that are inconsistent with that identity. In the case where this is the result of parental narcissistic investment in the identifications, the child is likely to remain fixated at the immature position wherein he demands approbation and reacts with rage to its omission.

The healthy identifications that are fundamental to the achievement of object constancy, the transmuting internalizations of maternal functions (Tolpin 1971, Giovacchini 1979), are not part of the false self. They are assimilated into the real self.

It is my feeling that this kind of individual is more difficult to treat than the person who uses the false self to protect the real, inasmuch as it may be far more difficult to tease out the identifications than to facilitate the emergence of the real self that has been kept in protective custody.

5. Lastly, in everyday life in the healthy individual, the false self is represented by adaptive social behavior—by politeness and behaving in ways that are appropriate to the situation. This individual has been able to accept the limits of society, however, without experiencing threat or the loss of the true self.

Winnicott points out that for the purpose of planning treatment, the recognition of the false personality is the most important aspect of the diagnosis.

CLINICAL EXAMPLE

Miss V. is a thirty-seven-year-old woman who negotiated life through her false self until the age of twenty. Away at college she had her first psychiatric hospitalization. Her mother was psychotic. Her father teased and humiliated her.

At the time I took over supervision of this woman's treatment, she had recently been released from the hospital. Her therapist was struggling not to be swallowed up by her demands and was intimidated by the potential rage. At the same time he was very drawn to responding to her needs. The issue of his needs versus her needs was in the forefront, resonating with her experience with parents, who from the start had little or no capacity to see her or respond to her apart from their own version of reality and their own need system. Her struggle to bring forth her true self into existence and into her relationship with her therapist was fraught with frustration on both their parts. His attempts to be "real" were experienced by her as an expression of his needs to which she must respond. The need for the analytic attitude is especially critical in this kind of situation.

Miss V.'s struggle back to sanity began paradoxically, two years earlier, with a psychotic episode in which she claimed to be pregnant with the Messiah. With this delusion began the birth of the true self buried within (ergo, her "pregnancy").

Because the true self had been overwhelmed with the impinging nature of the caretaking environment, it had never come into contact with external reality for which the object ideally constitutes a bridge. The false self, which was all of her conscious experience, remained in the forefront until the shut-off self-experiences, embellished with fantasy, became increasingly prominent and constituted the core of the psychotic reactions. Its mystical omnipotence took on the dimensions of the Messiah. The content of the psychotic experience reflects the organism's inherent drive toward organization.

The first goal in the current treatment plan has been to establish a bond between the true self and the therapist. Failures of empathy on his part and impinging intrusions of his own needs predictably evoked her anger, but there has been sufficient "good-enough" parenting on his part to carry them over these failures.

Miss V. is extremely well motivated to do the work of therapy. She uses writing to organize her torrent of thoughts and feelings.

Through her writing she beautifully spells out the environmental failure and its impact upon her development, as well as her recognition of what she must do psychologically to recover. She is the kind of patient who offers the therapist superb supervision if the therapist only pays attention. The following excerpts are good examples of this kind of material. The following was in one of her many letters to him.

> I'm going to change very dramatically and in a way I'm going to lose you because I won't *be* what you have liked.

There is potential object loss if the true self is expressed, since attachment is through the false self. (Marjorie isn't really timid and passive and helpless.)

> You're going to be very surprised by who I am, and partly there *is* guilt, there *is* wrongness; I have taken from you under false pretenses about who I *am*. You'll like the new me, but in a different way. I am really very strong. The submarine Marjorie, the real Marjorie, is really very strong. I have been feeding her and feeding her and making her strong.

The true self is hidden, but conscious and imbued with fantasy attributes.

> You make yourself so goddam vulnerable as though I'm not there. How can you pretend I'm not there? No matter what kind of pathological personalities people have, underneath they're all there, they have to be. There's as much aggression in me as there is in you. I don't use it, I don't show it, but it's there, and I see the world from it, how I can help it. I have no one to hold on to as I make this last change. What I want to ask you is to trust me. A Marjorie with aggression can be lovable too. How can a Marjorie or an anyone without aggression be loving? How can you be "good" when you have to hide your aggression from people; how can you like people when you have to hide your aggression from them? I am not just a receiver; I am an acter too. . . .

Marjorie tells us that expression of what originates within her constitutes aggression. The true self is the aggressive, assertive self. Fear of the anger associated with this healthy aggression is expressed elsewhere.

> Even a *baby* has aggression. . . . I have been lying about myself but there is some continuity to me and the continuous me wants to see you very much. I sound like some monster from a Japanese horror movie about to rise up out of the sea announcing itself. You'll like me, you will.

She tries to "cure" the therapist of his fear of anger so that he won't run from her and abandon her.

> The more your parents don't accept you, the more they are not there to you, the more you have to devise false ways of getting by in the world. All those years of therapy, all those therapists and none of them ever understood me. They couldn't partly because they wouldn't have wanted to believe who I was, what was really underneath.

Therapeutic and working alliances were with the false self.

> Children who don't have *anyone*, who are *totally* alone (and I was *totally* alone, there wasn't *anyone* there to me, to what I really felt), have to become monsters to survive.

The need to protect the survival of the self must be appreciated in the psychotic and borderline patients.

> My parents were out to kill me, not to *kill* me for the sake of killing me, not to be against me but to be for themselves; that was the only way they could feel loved, wanted, against the other's will. . . taking away all your control, all your volition, making you have to be against yourself in all other ways just to have contact, just to be wanted.

Object seeking and attachment takes precedence over need satisfaction.

> There are people who can only have by killing, only in that way can they experience *their* control of being wanted, by robbing the other of it entirely, making the other need them altogether, then giving you the right and withholding the right to love from you, then controlling it entirely. Only then do *they* feel "needed," when they control *you* completely. . . .
>
> My whole life has been a fight to own my own love, to control it myself, and with it to control my own life, because the first need, the absolute need is to love, and if we can't have that we have to sacrifice everything else to having it, to going after it and getting it, no matter what we have to do to ourselves in the process. I was prepared to do *anything* to have this.

She expresses the need to protect her good, and therefore loved (by her), self.

In another letter she describes in even greater detail her experience.

> It's not going to be five, ten, twenty years of "working through my separation problems." *I don't have an ordinary separation problem, not like in the books.* The sort of separation I have to do IS TO BE THERE AT ALL!

Interpretations must address the core pathology! There is an existential crisis.

> I was not alive to my parents! To them it was as though I did not feel at all, as though I had no feelings of my own, as though I did not have my own feelings of pleasure and pain, as though I did not have my own needs; they wiped out sentience altogether for me in how they viewed me, in how they interacted with me. They were both of them autistic. They "created" other people. They could not for the life of them recognize what other people felt as *real. They* decided what I felt or

should feel. I told my mother I felt something and she would tell me, no you don't, you feel such and such. . . . They acted on me, did to me, in complete oblivion to what I felt. That means annihilation. That means anything and everything can happen to you. That means you can be made to feel anything. If you are a newborn baby and the world acts on you ignoring what you feel, in complete oblivion to what you feel—what you feel has no impact on them whatsoever, it's as though what you feel didn't exist at all—you cannot control what happens to you!

This is a pathology of the attachment process itself. There is a failure to develop the most fundamental sense of mastery. Miss V. senses in her therapist an attitude that enables her to trust and to have hope. She wrote:

I've watched you with people, and in some vague way I can't pinpoint, you are there to what they want but don't expect them to be there for what you want, and in some way you are not there from what you want, as though someone extorted love from you.

Marjorie picks up her therapist's readiness to meet the other's needs and both identifies with him and uses this attitude in the service of the alliance (a combination of idealization and projective identification of the false self).

Marjorie's treatment will be neither short nor easy, but because of the superior intelligence that she brings to bear on the cognitive correlates of the object relations issues, the prognosis is relatively positive. Her therapist is in training, however, and it is not possible to predict the impact on her progress of his leaving at the end of his training period, should he be unable to continue with her. This will depend upon how much integration of the true self within the orbit of object relatedness has taken place by that time, as well as the availability of a good-enough replacement attachment figure.

DEFENSIVE DETACHMENT

I will mention briefly the patient who deals with conflicts that arise in the later stages of object relations development with the defense of detachment. When this happens, the overall process of object relations development is aborted. The consequence of that disruption will depend upon the point along the developmental continuum at which the defense becomes operative. It is important to distinguish other situations from the kinds of failures or disruptions of the attachment process that have been described in the last chapter. Nevertheless, the issues of attaching and detaching will be important to the treatment process in either case. But appropriate interventions and interpretations must be relevant with respect to whatever the core developmental issue is for any given patient. While this chapter has dealt with failures of attachment that interfere with the organization of an optimal stage of symbiosis, the following material reveals how detachment is used in the service of differentiation *out of* symbiosis. In the case of Miss R., material from later levels, including oedipal, was superimposed upon this earlier developmental incompletion. Development was not *arrested*, but was vulnerable to the resurgence of earlier unresolved conflict. Although the issues of this case relate to material covered in chapter 4, it is discussed here because of the attachment-detachment conflict involved.

Miss R. was a highly intelligent young woman who complained of depression and emptiness and who suffered from serious problems in self-esteem. She described her detachment as protecting her from "raw emotion," but her associations gradually showed that differentiation of self from other and the need for validation of that self was the core developmental issue that led to the use of detachment as a characteristic defense. What may have appeared, at times, as a wish for narcissistic and exhibitionistic gratification was, in fact, a manifestation of her need to have her separateness, and thus her existence, validated. She spoke of her detachment as a wall that others would have to come up against and would have to acknowledge. "It would force him to be aware of me." The detachment was especially important in the treatment situation. Not only did it protect the boundaries of her self, but it made it possible for her to be her real, initiating self rather than the false self who only reacted to me.

Clearly any attempt to break through the defensive detachment would have been experienced as a threat to the existence of the self. At this stage of her therapy, despite the defensive stance, both therapeutic and working alliances were excellent. Allowing her to be in charge of her protective wall in the context of an empathic relationship would gradually make it safe for her to relinquish the detachment and to then work on and through subsequent object-relational issues and impasses that are the result of this defense. These will be discussed in greater detail in the next and subsequent chapters. What is important for the purposes of this chapter is recognition of the central importance of attachment to the treatment relationship.

THROUGH ATTACHMENT TO SYMBIOSIS

Through the process of attachment, the child comes to the stage of normal developmental symbiosis. The process of cognitive organization of all aspects of inner and outer experience during these first months of life leads to the establishment of a cohesive true self and determines the quality and idiosyncratic patterning of the symbiotic stage. The earliest object relations scheme, the undifferentiated self-object representation, is the foundation for further elaboration of that mental structure and for its subsequent differentiation and integration.

Chapter 4

THE FIRST
DIFFERENTIATION:
THEORETICAL AND
CLINICAL ISSUES

Differentiation out of the symbiotic union with the object takes place in two stages: physical differentiation and psychological differentiation. The first stage is referred to as "hatching" by Margaret Mahler (1968). The second stage is that of the rapprochement phase of the separation-individuation process, and it is accompanied by the "rapprochement crisis." Each stage has its own danger of object loss, and each stage has its own characteristic resolution of that danger. In both situations resolution comes about as the result of further structuralization of the ego in general and of the self-representation in particular.

STRUCTURAL DEFECTS AND THE CHARACTER DISORDER

Defects in structuralization during this time span result in what we call the character disorder—a disorder of the structure of the character or personality rather than conflict within it, as is the case in neurosis. Giovacchini (1979) includes in the character disorders: schizoid disorders, borderline disorders, the character neurosis (including narcissistic disorders), affective disorders, and psychotic disorders. He writes (1975a, p. 28): "The importance of early object relationships becomes apparent in the genesis of faulty structuralization which many believe is the essence of character disorders." Faulty structuralization can take place anywhere along the developmental continuum, from attachment and symbiosis through the rapprochement period. It is my view that the pattern of integration (or its absence) in the symbiotic stage sets the stage of character disorders in general. This is in opposition to others, such as Masterson (1976), who view the borderline condition as the result of environmental failure at the rapprochement stage. Masterson writes: "the mother's withdrawal of her libidinal availability at the child's efforts to separate and individuate produces a development arrest" (p. x) at the rapprochement subphase. He highlights the threat of the child's individuation to the mother at this time. The mother who cannot tolerate the child's individuation at the age of eighteen months may well have found his self-assertive attempts much earlier as equally unsatisfactory. For example, she may have had to override his insistence upon feeding himself at the age of five months. Her inability to tolerate his being separate from her, to be a real self, as it were, would produce an impinging style of mothering to which the child could either react with chronic rage or with the development of a false-self identity.

The separation-individuation process will be viewed in Piagetian terms as described in the first chapter. Self- and object-representations are schemas that are enduring organizations, or structures, within the mind, which are the outcome of the several processes subsumed under the term organization—assimilation, accommodation, generalization, differentiation, and integration. These schemas change most rapidly over the first three or four years of life along with perceptual and cognitive development in general. They continue to be modified with subsequent developmental tasks and experiences, such as the assimilation of the changes of puberty into the self-representation. However, the basic structure of the self as a cohesive, integrated, and differentiated representation is laid down in the earliest years. Despite the hierarchical changes in the schema over time, earlier states can be reactivated under certain circumstances so that we may observe different levels of organization in the same patient. This is, essentially, what happens with "regression."

Giovacchini reminds us (1975a) that "regression in analysis is not identical with the corresponding fixation point. The ego does not revert totally to primitive patterns. . . . Usually the patient can still talk, maintain continence, and have sufficient reality testing to perceive, and communicate to the analyst" (p. 137).

We might speculate that the coexistence of different levels of organization in the same patient, which makes regression possible, is due to the manner in which the brain-as-computer registers the structural changes in the course of the evolution of the self-representation. One could instruct a computer, "disregard the previous information," without erasing from the tapes that information. We have to be careful not to understand the term *structure* too concretely. Once the structure of a building has been altered, it no longer has the shape of what was there before. We have to keep in mind that ultimately structure within the psyche comes down to organization within the central nervous system. Whether a "structure" is itself altered or whether it is joined by a new "radical" (as in chemistry) of information that, in effect, changes its overall form and quality, is a determination that would enable us to conceptualize the link between the organism and the psyche.

EMERGING FROM SYMBIOSIS

The separation-individuation process is that process through which the self-object representation of normal symbiosis (which itself was the outcome of organization during the process of attachment) is so modified. Continuing integration of new sectors of experience—e.g., the maturing autonomous apparatuses—is paralleled by increasing differentiation of self from object. There is a differentiation of the bad self from the bad object along with associated impulses, feelings, eventually thoughts, and the differentiation of the good self from the good object along with associated feelings, impulses, and thoughts. Finally there is the integration of good and bad self-images into a single, ambivalently experienced self and the integration of good and bad object images into a single, ambivalently experienced object. This comes with the achievement of representational intelligence, which unifies self-experience under the aegis of the "I" and which unifies object experiences under the aegis of the concept "Mama."

Most important to the process of differentiation out of the symbiotic orbit is the development of object permanence. This refers to the child's recognition that the object continues to exist even when it is out of the perceptual field. Object permanence—in the Piagetian sense—comes about toward the end of the first year. This coincides with the child's ability to distinguish his own actions from the actions of others. "At first he lives in a world without permanent objects and without awareness of the self or of any internal subjective life" (Campbell 1977, p. 65). "Decentering" results from the gradual coordination of sensorimotor behavior. Thus the child recognizes mother as having an existence apart from him and is able to connect her absence with the distress that accompanies the threat to his tenuous self structure when she is gone. At this point separation anxiety comes to be a specific danger for the child.

Lichtenberg (1975) writes about the development of the sense of self. As the child "hatches" from symbiosis, he has brief and repetitive experiences of object loss. When these experiences are tolerable, albeit painful, they promote the building up of an inner world of imagery that helps the child hold on to the experience of self vis-a-vis the absent object. The child gradually acquires a growing world of such experiential images. These are part of the development of structured representations of self and object and involve organized memory traces. With this achievement the child is able to evoke the image of mother at will. This inner, experiential life comes to compensate for the losses that the child incurs as part of the processes of separation and individuation. "The child therefore begins to 'live' a bit less in his body and a bit less in exclusive response to his outer world; he lives a bit more in his mind" (p. 461).

Anne-Marie Sandler (1977) relates eight-month anxiety to the child's growing awareness of mother's separateness from him. At this point the child fears the "loss of the heavily invested reciprocal dialogue between himself and mother" (p. 197). This dialogue is the essential maternal matrix within which the organization of the self takes place, and this organization is still indistinguishable from the matrix itself. Loss of the matrix at this very vulnerable point in time disrupts the still fragile organization. "His stranger anxiety (or stranger panic) reflects a normal developmental fragility at a critical period when self- and object-representations are beginning to be differentiated but are not yet well established" (p. 198). The child must continuously return to mother for "refuelling" (Mahler, Pine, and Bergman 1975) to reinforce the security of the existing structures. This is the period Mahler refers to as "hatching."

Sandler comments that eight-month panic "arises because the tenuous psychological schema or structure of 'mother-as-separate-from-me' cannot encompass the dissonant experience of the stranger's face" (p. 197). Whatever cannot be assimilated into the existing structure creates "perceptual dissonance" and disrupts it.

Sandler also points out that at a later stage in life "unconscious primitive strivings, and the wishes, fantasies and fears associated with them, may be extremely dissonant in that they are felt to be intrusive and disruptive, the instigators of conflict, and have to be defended against or dealt with by whatever means are available" (p. 198). In other words, the source of the dissonance may be internal as well as external. Those experiences that originate from within the person that were not integrated into the early self-object representations and that continue to be split off from the sense of self will lead to a state of disintegration when they are evoked.

In this situation the therapeutic task and its associated strategies will be to facilitate the integration of these split-off aspects of experience within the organizing matrix of the self-therapist dialogue. As always, the structural diagnosis allows for the formulation of appropriate therapeutic goals and strategies.

THE IMPACT OF PREEXISTING STRUCTURAL PATHOLOGY

The specific quality of the symbiotic experience will profoundly affect the ease or difficulty, the success or failure, of the changes in structure that go with differentiation. Pathology of the attachment process will have its own repercussions with respect to structure and pathology within the symbiotic phase and with respect to subsequent development. Giovacchini (1975a, p. 162) considers the symbiotic phase to be the first phase of psychological development. Emphasizing the importance of appropriate and nonintrusive mothering for the promotion of satisfactory symbiosis, he is concerned with the effect of the mother who fails in this regard. Instead of the gradual assimilation of good-mother experiences into the self as part of the self as differentiation proceeds, the disruptive experiences of the unsatisfactory symbiosis (and their associated feelings and impulses) remain as "unassimilated introjects." They are neither outside the self nor are they assimilated into the self, and they play a major role in the character disorder. They remain as remnants of the symbiotic phase and continue to be played out in later relationships in general, and in the transference in particular. For example: mother-experienced-as-bad-and-angry and self-experienced-as-bad-and-angry were of one piece. This unit, which begins as experience, becomes an inner structure that can be reactivated at any time in the future. Feelings and their associated impulses that were part of the original interaction are also part of this unit, as are concomitant physiological changes. In the instance of anger, the unit becomes bad-me-who-is-angry hating bad-mother-who-is-angry. If feelings of anger emerge, the bad self and hated-hating object are also activated. The hating will be attributed to the other person, who may be the therapist. The hating object is carried around intrapsychically as a counterpart to the bad, angry self and may be projected outward. The efforts of the patient to induce in the therapist behavior and attitudes consistent with the projection may lead to difficult countertransference reactions. One may, indeed, come to hate the patient who reacts and relates as though one is, in actuality, the hated object. The therapist becomes the "container" for the patient's rage (Bion 1963). The importance of maintaining an analytic attitude vis-à-vis this kind of patient is essential to the maintenance of a viable working relationship. In more serious disturbances this outward projection may be manifest in auditory hallucinations—accusing voices—or the bad other may be part of an organized delusional system. In psychosis there is a loss of the tie with external reality. The character disorder uses external reality to make what is intrapsychic concrete and real, and thus avoids psychosis. The relevance of this to masochism is described in chapter 8. The hating other vis-à-vis the bad angry self may also be expressed as self-hatred, as a harsh and punitive primitive conscience. Disagreement within psychoanalysis as to what constitutes the prime motivator of behavior—e.g., instinctual impulse or affect—may constitute a pseudo-problem. Insofar as the organizational unit consists of impulse, affect, and thought, the evocation of any one of these may serve to activate the entire unit, which then becomes manifest in behavior.

In any event, when the symbiosis is unsatisfactory, the process of separation and individuation will be compromised.

Severe pathology within the organization of symbiosis may also be walled off, and although a psychotic core remains, the individual may be able to function, although with certain limitations. We must consider that in the theoretical optimal stage of symbiosis, there are three states of being—three ego states. There are the good self-object constellation based upon pleasurable experiences in social interaction, the bad self-object based upon dysphoric experiences in social interaction, and the *core self-without-object.* This is based upon the parallel organization of self-experiences, which consolidates around the emerging autonomous functions. In the healthy organism, organization goes on with or without the object. This self-organization is connected with external reality, non-human reality (the cradle gym, the rattle, the child's own wiggling fingers, and what it perceives in the physical surroundings), although it is the reality of the nonpersonal world. In cases of failure of attachment in an organically competent infant, we see quite clearly the ability to organize nonhuman reality. An example of this is the affectionless psychopath. This ego-state can be seen as the anlage of the state of detachment, be it a pervasive character-ological detachment or a state that is used as a defense later on under conditions of interpersonal stress (Schecter 1978). It is what Guntrip (1969) refers to as the schizoid core. In general, the child does not need to invent its defenses actively; there are developmental anlagen to which memory has access.

I have observed the use of this particular defense against psychosis as well as against the anxieties of the borderline condition. Later on (chapter 10) I will discuss how the use of this defense interferes with the development of healthy self-esteem.

In some patients we see how recourse to this state in infancy—and still as an adult—serves the important function of supporting organization. When the object world, the people in the environment, actively interferes with organization with their intrusive, impinging, and even assaultive caretaking, the child may be able to organize itself and actually function at a higher level when alone. As an adult, this patient may deliberately seek solitude to cure himself of the fragmenting and disorganizing impact of others. It is likely that this may be the basis for some phobic reactions.

In one instance a paranoid core reflected the predominantly fear-and rage-filled self-object representation that remained from a grossly unsatisfactory early development. There was a series of nursemaids and a narcissistic, nonempathic mother. The patient recalls being locked in her room screaming as a disciplinary method. She reported that she had been told that she pulled some leaves from a tree, and that this meant what a destructive baby she was—while being carried as a babe in arms in the garden. In once-weekly psychotherapy I found I had to limit my goals and to avoid issues of transference. When I tried to explore her need to make me into a "doctor machine," she would become acutely paranoid. An inquiry about dreams would evoke an enraged, "That's none of your business!" She would sometimes jump into the corner of the couch (on which she sat) and crouch like an animal with its claws out if I said anything that transgressed the detachment. This was a young woman who managed to keep a job and support herself although she led a socially isolated life.

I was able to help her with reality testing around interpersonal issues at work, specifically with boundary structuring—what had to do with her and what did not. There were modest gains from treatment, and she regained an equilibrium that she had lost before she consulted me. With the boundary structuring and associated repression of the paranoid self-object image, I was able to help her make better use of the detached core self organization with its pleasure in the exercise of the autonomous functions (sports, reading, handicrafts, music, square dancing) and minimize their being flooded by affect and ideation from the psychotic, undifferentiated self-object. It was this situation that motivated her to consult me. She was doing quite well and abruptly left treatment when I was due to go on vacation. She left in good spirits, having successfully warded off the abandonment rage by means of the now more solid detachment. There was also a modicum of internalization of my therapeutic function. When in an anxiety situation she would say to herself, "What would the doctor say now?"

Although her life is quite limited, she supports herself with her skills and fills her leisure time with many interests. She makes maximum use of her autonomous functions, particularly those that involve the use of the body and the body ego, the self organized not only around the autonomous functions but also around the body and its kinesthetic experiences. The treatment goals in this kind of situation take into account that normal separation and individuation cannot proceed because of the severe pathology of the self-object representation of psychosis.

Kohut (1977) writes of the "primary defect in the self" and the difference between defensive and compensatory structures:

> I call a structure defensive when its sole or predominant function is the covering over of the primary defect in the self. I call a structure compensatory when, rather than merely covering a defect in the self, it compensates for this defect. Undergoing a development of its own, it brings about a functional rehabilitation of the self by making up for the weakness in one pole of the self through the strengthening of the other pole. [pp. 3–4]

In the case cited above, a strengthening of the defenses also brought about a strengthening of the compensatory structure.

Mahler (1968, p. 32) views the core disturbance in infantile psychosis as "a deficiency or a defect in the child's intrapsychic utilization of the mothering partner during the symbiotic phase, and his subsequent inability to internalize the representation of the mothering object for polarization. Without this, differentiation of the self from symbiotic fusion and confusion with the part object does not occur." In short, faulty or absent individuation from a pathological symbiosis lies at the core of the infantile psychosis. She regards "the issue of nature-nurture a moot one" (p. 47). I think the question in the long run is not moot at all. A defective organism which cannot use the mother in these important ways will not have intact autonomous apparatuses available for the building of the detached compensatory structure as described in the case above. Even with a gross failure of nurture, there may be sectors of functioning that will enable the individual to negotiate the environment with a degree of competence, albeit seriously circumscribed. The prognostic implications are indeed significant. Psychological testing of the seriously disturbed child will enable one to make this most important distinction.

THE ROLE OF AGGRESSION

In the last chapter I described Miss V., who struggled to bring her true self into relatedness with her therapist, the self that had been cut off from reality relatedness because of the gross failures of empathy in the caretaking environment. She had developed a false-self identity that carried her until she went to college, when the separation task of late adolescence stressed the pathological self structure beyond its limits. The true self emerged in its delusional form, the mad self unrelated to external reality.

Miss V. also struggled, in time, to emerge from her dependence upon her therapist to become a separate person. The possibility of a separate, reality-related self now seemed attainable. She wrote:

I never had the correct merger experience as a child, the merger experience that would permit me to evolve as a self. Don't ask me how I know this—perhaps it's obvious, but in the last few days especially I've come to realize that the correct connections within me and to the other were never made, why

I can't function as a separate person. I am undoing the faulty connections to others and in my own way going about getting the experiences from others that I failed to get as a child and that one needs to make connections inside. One can't "come into this world" alone. What I have going with you, for all my periodic rejections of you, has become inwardly essential to me. We need other people. Human psychological dependence on others is an incredible reality. I have the most primitive psychological dependency needs still in me. I am connecting to you correctly. It is the nature of the experience that it is a one-to-one experience and *you are the one I'm evolving in relation to*. . . . [italics mine]

I am much better now. If you leave me, I won't go psychotic. But psychological needs are very real. When I say I need you with the urgency with which I feel it you react as though I'm unwontedly "giving" myself to you, seeing in front of you a thirty-seven-year-old woman, but there's a desperately unformed child in one that *needs the other to form "against"*. [italics mine]

I use the term *aggression* to refer to the energy of the organism that is used to reach a goal. There is no inherent goodness or badness in this sense. "Coming up against the object" will be associated with aggressive impulses (with or without anger, depending upon the amount of frustration involved in the process), and the destructive aspect of aggression in this instance may relate to the "destruction" or dissolution of the primitive organism.

To define the self as separate by coming up against the object can only be sustained if the object remains available emotionally at this point. One can observe the infant pushing away from the mother's body with its feet. How she reacts to this behavior is critical. Does she stay with it, or put him down because he is being "difficult"? The mother who reports that her child did not want to be held may have reacted with feelings of rejection and a retaliatory withdrawal.

Since object loss carries the danger of dissolution of the self, the panic of this state is analogous to the eight-month panic of the young child. The demand of the mother for continuing merger (passive cuddling in this instance) presents the child with the alternatives of object loss or renunciation of differentiation. In either case, the evolution of an integrated and differentiated self is interfered with. The following verbatim material is from the sessions of Miss R., whose continuing difficulties with thinking were described in chapter 3. Her mother, in more recent months, advised her that if she really loved her boyfriend, she would not only comply with what he wanted or pretend to agree with him; she would, in fact, actually agree with him.

Miss R. attempted to use schizoid defenses in order to define her own existence. She defended against the ensuing separation anxiety with the mobilization of a grandiose self (chapter 5). This defensive structure was only partially successful.

There's a core of indifference in my relationship with Carl. I want to use my ability to be indifferent as a weapon. I'm fighting very hard to be in command of what I'm doing, both with Carl and my parents. I was thinking of how enthusiastic I'd been about the apartment. It flew out of my mind. I had to make an effort to recall, and it was only last week. (What do you mean when you say that you want to use your indifference as a weapon?) With Carl it's a wall that he would come up against and would have to acknowledge. It would force him to do something. It would make him aware of me. I have a power notion that my indifference would hurt him, would give me the upper hand, and also be a reminder for him that he doesn't have blind devotion to contend with, but there's a definite person there. With my mother, I'm defining myself, my territory, and expanding it. (It sounds like you use your indifference as a defensive weapon to protect your psychic survival.) I think of the weapon as a medieval wall. (Do you think of it as self-protective or as an offensive weapon?) More offensive with Carl. Finding himself against this wall would be an aggressive thing. (You seem to see your wish to survive as an offensive thing to do to the other person.) Yes.

The accretion of destructiveness to normal, inborn, goal-seeking aggression comes about as the result of the frustration of those efforts. If the attempt to define the self as separate from the mother is met with her resistance, frustration is experienced and frustration-anger is evoked. With this, aggression is fused with anger, and the self-asserting aggression takes on its dangerous dimension.

And in another session.

I'm enjoying making the apartment all mine. It bothers me that I feel like I'm withdrawing from the world, at how much I like being at home. I don't want a connection with anyone else. . . . I feel enthusiasm at eradicating my parents'—my mother's—influence. I'm thinking how unnerved she would be. I don't want to have to explain to her. Moving the furniture is living with the struggle and feeling the victory of the struggle, of setting up a separate existence from my parents. . . .

I need to take credit and let people know how important I am. I feel the need to be credited for having an impact at work. . . . It bothers me that I'm so critical. I should be able to stop this. (What triggers this behavior?) The feeling of not being noticed properly, of not knowing where I am in relation to others. The feeling that they don't give me a proper credit in a relationship. (Is it a matter of self-esteem or of validation of your existence?) The latter, the feeling of being separate, of pulling apart. The feeling of pulling apart to a separate stage and standing there in the spotlight. There's a terrible feeling of not being there and not being seen. I'm observing myself in a way to locate where the spotlight is to get separate from the rest of the scene. . . . What strikes me is how much I want appreciation for what I appreciate in myself. It helps me appreciate it in myself. Otherwise I couldn't. (Crying.)

The failure of the mother to acknowledge and mirror (Kohut 1971) the child's assertion of a differentiated self leads to an association of such assertion with object loss and the consequent dissolution of the self. Miss R. continues:

An observation I made in school: if the teachers thought I was great, I did and would do better and achieve what my abilities would allow. If they told me I was terrible, I would be terrible. (Do you have any hunch what was behind this?) I don't know. (Was it a matter of permission?) I don't do well in a vacuum. There is no intrinsic truth in doing well by myself. [Crying.] (It sounds like what is important is the connection. If there is no connection you are devastated.) I can't separate the connection from existence. I'm one hand clapping. (Yet it sounds like there is some shift when you are in your apartment. Is that so?)

By juxtaposing the recall of dissolution panic and the recent gains, I hope to bring about a degree of structuralization. The isolated core self is now brought into contact with external reality and thereby becomes itself, more real.

Yes. I minimize it to myself as just having the opportunity I never had before. [Continues to cry.] I guess I'm afraid it's just the opposite, and I'm afraid to believe it's a sign of strength. (Are you frightened of being let down?) [Nods.] I spread the plants out by the window. It's a symbol of what it will be when it's just mine. They're not cramped.

And a week later.

I know the problem for me is fighting the detachment. I see therapy as getting into the picture, not just observing it. Here things become more internal. It's not just something you get a big wrench to hammer the problems off [crying]. (It's not just to get rid of parts of yourself but to feel more integrated.) That's what you told me two months ago, and suddenly I know what you mean.

Miss R. had to use her wall vis-à-vis the therapist too, as a defense against engulfment and loss of identity. At this point in treatment it was necessary to the task at hand, e.g., differentiation within the therapeutic matrix. Because there was no psychotic core as in the earlier case, the detachment could be addressed and interpreted. However, it was carefully respected. The therapist's need to feel an emotional connection may motivate inappropriate and intrusive interventions. She still warded off other kinds of transference interpretations. In one session she presented a dream in which the couch figured prominently and that suggested anxiety over possible emergence of the negative transference. I only went so far as to wonder if the dream could have anything to do with therapy. In the next session she said:

> It bothered me that you mentioned therapy and related the dream to it. My first reaction was to feel resentful. It's not that important. There are deeper and more current things, and I wasn't thinking about therapy. (My comment negated your detachment. Did you feel like I was pushing myself at you or making a demand?) It definitely felt like that. . . . I resented it. I felt you came very close to me, next to me saying that— that it had altered the distance. It seems I can talk about it now because of the passage of time and the fact that I've told you once that interpretation is fixed and out on the table, so it's no longer me. It's out and separate from me, so I can accept it and it's not such a big deal. My reaction wasn't to the truth or falsehood, but what it was. I can deal with it because it's been separated from me.

Here we see how structuralization begins to make analysis of the object relations pathology a possibility. She struggles with transference and her defense against it.

> I was reading an account of psychoanalysis by Lindner. I was concerned that it would interfere with the relatively pure state I came here in. . . . The patient came in and tended to attack the therapist. It seemed to be more of a personal relationship. I was horrified by that, all the energy going into that part of it. According to the author, it is part of the process. Should I be doing that? Does it give the process more fodder? (You seem

to screen out your reaction to me.) Yes. (Why do you think you
do that?) It's mostly curiosity areas. I have a feeling I'm not
supposed to express that curiosity. I guess I have a very
clinical, laboratory image of what are the best conditions, that
somehow the curiosity parts don't fit in with the image. (So the
need to live up to an ideal comes into your sessions?) I guess
also in this account the personal attacks seemed childish. I
very much don't want to throw a tantrum. I want to be as un-
childish as possible. (I would think that that would sometimes
make your sessions feel like a burden.) I think the clinical,
depersonalized approach makes them easier. There's a lot of
demands the patient made by those verbal attacks, but they
also betrayed involvement she had with the doctor. That's not
required. (Perhaps you want a wall for me to come up against.)
I guess there's that and also the sense that having a more personal involvement would mean opening up and the more pre-
cious elements would run out. I'm not sure there would be
anything left when I wanted to close. [Tears.]

Now she speaks of the other danger, the loss of self through merger.

There's both the desire to perform well and the desire to keep
hold of whatever in me is involved in not becoming involved in
a personal relationship. . . . There is an overwhelming self-
centeredness which is protected by not becoming involved
personally. It allows me to be the acter and to be sure that you
are the reacter. The image I get of treatment doesn't accord
with your being the acter; I guess I have the feeling of being
the reacter too much outside. This is my one chance, and I
don't want to jeopardize it.

Miss R. now addressed the issue of the false-self identity through
which she negotiates many of her relationships—the self who only
reacts to the impinging other. She goes on:

I find my outlook on life as just expressed very depressing.
(You seem to see as the only alternatives a battle for who is to

be the survivor or to be alone.) It seems that the good possibilities are with me and that interaction will dissipate them with no possibility of replenishment. It's a lonely and bleak prospect. I was just thinking about building the wall for people to come up against . . . the teen-age rebellion I never went through. I was deprived of it earlier, even though it's unpleasant, even for me. I feel uncomfortable but continue in this posture. I will have to work through the attitude. (You're struggling to build your own boundaries.) Yes.

This patient's struggle to erect the boundaries of a differentiated self set for me the task of being as unobtrusive and nonimpinging as possible, yet to be present so that her struggle could take place within the matrix of relatedness, although this *relatedness was denied*. I spoke very little in the sessions, with my interventions aimed at facilitating the structuralization. My comments were sometimes aimed at mirroring the self-defining behavior. Some months after the previous session the patient commented:

I was thinking yesterday that you must be very different for different people and I had the sensation that you were more silent with me, that you do more talking with others. I guess it made me feel very special and cut off, that my problems were less desirable because the way to go about it is by being silent. (You feel cut off by my silence?) It makes the going more difficult. (Does it make me seem like your father?) Yes. I guess it makes me feel very separate from you—that for me the result of any kind of discussion is of closeness, but also of blending with the other, and by not having much dialogue, the separateness is reinforced.

Some months later, the following material emerged.

I had a dream Sunday night. I was supposed to walk along a beach, going away from a group of people. They see my back. I'm wearing shorts. I'm afraid I forgot to shave the backs of my legs and that I look unattractive. It seemed to indicate a great consciousness of myself as existing three-dimensionally. Before the universe was only what I could see. Now there's a realization that there's a back to me, where I've been, that there are things going on that I'm not aware of—in the back of my conscious—that can be seen by others. And I should understand that others may be reacting to this. . . . What disturbed me in your believing me is your picking up on not what I say explicitly but on what you can see. Not shaving the back of my legs is unattractive to me. I feel my negative feelings to Carl are unattractive-disloyal. (It's different from adopting your thinking. It implies that I have my own thinking. Both have their own kinds of distress for you, though.) Mmm. The other aspect of feeling I'm working against time—I've been thinking I should come here every day and speed up the process. I thought part of the desire was to totally monopolize you and make you a more integrated part of the process. I would reflect that I feel like I'm very alone and that it's a very uphill kind of thing.

At the end of this session I brought up adding an additional hour. She commented that it would seem to make sense and wondered if it will speed up the process. I commented that I had heard her feelings and felt that they should be acknowledged and respected, with which she cried. This intervention recognized and responded to her tentative letting down of the detached posture. In spite of the rationalization, the emotional reaching out for help was clear.

With the progress in differentiation and firming up the boundaries of the self, the defensive detachment can be put aside—at least a bit—and she can let the wish for relatedness come into awareness.

THE TASK OF TREATMENT

The technical problem of working with the patient who struggles to differentiate from the symbiotic fusion with the object is twofold: one must provide a matrix of relatedness so that, as differentiation proceeds, it is not equated with object loss, with its danger of dissolution of the self. In this case, separation panic may lead to a retreat from differentiation. On the other hand, the analyst must maintain an attitude of nonintrusion, allowing the patient to take the initiative, in order to avoid a situation in which the patient becomes absorbed into the therapist's reality and is engulfed once again by the object. This would necessitate flight into the defensive detachment, with recourse to the grandiose self to sustain the detached, objectless self.

The use of oppositionalism to ensure differentiation and identity may create an unresolvable paradox and therapeutic impasse. One young woman, in treatment with me for less than a year, realized that we were caught in this bind. She said that she felt the need to be in opposition to define herself as existing. Unfortunately this made her feel cut off (object loss) and anxious. She had a well-developed fantasy life, which both sustained her grandiose self and afforded immense gratification. At times she would present herself as helpless and pitiful in order to elicit pity and caring. When she succeeded in this, in her life she felt humiliated and angry at the responder, and once again the secret, grandiose self came to the rescue, this time to rescue her from humiliation. That is, the grandiose self counteracted both object loss and shame. Feeling caught, she decided to leave treatment, unwilling to trust herself to the couch because of a previous five years with a therapist who actively sexualized the situation, making it necessary for her to flee. Unless otherwise contraindicated, I find the couch is the treatment of choice with patients bound up in compliance-defiance interactions. The absence of cues presents the subtle acting out of these patterns vis-à-vis the therapist and the situation of an alliance with the false self. In the case of the patient above, after exploring the dynamics of her need to leave, I "let go" and simply said I would be glad to go on with our work should she decide to return. Stubborn and angry interpretation of resistance by the frustrated therapist in this kind of situation is experienced as coercion and a danger to the self, which is to be avoided. She was locked into this kind of stalemate with her previous therapist for two years and finally did not return or call him.

With the first differentiation and some degree of object permanence in the Piagetian sense, the child's focus shifts to the rapidly maturing autonomous functions—locomotion, perception, and learning. This ushers in what Mahler refers to as the practicing period. I view this as the developmental anlage of the grandiose self, which we observe clinically as a major defense against the dangers of object loss and/or shame and which often persists unconsciously even with the more evolved individual. Mahler (1968) writes: "He appears to be at the peak point of his belief in his own magic omnipotence, which is still to a considerable extent derived *from his sense of sharing in his mother's magic powers*" (p. 20).

Chapter 5

THE
PRACTICING PERIOD:
DEVELOPMENTAL ANLAGE
FOR THE GRANDIOSE SELF

When we carry forth the concepts of healthy organization, of the development of a cohesive, object-related, reality-related self, what are the implications of the normal practicing period as well as its distortions for this process?

The most significant new factor is the maturation of the autonomous functions: motility, perception, and learning. The question must be asked: how are these functions integrated into the self-representation as it is simultaneously in the process of differentiation from the object-representation? Is cohesiveness reinforced as the new capabilities are integrated smoothly, or is it disrupted by experiences that cannot be assimilated? Is there a preexisting lack of cohesion that is further stressed by their emergence? Does the mothering person mirror the child's pleasure in the exercise of these new functions adequately to bring them within the orbit of object relatedness? Are they associated with a detached state and associated with object loss, or are they integrated into a pathological, grandiose self-structure as described later in this chapter in the situation of Miss R.? And what of reality relatedness? Are the new functions assimilated into a false-self identity so that in their exercise the individual, as an adult, feels fraudulent for any recognition achieved through them? Or are they assimilated into a delusionally elaborated, secret real self?

When a patient complains of difficulties in the exercise of the autonomous functions, usually in the context of work or creative endeavors, we should at least consider the possibility of distortion of the organizing process during this critical period.

THE MATURATION OF THE AUTONOMOUS FUNCTIONS AND THE PEAK OF NARCISSISM

The practicing period, which overlaps and follows the first step in differentiation from the mother of symbiosis, spans the time between the age of ten or twelve months to sixteen or eighteen months. Mahler, Pine, and Bergman (1975) describe the two parts of the practicing period in which the child is first able to move away from the mother by crawling, climbing, or pulling himself upright, and the practicing period proper in which the child is finally able to walk alone. They note that the child's rapid body differentiation from the mother, the establishment of a specific bond with her, and the growth and functioning of the autonomous ego apparatuses in close proximity to the mother are interrelated developments that contribute to the child's first steps toward awareness of separation and toward individuation.

At this point the child's emotional investment focuses on the rapidly growing autonomous ego and its functions. "The child seems intoxicated with his own faculties and with the greatness of his own world. Narcissism is at its peak!" (p. 71).

This state of intoxication is interrupted now and then, however, as the child's awareness of the mother's absence introduces the threat of object loss. Mahler, Pine, and Bergman observed that during the practicing period proper children tend to become "low-keyed" when aware of her absence. They become less interested in their surroundings and seem to be preoccupied with what is going on inwardly. This is accompanied by a slowdown in gestures and performance motility. They add that the child is in a state reminiscent of a miniature anaclitic depression. They speak of the child's inferred "imaging" of the mother and interpret this behavior as "the child's effort to hold on to a state of mind that Joffe and Sandler (1965) have termed 'the ideal state of self' . . ." (p. 75).

It is likely that both are going on—that the child is attempting to hold on to its state of perfect narcissism as well as to the image of the mother, which is essential to that state. That is, the child is trying to hold on to the image to protect itself from the experience of object loss, from separation anxiety, and from that anaclitic depression. It has as a resource the developing object permanence (in the Piagetian sense) but not object constancy (in Hartmann's sense), which is not fully established until the third or fourth year.

Miss R., who struggled with issues of differentiation and whose thought processes had become involved with this struggle, demonstrates how the ability to control the object through imagining it protects from the loss of the real object.

> There's some comfort in being amorphous with a lack of boundaries. (It sounds like you don't like solid, concrete reality because it is outside you and you can't control it. If something is part of you, you can control it.) That makes sense in terms of the image I see—the thought processes or decisions of mind, like a ball of gas. I can't say that things at the outer limits are beyond my control, are separate from me. With a sphere things on the outer limit are separate, and making a decision is in a sense releasing something out to where you can't control it. . . . I guess my thinking processes, while I know they belong to me, are also foreign, alien, floating out there separate from me and not internal.

With the exercise of her autonomous functions so closely associated with object loss because of her mother's intolerance of her growing separateness, her intellect and imaging became caught up in the service of defending against that loss. By thinking, she could regain omnipotent control over the needed but unreliable object. If the thought becomes real and external in the form of a communication or decision, mother, in effect, becomes real and external and can no longer be controlled and the connection with her preserved.

I view this peak of narcissism, described by Mahler, as the developmental anlage for the pathological grandiose self-structure.

The distortions that lead to such a structure may occur for a number of reasons.

The mother may fail to mirror the pleasure of the child in his new sense of mastery with her own pleasure, or she may fail to support his continuing real dependence upon her. She may be angry at her own sense of abandonment by the child who now moves away from her, or her own separation anxiety may be mobilized. She may also be overly relieved at this ability to function without her assistance and may be unresponsive to his continuing needs. One might assume that these attitudes would have prevailed during the earlier stage of symbiosis as well. To the extent that the mother is able to respond empathically to the child from the start, she is likely now to respond empathically to either his autonomous strivings or his need for her support.

THE IMPACT OF PREEXISTING PATHOLOGY

Assuming the less than optimal symbiotic period, the child comes to the practicing period with greater or lesser pathology of structure. There may be a false-self identity organization alongside an isolated core true self. There may be an exaggeration of the separation between good and bad self-experiences vis-à-vis good and bad object experiences because of the unresolved, significant ambivalence of the primary caretaker. There may be a tenuously organized self as the result of a chaotic or disruptive environment. Whatever the situation with respect to the preexisting self-object representation, the new functions must be assimilated into this preexisting structure.

For instance, the organization of a detached, schizoid self that compensates for a fragmented object-related self (the outcome of grossly inadequate mothering during the period of attachment and symbiosis) may form the nucleus of the pathological grandiose self-structure. The emerging autonomous functions are assimilated into this relatively cohesive, schizoid self. Despite the severity of this pathology, it protects the individual from the disorganization that is associated with interpersonal relationship.

The grandiose self defends against and compensates for pre-existing pathology, and it is a protective base to which the child can fall back in the face of later environmental and developmental stress.

Whatever the nature of the maternal failure, the pathological, grandiose self may take into itself aspects of the autonomous functions, which then of course lose their autonomy. As they are assimilated into it, they reinforce it, and the development of a healthy, reality-oriented self-esteem is precluded (chapter 10).

Miss R.'s developing intellect became caught up in such a pathological structure. She spoke of a "state of grace," which referred to her felt ability to know things almost magically. Her high intelligence made it possible for her to sustain this illusion throughout much of her schooling. When confronted in graduate school with the need to study, with the need for hard work, in order to pass her courses, she experienced this as a "fall from grace," as annihilating the sense of the grandiose self. At this point she became extremely anxious and depressed. It is interesting to note that alongside the dependence upon the intellect to maintain the grandiose self, there was a failure to develop the motor functions. She felt ashamed that she had never learned to ride a bicycle, to swim, or to dance. She felt extremely awkward physically, fearful that she would be unable to move about at a party without bumping into someone. She is normal physically in every way, but the motor inhibition is notable.

THEORETICAL VIEWS

There is a theoretical disagreement as to the genesis of the grandiose self. Kohut sees fixation at the normal stages of the idealized object and the grandiose self as the basis for the pathology of the narcissistic personality disorder.

The idealizing transference . . . constitutes the therapeutic revival of that aspect of a developmental phase in which the child attempts to save the original narcissism by giving it over to a narcissistically experienced omnipotent and perfect self-object. Under favorable circumstances the child gradually faces the realistic limitations of the idealized self-object, gives up the idealizations, and . . . makes transmuting reinternalizations. . . .

In analogy . . . the grandiose self is . . . the therapeutic revival of that aspect of a developmental phase . . . in which the child attempts to save the originally all-embracing narcissism by concentrating perfection and power upon the self . . . and by turning away disdainfully from an outside to which all imperfections have been assigned. [1971, pp. 105–106]

From this point of view Kohut sees narcissism and object love as then having separate lines of development. It is my view that they may become separated in certain pathological situations. These situations are characterized by failure of object relatedness or by character detachment. In chapter 10 I describe the relevance of such a situation to pathology of self-esteem.

My own view is that the developmental basis for the grandiose self and for the idealized object are consecutive stages in the separation-individuation process. While the grandiose self is a derivative of the practicing period, the idealized object is a derivative of the next phase, the start of the rapprochement period in which the child recognizes more fully the separateness of mother and the relative helplessness of the self—the rapprochement crisis (chapter 6). Both normally build upon and come out of the cohesive, omnipotent, undifferentiated self-object representation of symbiosis. In pathological development the grandiose self is derailed, as it were, and goes off into a developmental cul-de-sac. It is with this derailment that narcissism and object love not only become split off from one another but also become fixated in this pathological state. I would agree with Kernberg (1975) that "pathological narcissism cannot be considered simply a fixation at the level of normal primitive narcissism" (p. 283). He writes of the genesis of the grandiose self:

Idealized object images which normally would be integrated into the ego ideal and as such, into the superego, are condensed instead with the self-concept. . . . The pathological condensation occurs after the achievement of the developmental stage which separates psychotic from nonpsychotic structures. [p. 282]

The assimilation of the power of the object, the mother of symbiosis, into the self-separating-from-object takes place during the practicing period after the first level of differentiation of self from object (chapter 4). The self-object representation, or schema, becomes differentiated in a distorted manner, with the power of the object "adhering" to the self. With this faulty differentiation the grandiose self as a pathological structure comes into being. As stated previously, certain aspects of the developing autonomous functions may also be taken into this structure.

The assimilation is facilitated by the preexistence of illusory omnipotence that comes with sharing the power of the object of symbiosis and by the "magically" unfolding autonomous apparatuses. I relate flying dreams to the experience of the toddler who now sees the world from the elevation of his new upright stance rather than from floor level. Flying dreams may often imply the activation of the grandiose self, at least in fantasy.

Kernberg notes that because the forerunners of the ego ideal and the mature superego—the idealized object images—are thus taken into the self-image and made a part of it in this manner, there is a failure to develop ideals and the superego as a mature structure. In such a patient, expressed ideals serve to uphold the grandiose self and are not easily amenable to modification. Nor are they true moral values, and we may see considerable psychopathy alongside a highly moralistic stance. That is, over time, there is an elaboration of the pathological self-structure, including the accretion of certain social values. They are characterized by their rigidity, and even fanaticism, and to the extent that they are part of the grandiose self, they may not be challenged. Since the grandiose self constitutes a cul-de-sac in development, healthy ideals and a mature superego cannot evolve out of the values adhering to it. Only a reversal out of that cul-de-sac in the course of treatment, with a return to the mainstream of object relatedness, can make this evolution possible. Kohut (1977) probably underestimates this aspect of his meaning for the patients in the "rehabilitation of the compensatory structures" (p. 58).

Later identifications may also be taken into this structure, as in one situation in which the woman's identification with her father was associated with the grandiose self. To the extent that she was male, the grandiose self was upheld; to be female was to be shamed and helpless.

It is important to keep in mind that later development and experience may be assimilated into the primitive structures, and what we see in the clinical manifestation of these structures is not a true reflection of the early developmental situation or its dynamics, but is a derivative of the interaction of the structure with experience. An example of this would be the sexualization of the early structure in which sexual excitement may be heightened by the excitement of regaining omnipotent control over the needed object. Later elaboration may also obscure the primitive structure, as, for example, when its elaboration is in political or philosophical terms.

However, if we have a clear picture of what goes on in normal development, we are in a better position to understand the distortions of development. And we will also be able to conceptualize the task of therapy to remedy the distortion insofar as it is possible.

ANALYSIS OF THE GRANDIOSE SELF

When we speak of the reactivation in treatment of the more primitive structures, it is well to keep in mind Giovacchini's observation (1975a) that we cannot equate regression in analysis with its corresponding fixation point. The patient does not, in fact, totally return to the more primitive level of functioning. Even though we may observe certain qualities that are characteristic of primitive development, the individual is still usually able to talk, maintain continence, and to communicate with the analyst (p. 137). Alongside the psychologically immature functioning there is still mature functioning in other areas.

The grandiose self is blatant in the case of many patients with a character disorder, but not always. In some it is quite secret, and its existence must be surmised and eventually probed for. This secret, grandiose self may be more or less conscious. The importance of theory and character diagnosis based upon theory is that it tells us about such hidden issues—much as the discovery of the planet Pluto came about as the result of theoretical certainty that it must be there. One can assume the existence of the grandiose self when there are serious disturbances of self-esteem, even though we may be presented only with the material representative of a self experienced as inadequate and devalued.

It is my experience that the uncovering of the secret, grandiose self is essential to the treatment of many individuals, whether its significance appears to be essentially psychodynamic (as when it appears in derivative form as grandiosity in the neurotic as ego defense) or whether its significance appears to be an indication of pathology of structure in the case of the character disorder. In the former case, since the grandiosity serves a defensive function in the face of intrapsychic conflict, interpretation and resolution of this neurotic conflict will usually bring about a resolution of its activity. Yet even in the more evolved character there are integrative issues at stake, particularly in the realm of the evolution of healthy narcissism, as well as a well-secured object constancy. It may be taken up into the competitive situation of the oedipus complex, interfering with its resolution. Although it is a vestigial structure as in this situation, its persistence will interfere with full integration of the self. This will be demonstrated in the case of Mr. R., in whom integration of his male sexuality and the capacity to mourn were at issue.

The following clinical vignette will illustrate the importance of analysis of the secret, grandiose self in treatment.

Mrs. J. was a very bright, articulate, thirty-five-year-old woman who was quite convinced of her intellectual inadequacy. She insisted that she could not learn, yet quite clearly she did. The presenting problem was depression. She had had five years of previous treatment with a reputable therapist, during which time she had apparently played the role of a good patient—an alliance with the false self—and the basic pathology had not been touched. She was too ashamed to return to that therapist and was concerned that her "failure" to have been cured in her treatment would make the therapist feel that she too had been a failure. If she did not support the narcissism of the object, she would be the recipient of that person's narcissistic rage. This information, coming in the first interview, reveals the nature of her interaction with her mother and what she would bring to treatment transferentially. Since the child who believes that he or she has the power over the mother's state of being usually has persisting illusions of omnipotence (Slipp 1973), we could hypothesize from the beginning the existence of a grandiose self on the basis of this information. We could also hypothesize the existence of a false-self identity as well.

Despite the extensive use of schizoid defenses, I did not view her as a schizoid character because of the quality of her relationship with her child, albeit narcissistically cathected, and her emotional aliveness vis-a-vis the nonhuman world. She complained of feelings of deadness, which were the counterpart of these defenses, of not feeling real, which was the counterpart of the false-self involvement, and of despair, which came of the profound sense of hopelessness with respect to the needed object. She was seen in twice-weekly analytic therapy using the couch.

I found myself talking a great deal more than is my usual manner of working. I answered her questions and explained my interpretations, which she professed to be beyond her capacity to understand. Happily, before too long I addressed my own unusual behavior and recognized it as my response to her acting out feelings of helplessness and inadequacy. This is an example of how the therapist may be induced into playing out the externalized role of an unassimilated introject, in this case, the omnipotent object. This interpretation was made, both the transference and countertransference components of what had been going on. She was angry, protested her impotence, and was enraged at my withholding my power. I had the power but would not give it to her or share it with her. This stance indicates that early development went forward into the rapprochement period. Since it could not be sustained because of maternal abandonment, regression to the grandiose self and its elaboration took place to defend against depression and separation anxiety.

An important aspect of what she presented was her physical behavior and attitude. She walked proudly—almost with that puffed-up appearance of the small child who is feeling important. It was clear that there was a cold pride, almost a haughty pride, alongside the doggedly determined assertion of inadequacy and slavish adoration of very brilliant women who also happened to be severely narcissistic and to whom she attached herself.

I confronted the issue of the contradictory feelings and states of being, of helpless inadequacy and of superiority, the latter having emerged in unguarded moments. I interpreted the existence of the grandiose self. She was able to acknowledge that this existed. It was not unconscious. Once we entered this area of exploration, the major issue of envy and envious rage came forth—her own envy of those she saw as powerful and her fear of their envy if they knew of her grandiosity and contempt. She came into one session reporting that she had wanted to tear up some scientific magazines I had in the waiting room, in a fury that I could understand them and she could not.

Melanie Klein (1975) sees envy as contributing to the

infant's difficulties in building up his good object, for he feels that the gratification of which he was deprived has been kept for itself by the breast that frustrated him.

She emphasizes that:

Envy is the angry feeling that another person possesses and enjoys something desirable—the envious impulse being to take it away or to spoil it. [pp. 180–181]

Despite my disagreement with Klein, who sees this situation as going back to the beginning of life, I do find her view of envy useful if put into the context of the rapprochement crisis at which time the illusory omnipotence of the developmental, grandiose self is lost. The idealized object upon which the self is dependent then emerges. If the object interferes with the process of transmuting internalization (Tolpin 1971), with the assimilation of maternal functions into the self, envy is evoked. The mother's competitiveness and the threat of maternal abandonment as punishment for steps toward autonomy created the situation of envy and its counterpart, the fear of being envied.

Subsequent analytic treatment was highly successful, with the evolution of a healthier self-esteem and Mrs. J.'s ability to act upon some of her ambitions at work, the giving up of the schizoid detachment that defended against a true dependency and its associated threat of object loss and depression, anger, and humiliation. The earlier stages of symbiosis and differentiation had gone reasonably well insofar as there was a cohesive self. The narcissistic mother had focused her attention on the little girl as though she were a doll. There was overgratification in certain sectors of the narcissistic realm with a failure to support other sectors, as well as frustration of her dependency needs.

When she was three years old a brother was born. He was colicky and sickly, and the mother turned guiltily to his care, almost excluding her daughter. The father was very detached and unavailable as a secondary object. Thus she was abandoned at the height of her felt dependency—after the full differentiation that ushers in the rapprochement stage and before libidinal object constancy. She turned to the more archaic, grandiose self to protect herself from both separation anxiety and humiliation. But this defense also mitigated against the evolution of a healthy, reality-oriented self-esteem.

The severity of the pathology of a grandiose self and the implications for treatment depend upon the extent of pathology brought forth from the symbiotic stage as well as the point of subsequent development at which the need for such a structure comes about. In the case of Mrs. J. the picture was not as grim as in the following situation. This patient's first year was colored by severe intestinal problems, and his mother was highly inconsistent in her attitude toward him, vacillating between overprotectiveness and assaultiveness. As a consequence, organization within symbiosis was compromised. He could not maintain an integrated or differentiated sense of self vis-à-vis the object but could in the position of the detached, schizoid, grandiose self. The developing intellect—the thought processes—was assimilated into the schizoid, grandiose self. He believed himself to be a genius. At other times he felt "stupid."

A middle-aged professional man, Mr. L. had many, many years of analysis or treatment with a long string of reputable therapists or analysts. Although there were brief psychotic episodes, none of which necessitated hospitalization, he was nonetheless able to function in his work, albeit below the level of his ability. There was a great deal of somatization. He presented himself to me as an emotional cripple, but there were flashes of his grandiosity in the intellectual sphere. Although I was not able to do any more than my predecessors, the importance of the grandiosity as a major source of resistance as well as a defense against disorganization did become clear.

He expressed his fear of destroying the analyst mentally if he let his true brilliance show. This would then bring (1) the loss of the needed object, (2) guilt, and (3) fear of punishment, of being killed in retaliation.

He defended against exposure of the grandiose self with a false-self alliance, by being whatever he believed the therapist wanted him to be. As his only female therapist, he brought to me the sickly child to whom mother might respond. Reciprocally, the grandiose self protected him from the loss of the sense of self that accompanied the false-self situation.

He used the grandiosity to defend against the recognition that the therapist was capable (and thus might have power over him— power to hurt as well as help him) with a genial "That's very good, Doctor," when he thought the therapist had been particularly "astute."

The inevitable failure of treatment led to a heightened grandiosity and contempt for the therapist which intensified the anxiety as well as intensifying the defenses, which further mitigated against the success of treatment. There was a subsequent rage at the failed idealized object with fear of retaliatory rage and the use of helplessness as a defense.

The entire process was a vicious cycle in which the grandiose self played a major role.

Here is another example of a secret, grandiose self that existed alongside an apparently dependent stance.

I had been seeing a middle-aged woman for a little over a year. She had had previous therapy, but seemed to have made little

progress. She came to me in crisis, caught in a masochistic relationship with her lover who wanted to end the relationship. She func-
tioned well in life, had a responsible job, but tended to complain
about the way she was treated by a number of people. Work was
done on the acting out of the masochistic triangle and on her need
to preserve the image of herself as all-good. Once the acting out
stopped, she made moderate progress in life, but we seemed stuck
in treatment. She did not seem to have the capacity to look at her
own mental processes or did not report them. I was plugging away
at the issue of the need to preserve the good self-image and the
necessity for splitting off and repressing whatever did not fit into
this image. Then one day she smiled sheepishly and said, "I'm
going to tell you something I never have told anyone else. When I
smoke grass I have this real inflated image of myself, as something
very wonderful." She came to the following session reporting a
dream in which there was a young man who was "creepy" and
seemed dangerous. "His whole physical image was strange, like
something from outer space. . . . The dream was frightening and I
didn't sleep well."

She began to work on the dream.

I'd say it was because of what we talked about last night. It
was myself as omnipotent. It's unreal, and I think it makes me
fearful. It's dangerous, and I think in my dream I also wanted
to kill this person. I was afraid it would kill someone. I
wanted to destroy it. . . . It's how this young man appeared to
me and how I felt about him, like I feel about myself when we
talk about my omnipotence and my behavior. I feel so un-
natural. I hate it! . . . It keeps me from being an entity, a
person. It keeps me from responding. Holding on to that image
I can't respond without anxiety. I would like to be able to
respond to things and people without having to have that kind
of control, and I hate what it must do to other people. . . . I
also feel a lot of times I'm on the opposite end of the stick—
helpless. It's probably why I felt that way for so much of my
life. Maybe in order to save myself I had to inflate my ego, and
I guess that scares me too. . . . To feel that all-powerful—I

have never been aware of this. I know what a fraud it is. I'm much more in touch with my neediness and helplessness and yet what I think about now is so many areas that fit in with being all-powerful—opinionated, dogmatic, judgmental. . . . I have certainly lost people in my life because of that. I'm also aware of the extremes—being Miss Goody-Good and Mother Superior. I can also be a mean son-of-a-bitch.

And later in the session, speaking of her ambivalence toward someone, she commented:

It doesn't really destroy your love for them. (Unless you are omnipotent, and then your bad feelings can kill. Your omnipotent self was your angry self, and you were afraid of it and had to repress it.) I guess that's what the person was in the dream.

GRANDIOSITY AS A DEFENSE IN THE PRENEUROTIC CHARACTER

Mr. B.'s presenting complaint was his inability to have a sustained relationship with a woman. He also complained of the inability to tend to the everyday matters of his personal business, such as the care of his apartment. He was highly successful in his work at the senior executive level, had many good friends, and was active and successful in competitive sports.

Grandiose fantasies were prominent in his mental life. He was able to tolerate and even enjoy the emergence of what would otherwise be shameful material in his sessions by using it as an indicator of his being a superior patient. Because of the prominence of the grandiosity and issues of power and control, my initial impression was that of a narcissistic personality disorder. However, it became clear that he had a neurotic character structure and that oedipal issues were central to his pathology.

He defended against the dangers of his oedipal strivings and the fear that he might not be able to control his sexual impulses essentially by a "self-castration." He also protected his father, whom he loved, from the danger of defeat and humiliation and himself from an associated guilt. He denied any warm feelings for his mother and related to her in a distant and hostile manner. He was angry at her "custodial" attitude toward him, although he solicited that attitude in women in general.

Because of the defense of ineptitude—"I'm just a little boy and thus no danger to either of you"—he felt ashamed and humiliated, and the grandiose fantasies that were fed by his real successes served as an antidote to this humiliation.

Th oedipal fears in the transference emerged sharply with the sudden death of his therapist's husband and the realization that he was alone with her in the apartment. He was anxious because the man was not there to protect him from the danger of acting out his sexual impulses. Although father was a barrier between him and mother, he was also protection.

He worked well analytically, achieving insight and gradually changing his behavior vis-à-vis women, no longer appealing to their need to be needed and no longer presenting himself as personally inept. At the start of his third year in treatment he reported an experience with a woman to whom he was very attracted, a situation in which he felt he had been able to affirm his manhood and his sexuality with full confidence that he could control it, confident that he was not a danger to the woman who appeared to be somewhat frightened of him. At this point he was able to understand fully the function of the grandiosity as well as how it interfered with his emotional life. He confronted the feelings of potential loss should the woman not return her feelings for him.

I feel now that I'm going through a process I view to be necessary. It's like I'm experiencing a mild form of grief. There's something satisfying about the grief—the feeling of pain and loss. I'm relieved that I feel them rather than some kind of abnormal exhilaration of previous days. There's something unnerving about that. If I adore this woman and have a question about the relationship, I'm uneasy about why I feel so good. As soon as I came into this room and lay down, I felt sad again. I was relieved to feel sad. It's consistent with my notions of what my feelings should be. (You recognize your exhilaration as a defense against the sadness in the past?) That's true. I think I'm aware of my tendency to stamp out what is unpleasant. . . . I do things which give me gratification and avoid what doesn't. Over time in therapy that has been reduced, though some remains. It's reflected in substituting certain pleasures to offset my losses in entirely different areas. I'm aware of that kind of substitution and feel better that it doesn't succeed. I'm anxious about being out of touch with my feelings and have a desire to integrate my life and not compartmentalize it to keep my equilibrium.

As a small child Mr. B. retreated from the dangers of the oedipal situation to earlier helplessness and passivity vis-à-vis his mother. Because of the shame inherent in this regression, he drew upon the developmental grandiosity of the practicing period to protect himself from the intolerable shame. This defense was so prominent as to obscure the true character diagnosis at the start of treatment. However it became clear that he was well-integrated, well-differentiated, evidenced no object splitting, and had partially achieved object constancy. This case illustrates how grandiosity as a defense mechanism in neurotic conflict gives way readily to the analysis of that conflict. Regression in the case of the more mature character structure is far more circumscribed and is not accompanied by a deterioration of object relations or of the structure of the self. It was, importantly, never accompanied by a devaluation of the therapist or of the object in his real life. The oedipal conflict was an impediment in the first steps to object constancy. This aspect of his treatment is described in chapter 7.

The development of a pathological, grandiose self-structure does create a point of fixation in that subsequent stages of the separation-individuation process are precluded so long as it persists. There will still be a predisposition to depression because of the failure to develop libidinal object constancy. There will be a predisposition to humiliation because of the failure to develop a healthy, reality-based self-esteem. Analysis of the grandiose self is essential to the freeing up of the autonomous functions in the service of productivity and creativity. Only values and goals that are consistent with reality are attainable. The unpublished paper, the unfinished dissertation, and the unwritten book are freed from the anxiety associated with the potential destruction of the grandiose self. And analysis of the grandiose self is essential to a healthy object relatedness insofar as the positive qualities of the object are returned to it. The concomitant analysis of the idealized object and a working through of dependency issues make possible the achievement of libidinal object constancy, which comes with the internalization of these functions of the idealized object that provide a sense of security and self-esteem.

THE VULNERABILITY
OF NARCISSISTIC STRUCTURES

The following case illustrates the intrinsic vulnerability of the narcissistic structure—the grandiose self and the idealized object—even when they appear to work well for the individual.

After seven years of outpatient therapy, a sixty-five-year-old woman was presented for assessment of her current status. She was very attractive, well-dressed, intelligent, articulate, insightful, and eminently sane. When she had first come to the clinic, she was filthy, living in seclusion, and speaking "word salad."

Mrs. N. came from a cultured, well-known family with a wide circle of friends. She married and had a son, who was also artistically accomplished. Three major traumatic events had led to her eventual disorganization. When in her twenties she was powerfully confronted with her sister's envy and hostility toward her. In middle age her husband died suddenly, and she was confronted with the existence of his beautiful, young mistress. And a few years after that, her son was diagnosed as schizophrenic and hospitalized. The hospital noted at that time that she was very paranoid about the hospital.

She was treated by one member of the staff for the entire course of treatment, a very important factor in her recovery. Her therapist started by giving her small tasks aimed at restoring her day-to-day functioning. The patient responded well to this highly structured

approach. She recalled that the turning point for her was her acceptance as part of a community social program (not a mental health
setting). Having been able to "sell herself," she regained her self-
esteem. Her therapist reported that the work became increasingly
analytic with the achievement of some insight into her life. She had
been psychoanalyzed in her youth. She was aware of the extent to
which she had denied evidence of her sister's hostility as well as of
her husband's infidelities over the years. By and large it was clear
that her relationships in general were idealized. When asked about
her relationship with her son, she commented glowingly that it had
not changed from the day he was born, that she essentially idolized
him. It was also evident that Mrs. N. highly idealized her
therapist. Sessions had already been reduced to once in three
weeks, and she wanted to cut them down further, yet maintaining
the connection.

The questions were asked, what caused her breakdown and further, what could her recovery be attributed to? We can hypothesize
from the data the nature of the premorbid character structure, the
dynamics of the decompensation, and the dynamics of her recovery.

There is evidence of the idealized object-representation that was
rigorously protected with denial of certain realities. A secret (or
unconscious?), grandiose self-structure was projected on the son at
his birth. With his identity building around this projective identification, his pathology was set in motion.

The three major traumas devastated both the object- and self-
representations with consequent disorganization. Developmentally, a
failure of integration during the symbiotic phase set the stage for the
evolution of the pathological self- and object-representation with the
expected subsequent failures of differentiation.

The therapy reversed the malignant procession. With the structured approach and organizing presence of the therapist, she
reorganized. With the restitution of the idealized object in the person of the therapist, she was once again able to function and to
recover her self-esteem. The fact that she had one therapist during
the entire time (unusual in a clinic setting) provided that organizing
interpersonal matrix analogous to that of the symbiotic phase of
development. The son had recovered and become highly successful

in his field, making him accessible once again for the externalization and realization of her grandiose self.

Her recovery quite probably represents a return to the premorbid structure, which appears successful despite its pathology. The maintenance of the idealizing transference, although at a distance, the self-esteem based on the realities of her current accomplishments, plus the maintenance of the grandiose self through the son are operating together to allow her to function at her maximum potential. Only time will tell whether this will continue to be successful. If she were younger, one might consider analysis of the pathological narcissism. In this case it makes less sense, and even to suggest that she "needs" more treatment would be a severe narcissistic wound. Like the artist, the therapist has to know when to stop.

The practicing period comes to an end with the child's fuller recognition of the mother's separateness, psychological as well as physical, and the recognition of the limitations and relative helplessness of the self. It is a time of renewed separation anxiety, potential shame, and depression associated with loss. It is the time of the rapprochement crisis.

Chapter 6

THE SECOND DIFFERENTIATION: THE RAPPROCHEMENT PHASE OF THE SEPARATION-INDIVIDUATION PROCESS

Once again our concern, as with each subsequent stage of development, is with the effects of maturation, experience, and learning on the ongoing process of organization. There should be an increasing differentiation along with an increasing integration. At this particular point we pose the question: what is the import of the rapprochement phase and of the rapprochement crisis for the structuralization of the ego in general and for the evolution of self- and object-representations in particular?

Clearly to answer this question with respect to any given individual we must take into account the preexisting structure that has come about as the consequence of the vicissitudes of attachment, symbiosis, early differentiation of self from nonself, and of the practicing period with its rapidly unfolding autonomous apparatuses. Failure of attachment, of integration, and of differentiation during any of these critical periods of organization set the stage for further pathological development. The rapprochement crisis may stress a brittle structure making defensive or restitutive mechanisms necessary for the maintenance of structure, while brittle structure impedes the achievement of developmental tasks of rapprochement with the outcome of arrested development.

THE RAPPROCHEMENT CRISIS

Let us begin with a review of what is meant by the rapprochement crisis in the course of normal development. Mahler, Pine and Bergman (1975, p. 76) characterize the acquisition of free upright locomotion and the beginning of representational thinking and speech (Piaget 1936) as "the midwives of psychological birth . . . [the] stage . . . of being a separate individual entity." The maturing of autonomous functions brings with them the awareness of the separateness of self from the object with concomitant loss of illusions of omnipotence. With the loss of omnipotent control comes the corresponding awareness of the relative helplessness of the self.

Rapprochement overall spans the period between fifteen to eighteen months up to around three years. The critical switch point, "the rapprochement crisis" proper, is set at about eighteen to twenty-one months of age and sometimes beyond. It follows closely upon the elation of the practicing period in which the world is the child's "oyster," in which he is at the peak of narcissism.

At this point the child may become sad or anxious, alternately clinging and pushing away, or attempting to regain omnipotent control over mother. He is torn between wanting to exercise his growing individuation and anxiously returning to his mother's side. He is now concerned less with object loss per se and more with the loss of the love of the object. He tries to "woo" mother, and there is an internalization of rules and demands, the beginnings of the superego (Mahler, Pine, and Bergman 1975, p. 101).

The mother of a two-year-old boy observed his continuing struggle with the realities of his limitations and the disruptive potential of his frustration and anger. As during the less turbulent period of symbiosis, she responded to his distress in a manner that mitigated the negative aspects of his realization of helplessness.

He wants to do everything for himself. Douglas do it! is his catch-cry for everything. This includes going to the refrigerator and getting himself a pickle from the jar or filling his own bottle. Some things, like the latter, are impossible for him to manage, and when I try to do it for him he goes into a lengthy tantrum. He's so miserable, and even when he's screaming and stamping his feet, he's saying "mummy" and "uppie" between cries. (Although when I try to cuddle him he fights me.) He really doesn't know what he wants. Eventually I calm him down, and he has a bottle on my lap.

The traumatic effects of helplessness continued to affect Douglas in this manner off and on for the next year and a half. He frequently dealt with it by attempting to regain omnipotent control over his parents with tantrums. By the time he was four years old he was usually able to view himself more realistically and ask for help when he needed it.

At the beginning of the rapprochement period the child begins to widen his world, extending it to include others besides his mother, primarily his father. Insofar as he is related in much the same way as is the mother, he is not fully outside the symbiotic unit. But insofar as he is not included in the self-object representation of symbiosis, he is not fully part of it either. As he brings more of that which is unique to his own style of relating, he will become more clearly differentiated from mother and will increasingly constitute a bridge between her and the external world beyond the symbiotic orbit. The importance of the father in the separation-individuation process is not to be underestimated.

Between the ages of three and four, Douglas reported many dreams in which his father rescued him from a threatening monster. The monster, representative of the bad mother and his anger toward her, was less threatening because of the availability of a loving father from the very start. It did not become necessary for Douglas to develop pathological defenses against the bad mother, although his ambivalence was clearly troublesome to him. With the achievement of ambivalence that comes with the integration of good and bad self-images and good and bad object images, the primitive bad-object image still emerges in fantasy and dream.

The child also develops relationships with others in the environment. The recognition that other adults, or even older children, can also meet the needs of the self serves to mitigate the anxiety over mother's separateness and thus her potential unavailability. Others can be approached and appealed to.

Mahler, Pine, and Bergman point to the growing individuation that makes it possible for the child to function more and more away from the mother. One aspect of this individuation is the development of language and the ability to express wishes verbally, to make the self understood. Secondly, the internalization process, with higher-level ego identification and internalizations of rules and demands, as well as mechanisms for mastery, increase both structure and autonomy. And thirdly, progress in the ability to express wishes and fantasies through symbolic play opens an avenue for the mastery of developmental tasks and their intrinsic traumas and stresses.

Thus the losses inherent in the awareness of separateness are attenuated by new gains. For example, the loss of illusory wish fulfillment is counteracted with the availability of a reality-oriented technique—verbal communication. We sometimes observe in our borderline patients an expectation that their minds will be read and their wishes fulfilled. To have to "put it into words" constitutes an assault upon the illusory omnipotence, with its implied persisting merger. The too-understanding therapist who tolerates vagueness in the attempt at empathic understanding and who is reluctant to ask the patient for clarification may be reinforcing this illusion. The desideratum of empathic understanding on the part of the therapist does not imply mind reading.

Winnicott (1965) writes: "The term 'holding' is used here to denote . . . the total environmental provision prior to the concept of *living with*." He goes on to say, "The term 'living with' implies object relationships, and the emergence of the infant from the state of being merged with the mother, or his perception of objects as external to the self" (pp. 43–44). He notes that the infant is maximally dependent in the holding phase. As differentiation proceeds and the child gradually becomes aware that mother and self are separate, there is a parallel change in the attitude of the mother. She realizes that the child no longer needs her to "magically" understand its needs, that it can wait longer, and that it becomes capable of using communication to summon her and to inform her. In fact, it is very important that she make this shift: "if now she knows too well what the infant needs, this is magic and forms no basis for an object relationship" (p. 50).

Winnicott goes on to stress the importance of a similar shift in our analytic work. The important feature of the child's beginning separation out of merger is that he has to give a signal. This same subtle change will be manifest in the transference. "It is very important, except when the patient is regressed to earliest infancy and to a state of merging, that the analyst shall *not* know the answers except in so far as the patient gives the clues" (p. 50).

Mahler, Pine, and Bergman (1975) also observe in the nursery that by the twenty-first month "the vicissitudes of their individuation process were changing so rapidly that they were no longer mainly *phase specific, but individually very distinct, and different from one child to the other*" (p. 102).

NEW GAINS IN ORGANIZATION

The rapprochement subphase culminates with the organizational achievement of a unified self-representation that is clearly demarcated from a blended and integrated object-representation (Mahler, Pine, and Bergman 1975, p. 108). I would add that there is at this point a fully cohesive (well-integrated), reality-oriented (versus delusional), object-related (versus schizoid or detached), and differentiated self.

One of the most important aspects of this final phase of separation out of the symbiotic self-object unit is the assimilation of maternal functions into the separating-out self-representation. In terms of process this is analogous to the pathological assimilation of the power of the object into a grandiose self-structure during the previous practicing period. However, what is assimilated now is based upon reality experiences with a good-enough mother rather than upon illusions of omnipotence. The later assimilation of attributes of the object into the separating-out self is to be desired inasmuch as it is basic to the capacity of the self to nourish itself and to sustain its emotional and narcissistic equilibrium from inner resources, thus achieving a far greater degree of emotional autonomy.

And in the later, healthy process of assimilation, the object relationship is maintained.

Tolpin (1971) writes of this process of "transmuting internalization." She describes the role of the transitional object (Winnicott 1975) in this process. The child, through the use of his blanket or his teddy bear, actively creates something to restore or improve his inner equilibrium. This creative achievement usually takes place when the child has emerged sufficiently from the symbiotic state to be able to perceive his mother as the chief instrument of his sense of well-being and of his relief from distress. With the help of the transitional object the child is able to become increasingly independent from mother by virtue of his own mental activities. The blanket or teddy bear eases the stress of the transition from symbiosis through separation to object constancy, since it helps to preserve the mental organization that is associated with the good-enough mother who mediates structure during the time that this structure is not yet formed "inside." Even as it substitutes for structure, it promotes structure. That is, "it promotes internalization of the mental structure on which object constancy depends—the inner structure now performs for the self some of the equilibrium-maintaining regulations which depended at first on the need-satisfying object . . ." (p. 328).

The twin processes of accommodation and assimilation, which go hand in hand, continue to modify the self-representation, or schema. Accommodation is that process by which the self-representation is altered by virtue of adaptation to external reality. Awareness of separation or differentiation is an accommodation to what is perceived of that reality. Omnipotence is modified by the experience of helplessness. Assimilation is that process through which the self-representation is enlarged or enriched by what is taken into it, such as the maternal functions, which undergo transmuting internalizations as described by Tolpin.

The autonomous functions of the ego in healthy development continue to be assimilated into the self-representation with a resulting sure sense of one's realistic capabilities. This integration assures increasing cohesiveness and the capacity for autonomous functioning of the self. They may, on the other hand, be assimilated into a pathological grandiose self-structure with a less salutary outcome (chapter 10).

SEPARATION-INDIVIDUATION AND GENDER IDENTITY

Gender identity, the sense of maleness or femaleness, is even more complex. Mahler, Pine, and Bergman observed during the rapprochement phase

> a rather significant difference in the development of the boys as compared with the girls. . . . The boys, if given a reasonable chance, showed a tendency to disengage themselves from mother and to enjoy their functioning in the widening world. . . . The girls seemed . . . to become more engrossed with mother in her presence; they demanded greater closeness and were more persistently enmeshed in the ambivalent aspects of the relationship. [p. 102]

They also observed that boys were "more motor-minded . . . and more stiffly resistant to hugging and kissing, beyond and even during differentiation" (p. 104).

Greenson (1968) notes that he has found men to be far more uncertain about their maleness than women about their femaleness. He attributes this difficulty in men to the early identification with the mother in the symbiotic period of development. He uses the term *disidentify* to describe the boy child's attempt not only to differentiate out of the symbiotic unit as a separate self but also to replace the primary object of his identification, the mother, and to identify instead with the father. This is necessary if he is to develop a male identity during this critical period. Rather than viewing this process as the outcome of the resolution of the Oedipus complex, Greenson sees it as taking place earlier in the service of differentiation and establishment of gender identity. He stresses the importance of the attributes of both mother and father in this process. The mother must be willing, and the father must be available. He attributes the prevalence of disturbances in the gender identity of males (to a greater or lesser degree) to the original primary identification with the mother of symbiosis. The self-representation of the little boy must accommodate to the reality of the difference between himself and mother, and it must be able to assimilate the higher level of identification with the father. The mother's pleasure in this course of development makes this shift possible without its becoming associated with loss of her love, which would interfere with the parallel process of transmuting internalization of maternal functions. It is my view that detachment is more common in men than in women and that this can be attributed to the early defense against the regressive, gender-blurring pull toward the preoedipal mother and the need to resist it. Greenson relates the facts that fetishism is almost 100 percent a male disease and that between two-thirds and three-quarters of all transsexuals are also male. And he adds, "The fact that transvestism is almost exclusively a male disease . . . is a more impressive testimonial for man's dissatisfaction with maleness and his wish to be female" (p. 307).

The relevance of gender identity disturbance to the separation-individuation process is exemplified by the case of a twenty-five-year-old man who had been hospitalized in a state of panic with the feeling that he was turning into a woman. His father had abandoned the family when the patient was one year old. He slept with his mother until he was ten. He developed elaborate, idealized fantasies about the absent father and identified with them. There was an older brother to whom he was attached. The precipitating event leading up to the hospitalization was the marriage of this brother. Psychological testing revealed a prominent, grandiose self alongside a poorly differentiated, helpless self. Even as the grandiose self protected him from the identification with the mother of symbiosis, it also isolated him, leading to a state of despair. Since the grandiose self partly derived from a relationship with a fantasy figure, there could be no true parental function to internalize. He tended to relate on the basis of gross identification and wanted a male therapist who could live up to the image of his intellectually idealized father—that is, someone who was as "brilliant" as the father and his own grandiose self. His intellectual level was in the superior range. Since he would identify with the therapist, the therapist's brilliance was essential to the maintenance of the grandiose self.

The fact that this young man's sense of maleness had always been tenuous was attested to by the fact that he had always been anxious in gym class as a boy with the fear of being seen by the other boys, although he was physically robust. He had erroneously been diagnosed as schizophrenic and had been treated accordingly for two years. With a change of diagnosis as the result of review and psychological testing, medication was discontinued, analytic therapy was begun, and structural issues addressed. Understanding the pathology to have arisen in the separation-individuation process in the context of a relatively cohesive, albeit grandiose self, enabled the development of an appropriate treatment plan.

FROM OMNIPOTENCE TO DEPENDENCY

This critical switch point—from the elation of the practicing period in which "the world is his oyster" to the ignominious status of a dependent baby—brings with it the anxiety of the potential loss of the needed object, or the love of the needed object, who is now perceived as such. It also brings with it the potential for the anxiety of helplessness itself and for the shame that goes with the loss of the illusory perfection. It is at this point that the importance of the maintenance of object relatedness to the development of healthy self-esteem becomes apparent. I do not agree with Kohut (1977) that there can be a healthy development of self-esteem separate and apart from object relatedness, inasmuch as the transmuting internalizations of which he writes depend upon the continuity of relatedness. I write further of this in chapter 10.

The switch point—from illusory omnipotence, the nucleus of the grandiose self, to helplessness and dependency upon the powerful, idealized other—will be identified as a core issue in many patients who may be diagnosed as borderline, narcissistic personality disorder, schizoid character, or even neurotic with significant narcissistic features. Wherever the conflict between dependency wishes

and shame is intense, we can be quite sure that we are seeing the
continuing reverberations from this developmental crossroads. It
will be the source of one significant form of transference resistance
in the treatment situation. Analysis of the shame of "needing
therapy" is often a necessary first step in treatment. We can also be
quite sure that this developmental crisis marks the genetic basis for
the massive shifts in self-esteem reported by some patients.

The following dream was reported by a middle-aged woman who,
although having an essentially neurotic character structure, still
struggled with the narcissistic issues of the rapprochement crisis. For
most of her life Mrs. G. had adamantly denied dependency wishes
and suffered from feelings of intense shame when she could not live
up to her idealized "grown-up" image of herself. These unconscious
dependency wishes and the anger toward the object whom she could
no longer control and who had ultimate power to meet or refuse to
meet those needs emerged in the following dream in which her older
sister was associated with the denied mother.

> I smash all the windows in my sister's room. I go back later,
> and she's picking up the glass. I explode and say something
> about her having power over me. I say that I could always kill
> her. I could come in when she's asleep and put a knife through
> her heart and thus have ultimate power over her. She leaves
> for a moment and comes back, and I go on with my tirade. She
> has turned into G. L. (a woman who was telling me how angry
> she is at her older sister who died for not helping her as much
> as she had wished. She couldn't tell her about her resentment
> because she was dying). She comes up close to me, and as I go
> on, she puts her arm around me, and from the back puts a
> knife into my back, and then I woke up.

Her anxiety is stirred up with the emergence of the repressed
dependency needs, the frustration of the need to control the needed
object, and the fear of retaliation for that anger. She does not really
want to destroy the object—only control it.

An overview of violent patients in a large metropolitan hospital's
psychiatric department led to the conclusion that these patients

were saying, in effect, "Take care of me or I will hit you." These patients were fighting to be admitted, not to be discharged. This violent behavior directed at the staff reflects the kind of rage experienced by the toddler of the rapprochement crisis who experiences his helplessness vis-à-vis a separate, needed, powerful, nonresponding parent. It also reflects the child's attempts to regain omnipotent control over the object.

The need to regain omnipotent control over the needed object who is personified as "Lady Luck" is probably the central dynamic in the situation of the compulsive gambler. In another case apparent psychopathy was a manifestation not of absence of conscience, but an expression of rage at what was withheld by the powerful object and the attitude of entitlement to restitution. This took the form of "ripping off" insurance companies and eventually leaving treatment without paying the bill. This man would attempt to induce guilt in the therapist who brought up issues of money.

The feelings attendant upon the rapprochement crisis were described by a thirty-five-year-old man in association with a dream fragment.

There was a baby at the office. That's all I can remember. (What were the feelings in the dream?) Feelings of helplessness, abandonment, fear, belonging to no one, isolated, being separate, incapable, at the mercy of adults.

Unlike Mrs. G. who had a warm and loving relationship with her father and an older brother, this young man had no alternatives to the primary object. His father was distant and feared because of his explosiveness. Issues of the shame of needing, the rage at the power the needed object had over him, as in his current relationships with women, and the anxiety of abandonment were central to his struggles. Yet even in the instance of the better developmental outcome of the woman dreamer, we see how the issues vis-à-vis the primary object remain, albeit unconscious and only accessible in dreams.

This is an important distinction. We have ample clinical evidence that memory of the primitive stages of object relations development is retained, although unconscious, inasmuch as these images and associations do appear in the fantasy and dream material of the neurotic patient as well as of the nonpatient. The creative process often draws upon these common human experiences to express what are sensed as universal truths. Jung's concept (1928, p. 162) of the "collective unconscious" comes to mind here. However, in the more evolved individual these primitive aspects of development are no longer manifest in structure. They are not central to the character structure as they are in character disorders.

THE ROLE OF THE FATHER
IN SEPARATION-INDIVIDUATION

The impact of the father in the separation-individuation process will depend upon the extent to which he participates in the caretaking relationship with the infant and toddler. This will determine whether he is experienced as a stranger or not at the point of eight-month stranger anxiety. The quality of the father's relating, either primarily nurturant, primarily social (play), or a combination of both, will affect whether he is perceived as definitely not-mother, as primarily a mother-equivalent, or as a bridge between the two. It is probably more difficult to characterize the role of the father at this stage of development beyond broad, general guidelines because of the wide variety of interactional styles that may obtain. There is a general agreement that "the father's first role is to draw and to attract the child into the real world of things and people" (Abelin 1971, p. 232). His early role is to facilitate and enable the separation and individuation from the primary maternal object of symbiosis. Abelin writes further:

> The symbolic representation of the father must be distinguished from the actual relationship with him. The rapprochement crisis is at first centered solely on the representation of the self and the mother. A few weeks later, the father begins to appear in the fantasy world of the toddler as the other, more powerful parent. This father image may be necessary for the satisfactory resolution of the ambivalent rapprochement position. [p. 247]

Douglas's dreams in which the father saved him from the threatening monster reflected the extent to which, for him, the father image did thus enable him to master his ambivalence toward his mother.

The role of the father would seem to be particularly important during the late practicing period and during the rapprochement crisis, at which point the father functions as a human support for the child as it moves away in time and space from the mother. When the child has such a human support, the unfolding autonomous apparatuses do not become associated with the anxiety of object loss necessitating a defense against that loss. One such defense, clearly, is renunciation of competence and return to the safety of the maternal orbit. The other defense will be dependence upon the grandiose self.

As Abelin points out, the father is clearly perceived and defined as "other" following the rapprochement crisis. Whether once again he becomes an enabling figure, or if instead he becomes a rivalrous figure, will depend upon marital dynamics. Abelin comments: "It is only when the relationship between the 'one' and the 'other one' has been sufficiently apprehended, that this 'other one' can become 'the one who wants the same one I want'" (p. 250). This development is quite clearly a necessary forerunner of the Oedipus complex.

Once established representationally, the father becomes available for externalization, acting out of the split in object representation, and the emergence of the masochistic character. In this instance the father, clearly separate from self, becomes the recipient of the good-object projection alongside the still undifferentiated bad self-object attachment to the mother. And in parallel fashion the split may be acted out in the opposite direction, depending upon the quality of the father's attitude and behavior toward the child. He may be the recipient of the separated-out, bad-object projection, while the mother becomes the idealized, nondifferentiated good object. In this case the child is likely to be fearful of moving away from mother, reinforcing the symbiotic tie with her. On the other hand, the father's absence or unavailability at this point in development may fixate the child's attachment to the highly ambivalent maternal figure, and the intrapsychic world becomes more intensely conflicted and split.

A number of hypotheses may be drawn from this formulation, to be validated with clinical evidence. For example, the male homosexual who turns to abusive sex partners may experience this return to the separated-out, bad-object father as his only defense against the engulfment and loss of gender identity that goes with the loving but undifferentiated relationship with women. I have observed this highly idealized attitude toward the "angel mother" in several such men.

The availability of the father as recipient of either the good or bad object projection—depending upon the quality of his interaction with the child—may protect the child from the dangers of psychosis, from getting lost within the intrapsychic world, inasmuch as he is clearly separate from the self and is a representation of external reality. He may mitigate the pathogenicity of the mother. The tenacity of this defense, the externalization of one side of the split, must be understood relevant to its importance for structure, for differentiation of self from object—at least partially—and as a defense against psychosis. The difficulty of treatment in this situation is proportional to its importance in the maintenance of the sense of the differentiated self. The reactivation of the core pathology vis-à-vis the mother, the primary attachment object, may result in a psychotic transference.

Kohut (1977) addresses this issue in his discussion of primary versus secondary, or compensatory, structures. Discussing a case in which the compensatory structure of the personality was built on the relationship with the father, he says:

> Here I shall only say that, despite its shortcomings, Mr. M.'s relation with his father (and thus the compensatory structure of his personality that had arisen from the matrix of this relation) had been at least partially successful in providing him with narcissistic sustenance. [p. 51]

In some instances Kohut notes that the defect in the primary structure is not treatable and that we must instead address ourselves to a "rehabilitation of the compensatory structures" (p. 62).

THE RAPPROCHEMENT CRISIS
AND THE EMERGENCE
OF PREEXISTING STRUCTURAL PATHOLOGY

It may appear that the rapprochement crisis is responsible for all subsequent developmental pathology since symptomatology may begin at that time in the child. However, it is my view that, most importantly, the rapprochement crisis and the awareness of separateness on the basis of the developing autonomous functions lays bare the preexisting pathology of organization within the symbiotic phase and exacerbates it. It is not only a developmental crisis in its own right but also a stressor with respect to earlier structural pathology. For this reason it has been pinpointed as the bete noire of development.

Failure of the environment at this point has been identified by some (Masterson 1976) as the primary etiological factor in the pathology of the borderline patient. He writes:

The object relations theory suggests that the mother's withdrawal of her libidinal availability at the child's efforts to separate and individuate produces a development arrest at the phase of separation-individuation (rapprochement subphase). This arrest or fixation occurs at exactly that time because the child's individuation constitutes a major threat to the mother's defensive need to cling to her infant and causes her to withdraw her libidinal availability. [p. x]

He adds:

The twin themes of this interaction—reward for regression and clinging, withdrawal for separation-individuation—are introjected by the child as self and object representations and thus become the leitmotif of his intrapsychic structure—the split object relations unit. A split ego develops along with the split object relations unit. These structures are then recapitulated in the therapeutic transference.[pp. x–xi]

I believe that it is seriously oversimplistic and highly reduc-
tionistic to conceptualize the borderline in terms of the kinds of
maternal failures associated primarily with this stage of development. If development has been optimal up to this point, there
already is a high degree of integration of various aspects of the self,
with a structuring of affect and impulse and some assimilation of
the autonomous functions into the self-representation.

I agree with Giovacchini (1979), who sees the failure that comes in
the early stages of separation and individuation as leading to the
formation of what he refers to as the character neurosis—which
includes the narcissistic personality disorder. He writes:

> The ego of the character neurotic distinguishes rather well be-
> tween the self and the outer world and has the capacity to form
> a fairly stable mental representation of external objects and
> adaptive experiences. This represents a very significant advance
> from the schizoid and borderline disorders. . . . There has been
> considerable psychic integration and cohesion. . . . [p. 208]

He adds that whatever the quality of narcissism in the character
neurosis, anger is well structured and hostility is manifest. This is
not the case with the schizoid and borderline patients. Their inadequacies dominate the picture (p. 229).

Furthermore, the patients who have character disorders tend to
externalize their problems. There is some capacity for object relations, although these may be characterized by their involvement in
the acting out of the intrapsychic problem.

The preexisting structural pathology that is morbidly stressed by
the rapprochement crisis lays the groundwork for what is designated the borderline personality. There is a failure to develop a
cohesive, integrated self-object representation in the symbiotic
phase. Islands of experience cannot even coalesce into cohesive,
well-delineated good self-object and bad self-object schemas.

It is useful to recall here the innate propensity of the organism to
organize its experience from the very beginning. The extent of
disparities in the environment and the concomitant disparities in
the self-experience will inevitably affect the overall organization.

The questions are asked: "Are there unintegratable islands of organization as in the case of Miss O., or is experience largely organized cohesively around predominantly good-enough experiences vis-à-vis the mother?" What has been excluded entirely from organization—e.g., rage or terror?

Giovacchini writes also that

> the symbiotic phase is crucial for the acquisition of communication skills. . . . [the patient] will not have achieved the ego integration that promotes the formation of introjects and the ability to construct symbols in a meaningful communicative pattern. [p. 122]

He writes of those patients who have not been

> able to assign proper feeling to situations and relationships that, at the time they were experienced, were only perceived in vague somatic terms. [p. 127]

Giovacchini points out that the borderline patient feels he is missing some vital psychic elements and thus his basic integrity as a person is vulnerable. This is not true of the individual whose developmental symptomatology can be pinpointed as arising out of the rapprochement crisis proper.

The failure of successful organization during the symbiotic phase may lead to the formation of "unassimilated introjects." An introject refers to experiences and objects that have become part of the ego during the symbiotic phase but have a structure of their own that distinguishes them from the rest of the ego as a result of partial differentiation (p. 166). When they are subsequently integrated into the ego as adaptive techniques in healthy development, they "lose their introject status." They become assimilated into the self-representation. When introjects are disruptive or traumatic, they cannot be assimilated into the ego but remain neither as part of the self nor as outside the self. Miss R. reported a dream in which the unassimilated introject was clearly represented by a tapeworm.

(What comes to mind about a tapeworm?) It's hard to get rid of
and it's voracious—a kind of external-internal thing that
substitutes its appetites and desires for your own, so maybe I
feel my motivation for being with Carl is a foreign object and
not really me. (That his appetite takes the place of yours?) That
my need to be with him comes from a foreign source. The other
part is that it satisfies the foreign source but doesn't satisfy me.
I'm trying to remember if the tapeworms were supposed to
come from me or if we found them out there. (In the dream you
took something from inside and put it outside where you could
look at it.) . . . I have a feeling I'm being forced to go out into
the world, and it seems like my fears about being on my own
were there (in the dream) as well as the fear to escape it
somewhere with someone in control or in charge.

The separation anxiety, as she worked on differentiation from her
mother, was defended against by involvement with a man who
played out the role of the now-projected, unassimilated introject,
the "voracious" tapeworm.

It is during the rapprochement phase that, optimally, early introjects become assimilated into the self at the same time as they are
being differentiated from the self. This is the essence of the
rapprochement phase of the separation-individuation process.

Within the ego, boundaries form around the maternal representation. These boundaries mark the beginning of the psychic
separation of the child from his mother. As the ego begins to
differentiate itself from the maternal introject, the child sees
himself as separate and distinct. At this point he becomes aware
of his dependency. . . . [Giovacchini 1975a, p. 166]

By the process of assimilation, or of transmuting internalization
as Tolpin refers to it, we see that the child makes mother's adaptive
techniques his own, achieving further separation and strengthening
the boundaries of the self. Coming from a harmonious symbiosis
and continuing to promote psychic harmony, the maternal introject
is not a danger to the developing self and does not have to be

defended against. "As the maternal introject is 'absorbed,' it helps to structuralize various ego systems, such as the integrative and executive systems. . . . [The maternal introject] *is no longer a distinct entity but has become a modality*" (Giovacchini 1975a, p. 167).

When the child cannot use the maternal introject (the object-representation coming out of the symbiotic phase) for transmuting internalizations of helpful maternal functions, there is a deficiency in structuring and autonomy is impossible. He must turn to outside relationships later on to provide what he cannot provide for himself. "The child . . . turns to the outside world for anaclitic nurture and salvation from a raging, self-destructive self" (p. 170).

Miss O. was a thirty-two-year-old woman who worked in a responsible position. The organization of self around the autonomous functions, maintained through detachment, which allowed this sector of functioning, protected her from the pathology of her inner object world. Her level of anxiety was so intense that she often paced about the room. She was terrified that I might touch her even just to shake hands. She felt that were I to get too close she might literally disappear. It is important to note that this young woman had friends and was not a social isolate.

Miss O. was able to observe her inner psychic world and write a play in which the various representatives of self and corresponding "unassimilated introjects" played parts. There were five manifestations of self: She, Good Self, Bad Self, Self, and Un-Self (referring to conscious fantasies the self finds disturbing and does not want). The five characters comprising the parallel splits perceived in the therapist were assigned roles of the prosecutor, the setter of limits, the masochistic and punishing one, the all-good object (given the name of a bridge), and the one she equated with "mother-potential." This last was the main target of the "defendant's" hatred and rage, and the one they most wanted done away with. In this courtroom scene the judge was given a variation of the therapist's husband's name. The time of the scene was set at her appointment hour and the place, "in my head." The script was introduced with the following synopsis.

A melodrama involving the prosecution and stalled execution of five parties guilty of being who they are and attempting to reconcile the difference among them, to avoid death by the principle, unprincipled plaintiff—Ella ("mother-potential").

Miss O.'s inner world of unintegrated islands of self-experience and unassimilated introjects makes the tasks of rapprochement impossible. "Mother-potential," the danger of psychotic transference that would lead to the annihilation of the self (selves) must also be defended against.

I view this sort of situation as the basis for the multiple personality when each of the introjects, split off from one another and cut off from consciousness, continues in interaction with the corresponding islands of self. Each combination becomes further elaborated as subsequent experience is classified and assigned, as it were, to the appropriate and corresponding self.

A certain amount of work was done around boundary structuring and issues of autonomy. She was very skittish about treatment and fearful of the potential psychotic transference, the "mother-potential." She did not want me to comment on the play, which is too bad, as integrative work might have been done with it as a focus. She was in once-a-week, face-to-face treatment, and after two years decided she wanted to "try it on my own." She agreed there was more work to be done and suggested that she might return at some future time. In general, when the borderline patient arrives at this juncture, I do not confront with interpretations of resistance since such an approach often exacerbates the potential negative transference rather than resolving it, and indeed may create an intractable stalemate. I prefer to be a "good-enough" therapist-mother of rapprochement, making it clear that I am still available even as the patient defines herself as separate from me and not needing me (or wanting to need me) at that time. I have found that this kind of patient frequently continues to use the positive introject of the good-enough therapist toward further structuralization, with a gradual transmuting internalization of the adaptive techniques learned from the therapist's attitude and from the working alliance.

Quite clearly, as the child is brought to the rapprochement phase by virtue of the maturation of the autonomous functions, the tasks of rapprochement will be impossible in the face of such preexisting structural pathology. Thus it is my view that it is incorrect to define the borderline syndrome as due solely to the failure of the mother to sustain the developmental thrust of a normal rapprochement crisis.

The developmental split between good and bad self-object experiences and their associated representations, or schemas, arising during attachment and symbiosis, begins to be integrated with the achievement of representational thought and speech. The acquisition of "I" begins to bring together and thus to integrate the experiences of self (Mahler, Pine, and Bergman 1975). The acquisition of "Mama" begins to integrate the images of the object as well (Sullivan 1953, p. 189). Thus the rapprochement period marks the shift from normal, developmental splitting to the capacity for ambivalence toward a single object, although the consolidation of this capacity does not come about until toward the end of the separation-individuation process.

AMBIVALENCE AND FIXATIONS OF RAPPROCHEMENT DEPENDENCY

The patient in whom reverberations of the rapprochement phase proper are central may tend to view others, including the therapist, as powerful parent figures who must be pleased, placated, or bribed. The dependent stance is dominant, alongside a need to control the source of supplies. There are subtle and not so subtle demands for approval and permission, but the need for omnipotent control may not be apparent. Departure from analytic neutrality in the interest of "encouraging" such a patient in his or her outside life activities, interferes with the resolution of this dependent relationship vis-à-vis the object, inasmuch as such encouragement is taken as *permission*, reinforcing the relationship set-up. At one point in the treatment of Miss F., it became evident that she took the therapist's "mhms" as approval of what she was saying.

Miss F. talked about how she put the therapist on a pedestal. It should be noted that in this kind of situation, the perceived disapproval of the therapist or empathic failures that may be interpreted as criticism do not lead to the return of the grandiose self with concomitant denial of the importance of value of the object. The patient tries even harder to "be good."

In these situations, although we cannot accurately say that there is object splitting, there is a high level of ambivalence that interferes with the final step in the separation-individuation process— the achievement of object constancy, which comes about with the transmuting internalizations of maternal functions. Thus, the individual continues to be dependent upon the object for the maintenance of narcissistic equilibrium. The danger is no longer one of object loss per se, but of the loss of the object's support, love, and approval. The closer we get to the close of the separation-individuation process, the closer we come to that structure designated in patients as neurotic. With the assimilation of parental love into the separating-out-self of rapprochement, what Schafer (1960) referred to as the loving and beloved superego emerges. To the extent that the anger toward the ambivalently experienced object interferes with this process, the child will continue to need the external object to provide love for the self and to reassure the self that it is not bad and hated.

This kind of patient has to be distinguished from the masochistic patient who externalizes and acts out the split object situation. In the latter instance, activation of the bad self that is *not* differentiated from the bad object of symbiosis leads to a loss of differentiation and consequent annihilation of the self.

In the more evolved patient the degree of ambivalence that persists speaks to some maternal failure during the rapprochement phase, but not total failure. Maternal ambivalence, inconsistency, or unreliability at this stage generates frustration and frustration anger, which is structured and focused upon the frustrating object as such. When the angry self is mobilized, there may be some depression with feelings of unlovableness, since the unlovable self is associated with the unloving object. Schafer says that in the hostile aspect of the superego, object hate is turned around and transformed into self-hate while in the benign aspect of the superego, object love is turned around and transformed into self-love. The transmuting internalizations of the rapprochement phase of the separation-individuation process are colored by the existence of significant ambivalence, resulting in an ambivalently experienced superego as well. The ambivalence precludes the achievement of the more unified self- and object-representations of the healthy stage of object constancy and identity.

The following material is from a session of Mrs. N., a middle-aged woman who presented a year and a half previously with depression around the breakup of a marriage with an alcoholic husband. The positive transference had continued from the first session on, when she had felt "understood" by the therapist. Negative feelings for the therapist had been notably absent. This session reflects the resolution of an idealizing transference characteristic of the patient who, although essentially neurotic, still had problems left from the rapprochement period. These problems have to do with dependency upon the object for self-esteem.

> I'm not judging myself for what I feel and not coming to moral conclusions about my feelings. I've been thinking about this business of being good. There's nothing wrong with wanting to be a good person, but it's out of proportion, my concern with being good in some situations. I would rather be effective and get life for myself. I'm feeling good about me, taking care of myself effectively—not going for approval. What I do is not appropriate, as though being good will get me what I want. You don't get paid off for being good. I had a dream, a large thermostat. There was a lock next to it. Harold (her husband) wouldn't give me the key. My mother was there. I told her Harold was treating me badly and to please tell him to stop. She walked over to the thermostat, took out the key, and put it in the lock. I said the key had nothing to do with the lock and that I'd handle it. I asked her again to protect me, to tell Harold off . . . .

He withholds his love, which is the "key" to her self-esteem. And she rejects identifications with her mother and thus continues to be dependent upon the object for protection.

I took seriously what you said about idealizing you, about not being frank with you. You're human and I'm less than honest. I needed you to be perfect because of my dependency on you. In a sense I protect you for my need. But I want to get on my own feet. I need help from you but don't need you to take care of my life—only I can do that. I do have mixed feelings about you. I did feel jealous when you were going out that night. I've felt different since then. Suddenly you were a female, not just a doctor taking care of me. I was positive you were involved with a man. I stopped myself from thinking that. Because I have certain expectations, I have to see you in a certain way. But how I see you has nothing to do with how effective you are. I don't need you to be pure and wonderful. I have to be able to open up to you. It scared me when I began to see you as a separate entity. It scares me that I see myself as a separate entity. The woman's group has been helpful. Part of myself was lost, especially since the split with Harold—a softness. I noticed how soft I was in this group. I started to feel good because I didn't want to lose that part of myself—I hadn't killed that part. It's not a situation I'd figure I'd be that way in. I've stopped judging and just pay attention. I feel soft and not frightened—open but not pushing. When I have had these soft feelings I said it must be the real me. Then I realized it was only one part of me—not the real me any more than the tough me is—the real me is all of them. . . . Others see the real you in terms of what they need. No one knows the person better than the person himself. You couldn't feed the data of the entire organism to someone else. It's important that *I* feel and understand me. I was hoping you would. But you couldn't. Anyway, you're not going to be with me the rest of my life. I learned more in resentment and resistance when I realized you would not let me continue in this way. I hated you for destroying this. I felt I didn't have a prayer, like when my mother went away (a traumatic two-week absence when the patient was three years old).

The dream represents her continued resistance to an identification with (transmuting internalization, assimilation of) the mother's strength and capability—her executive functions and valuing functions—since these were so closely associated with her mother's aggression, which was turned against her from time to time. The hatred of the sometimes literally assaultive mother would be experienced as self-hate were she to accept the identification. She will not permit the internal mother to assume control of her internal regulator, so she cannot, and still is dependent upon external supports. She says:

> When I feel hatred to Harold I get the image of my mother's face, and I feel just like her. I feel it as very threatening. It means I'll get hit.

Even though the dream reveals that the changes realized in treatment are still to be worked through, the session itself suggests that this process is in motion. It is important to note that with the renunciation of the idealized image of the self as all good, there is a superego that says, "There's nothing wrong with wanting to be a good person." Her idealization does not reflect the kind of idealization we find with the more primitive organization with self and object splitting, as much as repression of the negative arm of her ambivalence as a defense against intrapsychic conflict. In the more primitive patient one must be careful that in the resolution of the idealized images of self and object, one does not destroy the only existing nuclei of the superego. I have seen more than once how a therapist's efforts to relieve the patient of the pressures of the primitive, punitive superego has led to the premature termination of a now quite psychopathic individual, with a perceived therapeutic sanction for acting out narcissistic rage, the attitude of entitlement. In the patient described above, it was clear that there was a well-developed reasonably mature superego. Those maternal qualities that could not be assimilated into the self were related to the appropriate use of aggression and to issues of self-esteem.

I view the situation as preneurotic insofar as there is not yet a fully integrated, autonomous self, nor is there fully established object constancy. But by and large, this kind of patient looks more neurotic than characterologically impaired. It is more and more my belief that an incomplete resolution of earlier developmental issues underlies all later neurotic disturbances, and that psychotherapy and psychoanalysis must address themselves to this resolution. If such exploration is not undertaken and early developmental impasses are not resolved, treatment may go on and on, with certain isolated derivatives of these impasses continuing to interfere in the person's life and relationships.

I have observed a number of situations in which the identification with the mother is refused in a way that leads to a continued dependent stance vis-à-vis the object. Most often I have found this to be a woman who is dependent upon a man who will provide for her her own disavowed strengths and self-esteem. In the absence of someone to depend on in this manner, the symptom of depression usually develops.

In one instance, the reluctance, or refusal, to internalize maternal competence (her own coping strategies would wax and wane) was accompanied by a parallel, conflicted identification with her depressed and inadequate father. As a child she had allied herself with him in the context of marital schism. The triangulation—heightened by oedipal strivings—the alliance with father against mother, continued intrapsychically, so that insofar as she would begin to do well in her career, the inner experience was one of betrayal of father, betrayal of the identification with the depressed, inadequate father, and she would begin to falter in her work.

She reported two dreams that revealed this struggle. In one she was having intercourse with a man, and she thought that she must not let her father see. And in the next she was trying to find a place to make her father comfortable and awoke relieved, realizing that he was dead and that she didn't have to worry whether he was comfortable. The abandonment of the father—and to some extent the loss of her loving connection with him as a result—led to guilt and depression.

In the situations with both these women, women who were actually extremely competent, able, and decisive, the identification with the strong mother—strong with respect to effectiveness of executive functions and in negotiating the environment—was rejected. In both cases the mother used her aggression against the daughter from time to time, so the aggressive mother was hated from time to time. In the session notes cited above, the patient reports how she feels she is turning into the feared and hated mother. With the second patient the threatened emergence of her own hostile, aggressive impulses led to attacks of severe anxiety. The mother who could use her aggression protectively also used that same aggression against the child. Identification with the protective mother meant identification with the dangerous and hated mother. The capacity to protect the self was not achieved, and the child remained dependent in this manner. The thermostat dream illustrates this.

I must emphasize in both instances there was no object splitting. The mother and other objects could be and were experienced ambivalently. The attempts to idealize the self and the object—the therapist in this instance—was an attempt at repression of the negative feelings to avoid conflict. The significant issue here is the interference with the process of transmuting internalizations. On the basis of a reasonable, mature superego, obviously the process was only partially deficient. This kind of situation can clearly heighten the dangers of the oedipal situation and can complicate its resolution.

The extent to which women who continue to be drawn to the oedipal father in their relationships with men are dependent upon these men, I believe is the outcome of the refusal to identify with the mother in some significant way, so that an integrated self and object constancy are not secured. In more classical analytic terms this may be interpreted as her anger that the mother did not give her a penis and that the preferred identification or alliance is with the father. Yet I have seen enough cases in which it was the mother who was seen as strong and the father as weak and in which that very strength was a danger to the self to suggest that one must look further for the factors that interfered with the process of transmuting internalization to be sure that the interpretation fits the patient instead of trying to make the patient fit the interpretation.

A parallel situation with a male patient showed that the failure to achieve object constancy because of the resistance to identification with the mother also involved a resistance to identification with the father. He was both afraid of the father and deeply ashamed of him, rejecting him as a model. Without the identification with the father to secure his gender identity, resistance to identification with his mother served, in part, to protect his sense of maleness.

Schecter (1968) examines the relationship between identification and individuation. He defines identification as "the means by which part of the psychic structure of one person tends to become like that of another to whom he is emotionally related in a significant way" (p. 50). It is a "relatively enduring modification of the self in the direction of similarity to the object. . . ." He remarks upon Freud's idea that identifications were both out of loss and were substitutive phenomena and Freud's later thoughts (1923) that "it may be that this identification is the sole condition under which the id can give up its objects," that "alteration in character occurs before the object has been given up" (pp. 29, 30).

Schecter concludes:

Identification may then be conceived, at least in part, as growing out of primarily active, relatively conflict-free individuating processes, and as contributing to the ego structure ("strength") required for gradual relinquishing of the more primitive object ties. [p. 63]

Schecter's conclusions are in harmony with the concept that the achievement of object constancy, the culmination of the separation-individuation process, is dependent upon the internalization of (identification with) the object.

He points out that:

During psychotherapy and psychoanalysis, identification is as inevitable as transference love and hostility to which it is obviously and intimately related. . . . [p. 57]

He goes on to remark upon the difference between growth-promoting identifications with the analyst and "the patient's tendency to passive-submissive patterning of his self after an authoritarian model" (p. 58). This is another manifestation of how the relationship with the therapist within the therapeutic matrix (chapter 13) is analogous to the early maternal matrix. Like the early object, the therapist is the mediator of organization. And as the transmuting internalizations of maternal functions result in autonomy vis-à-vis the object, so certain identifications with the therapist bring the patient to eventual termination and an autonomous life.

RAPPROCHEMENT ISSUES IN THE TERMINATION PHASE OF TREATMENT

Rapprochement issues are often evident in the termination phase of treatment. This is demonstrated in the sessions of Miss H. I started seeing her when she was twenty-five years old. She was extremely obese, unkempt, a social isolate, chronically depressed, and abusing alcohol. She was also an underachiever with respect to the work she was doing. She was self-supporting and reliable in her work, however.

I saw Miss H. for seven years in once-weekly, analytic therapy. The last four years were on the couch. Two years prior to termination she gave up alcohol and became active in Alcoholics Anonymous. She could only do this when she stopped identifying the therapist who wanted her to stop drinking with the mother who wanted to deprive her of gratification. By that time she had lost 140 pounds and was no longer unkempt, having analyzed the rage and aggression behind that behavior—what was dubbed "the dirty diaper syndrome."

It became clear that we were moving into the termination phase as her investment in peer relationships and in her schooling started to come into conflict with her involvement in treatment and with her therapist. A termination date was set four months in advance. The following verbatim material is from this period.

My ways of showing love and affection are my mother's ways. I'm getting more physically affectionate. It's coming more naturally. With all these changes—there was a brick wall around me. There's layer after layer—like an onion skin. Why is the pain so present? My father died twenty-six years ago.

I've been mourning him all my life. Not only did I never get that kind of affection—I probably never will. It hurts more—I'm not going to get another father. (Do you think your thoughts about his death may be related to the thoughts of ending therapy?) It'll be a hard separation for me. . . . Why do I find this so hard to say? I have a great deal of affection for you—part friend and older sister—and I've come to rely on you. If it gets too bad, part of me is saying, "You've gone most of the way—you have to stand on your own feet." It's like an adolescent separation. I'm a long way from the person I was when I came in. (Yes.) I remind myself that I'm not alone, though I have to stand on my own and do it on my own.

With the structuralization of the ego and the internalization of the good-enough therapist-object, the real therapist can be perceived rather than the transferential preoedipal mother.

I'm going to miss you. [Tears.] At the meeting the other day there was a theme of loneliness. One friend wants to visit her mother and be taken care of. I feel David's presence and have the image of the coffin going out the door. I haven't accepted my father's and mother's death. I really am alone. But I don't have to do everything alone. I have friends. In reality my mother couldn't help me today. I've been thinking about the hospital where I was when I was eighteen [She had been hospitalized for six months for depression.] (Why do you think you dream about the hospital now?) I felt safe there. I hated it. I'm feeling frightened, so I go back to when I felt safe. It was a pleasant prison—nothing was expected of me. . . . I'm frightened of leaving therapy. I have a lot of fear and don't know what to do with it. (So your dream represents your wish to regress and be taken care of.) That's in my unconscious mind. Consciously I want to prove that I can do well in school, get a new job, leave therapy, make friends. Maybe knowing what I have to do will help. There won't be any miracles. My deepest goal is to live more happily and comfortably with myself. . . . Everything seems related (related to leaving mother and safety. You also seem to be afraid that mother will be angry that you want to leave her, so you make money an excuse.) Rather than say I don't want to come. I don't feel the same anger to her. (Any thoughts why?) Because I do feel I don't need her because I feel better about myself. I've let myself see my own contribution and realize it wasn't as one-sided as I thought it was. You told me many times that when I can stop being angry I could enjoy the pleasant memories with her.

As she relinquishes the last vestiges of the split between the good and bad object and achieves a unified image, she is also able to do the same vis-à-vis the therapist and can thus assimilate that which was good into herself as part of the separation-individuation process. Many early memories also emerged during this time. The theme of the need to regain control over the abandoning object emerged in the form of memories and would come out with respect to the therapist as well. Even though it was her own idea and wish to leave treatment, it still felt, at times, as though the therapist was leaving her.

It's so clear to me now. Until I was eight years old I wouldn't wash or dress myself. My mother had to do it. She tended to my physical needs. (You found a way to force her to do that.) Yep! (And if you imagine that now I am unavailable, you think about stopping taking care of yourself.) Yes. You have so much power. My heart is beating fast. It's so ancient, the feelings. . . . I can't deal with the feelings now. I have a class tonight. It's funny—I'm remembering that it was at this exact period that my mother took me to school and they said I needed psychological help. This was my reversion period. The school recommended someone. They took my mother but she wouldn't keep it up. She told me after that it made her depressed. But she *was* depressed and angry, and she had to go to work. It wasn't her fault. She had to survive. I guess it doesn't matter whose fault it was; it's how I reacted.

At this point she is able to form a more realistic and integrated image of her mother, and thus to differentiate fully from it. The mother's anger and depression had nothing to do with her, and she was not the bad counterpart of it.

Last night there was a fire down the block. I was scared. When I was little, there was a fire in our house. Mama put a coat on me and her. We stood in the street while the firemen battled the blaze. I was so sleepy. She dragged me downstairs. It was cold—midwinter. I don't know why I remember that. It makes me want to cry. It was very frightening. Mama was very calm and did what she had to do. (And last night you were aware that she wasn't there to take care of you?) Yup. [Crying.] . . . to reassure me that everything would be O.K. I remember her being so strong, to the last years of her life. She never seemed frightened. She was at her best in a crisis and knew exactly what to do. (I wonder if all this has anything to do with our coming termination?) That's another separation for me. I'm lying here feeling that it hurts that I have to live the rest of my life without my mother. It seems to—a lot of—toward you. The Pillar of Strength.

And three weeks later.

I'm telling myself I'm not the only one sloshing through slush. Big deal! We all do it. It has nothing to do with me. I don't have to like it—just accept it. I have to face that I don't have control of what happens after I take an action. I don't like the feeling of powerlessness, having to depend upon what the other feels. I spoke to a woman who left therapy a month ago. I asked her how it felt. She refused to deal with it until the last session and found herself turning the next week to go to his office.

It's frightening, but it feels good. It's like a certificate that I'm grown up. I feel a little less panicked. . . . Something's going on. I feel like sitting up. I remember talking to someone about you saying it was no use competing with her. She'll always be ten years ahead. Do I feel competitive right now? It must be. (When did it start?) When we were talking about that business with love. (And I put what you said in different words.) That could be it. I was groping to express it, and you were able to say it—you said it for me. (And you are angry at me for doing that.) I guess I am. My head says that's her job. The whole thing with competitive feelings came up. That's how I'd like to be someday, talking about you. I have some idea what you're like, though it's in my head. I say to people, talk about the power of example in A.A. It's funny, now I feel sad. I don't know where it's from. In the program they say if you admire someone, don't develop their life-style, just their attitude, their viewpoint on life. That's what I mean about you as a role model. I don't want to be a therapist and have a house in the country like you do. I don't want the details. I do want to feel what I feel you have going for you inside. (I guess this relates to our ending too.) I suspect *everything* has to do with that. There's a real feeling of loss.

As Miss K. differentiates more fully, she begins to assimilate aspects of the idealized object into her self in a healthy way, quite unlike the gross identification that we see with some more primitive patients. Her individuation-promoting identification with the therapist set the stage for the achievement of identity and object constancy.

Dealing with loss and its attendant sadness is part of every step toward independence. Miss H. has dreams.

Grief and loss, grief and loss. It must relate to you. A person leaving a daughter. I turn it around and feel like I'm losing my mother for the second time. What else could the dreams refer to? Someone is stricken with grief because she is losing her daughter. Someone I spoke to about this is on a perpetual search for a mother. I said I don't want a mother. I realize I don't look for one because I've made you my mother.

In her next to last session she went on:

I'm increasingly anxious as we get closer to termination. I have the same dream—a couple who loses their daughter. The husband talks about how to cope with it. You asked last week why I had to tell you everything that's going wrong. *I* decided but I'm feeling that it's you who is throwing me out. (So if you can make me bad enough you won't mind leaving.) I can't make you dead if I owe you money. I decided that at the last session I would hug and kiss you whether you liked it or not. [Laughs.] (What's the laugh about?) I always had trouble saying, "Gee, I really like you." I made it sound like an act of aggression. I feel saner somehow, now that I've said that. I feel I can accept not being a little girl—I can accept being a woman and taking care of myself. I have a sadness that I'll never be able to make amends with my mother in a direct way. Now I don't have to pull her memories over the coals. [Telephone call, which I answer briefly.] Why is there always a telephone call in the middle of a session? (Always?) I like to think that at the very least I'm getting your undivided attention. You could be thinking about what you're having for supper. I wonder about this anger. I want to push you away so that I won't have to deal with leaving. I'm turning you into a bad mother. (It also involves giving up the claim to total, undivided attention.) Yeah! It's a form of power—hard to give up. The more I try to be in control, the less I am. There are better mechanisms for dealing with loneliness—to admit I need people, I give up a lot of power, or the illusion of power. I'm giving up the illusion of power for the reality of friendship. . . . I seem to be emphasizing my independence—both ways of dealing with separation. . . . I've been tempted to put on make-up—part of my self-improvement program. I still go from one extreme to another with my self-image, but the extremes are closer together. I'm permitted to be imperfect, to be fallible. I've struggled so hard with myself—I don't have to be right all the time. There are no extreme highs or lows.

Issues of relinquishing omnipotent control and the integration of the split between good and bad object are rapprochement issues that emerge in the termination phase of Miss K.'s treatment. She is able to hold on to the loving feelings toward the good object, even in the face of symbolic abandonment. She had dealt with separations before by making the object "dead." The gradual internalization of the good object, the step toward object constancy, is now possible for her. Her chronic depression is a thing of the past. Now she experiences a reactive sadness that is appropriate, related to the reality of her life, and that can end as the process of internalization goes on. Paralleling normal development, the end of the rapprochement phase brings the individual to the stage of object constancy and a well-established identity. This is not a phase but an end point in one line of development. There will be a further elaboration of both self and object structures throughout the rest of life, but at this point structural stability has been attained.

Mahler, Pine, and Bergman (1975) note that toward the end of the rapprochement phase of development in young children "the vicissitudes of their individuation process were changing so rapidly that they were no longer mainly *phase specific, but individually very distinct, and different from one child to the other*" (p. 102). What became important now was not the realization of separateness per se, but the impact of that realization on the mother-child relationship and on the father-child relationship, as well as the integration of the child's total personality. Mahler notes that

this very important "final phase" of rapprochement as intrapsychic development seemed to be the summation of the solution of the many maturational developmental tasks that each individual child had arrived at during the course of his particular subphase development. . . . [p. 104]

Chapter 7

THE CONSOLIDATION OF IDENTITY AND OBJECT CONSTANCY

The overall process of object relations development (along with the general ego development to which it is central) ideally culminates in libidinal (emotional) object constancy (Hartmann 1952) and a consolidation of individuality (Mahler, Pine, and Bergman 1975). Burgner and Edgcumbe (1972) understand the concept of object constancy as "the individual's capacity to differentiate between objects and to maintain a relationship to one specific object regardless of whether needs are being satisfied or not . . ." (p. 315). It is the "capacity to recognize and tolerate loving and hostile feelings toward the same object; the capacity to keep feelings centered on a specific object; and the capacity to value an object for attributes other than its function of satisfying needs" (p. 328). Mahler describes object constancy in terms of the internal good object, the maternal image that is psychically available to the child just as the actual mother was previously available for sustenance, comfort, and love.

Mahler, Pine, and Bergman (1975) point out that "the constancy of the object implies more than the maintenance of the representation of the absent love object . . ." (p. 110). Good and bad object-representations become integrated into a single, unified representation. With this the hatred felt when the object is experienced as bad is tempered by the positive feelings associated with the same object under other circumstances. When the object is experienced as nongratifying, it will not be rejected or exchanged for another. When absent, the object will be longed for and not hated.

These authors comment that object constancy seems to come about during the third year, and that with this achievement the mother can be substituted for in part by the now reliable internal self-image. They also point out that in the third year object constancy is still a "rather fluid and reversible achievement. It is still . . . a matter of degree. It is dependent on the context of the many other developmental factors, the prevailing ego state, and the environmental affective response of the moment" (p. 112).

The further delineation and enrichment of self-representation goes on at this time, and the establishment of individuality is the developmental task that is paired with the achievement of object constancy. Mahler, Pine, and Bergman note that this subphase is "characterized by unfolding of complex cognitive functions: verbal communication, fantasy, and reality testing" (p. 117).

The self-representation is also enriched with the assimilation of maternal functions into the self. Giovacchini (1979) remarks:

> The connection I am focusing upon is between the self-representation and the maternal introject or . . . the nurturing modality. The evaluation of the ego's functional capacity becomes incorporated into the identity system and contributes to the self's feelings of confidence, security, and esteem. Thus the registration of caretaking activities becomes an important factor in both the structuring and equilibrium of the self-representation. [p. 276]

The self-representation also comes to include access to the autonomous functions and the sense of mastery that they provide. In certain situations the autonomous functions are instead assimilated into a pathological, grandiose self with resulting disorders of self-esteem and deficits of object relatedness (chapter 10).

The end of the separation-individuation process is marked by the assimilation of maternal (or parental) functions into the self even as the object is separated out as fully differentiated from the self. This involves the assimilation of nurturant and executive modalities (Giovacchini 1979) and the assimilation of the imperatives that lead to the structuring of the superego.

Schecter (1979) speaks of the formation of the superego as "the organization of experience in the imperative mode." The ego ideal and its associated affect—shame—is paralleled by the conscience and its associated affect—guilt. Shame accompanies experiences of failure or inadequacy, while guilt accompanies transgressions of the shalts and shalt-nots. Schecter describes masochism as the interplay between the self vis-à-vis the loving and persecutory superegos. Like the masochism that reflects the externalization of object splitting in a triangular fashion in a more primitive character structure (chapter 8), masochism vis-à-vis the superego is also a triangular situation, albeit now with conflicting aspects of the self.

Giovacchini (1979) states that "the formation of the self-representation accompanies a consolidation of the general ego organization" (p. 269).

Introjects have been differentiated from the self and their significant functions assimilated into the self. The synthetic function of the ego is not overridden by unassimilable, traumatic states. Affects and instinctual drives are structured and integrated not only into a cohesive self-representation but also vis-a-vis the object, and are subject to both ego and superego controls. The autonomous functions are conflict-free, are also integrated into a reality-related and object-related self-representation, and are a source of realistic self-esteem as well as reliably available for the mastery of reality demands. Reality testing and the sense of reality are secured. The thought process is not dominated or disrupted by primary process thinking but is consistent with reality and logic. And there are adequate adaptive defenses against anxiety. Anxiety acts as a signal for defense rather than constituting an overwhelming trauma.

CLINICAL ISSUES

By and large, the individual who has fully achieved both object constancy and a well-integrated, nonconflicted identity or individuality is not likely to present as a patient. One does meet with issues of object constancy and individuality in patients who still manifest the "waxing and waning" described by Mahler et al. Dependency and depression and/or shame are likely to be issues. These were described in the previous chapter, also representing as they do issues of the end of the rapprochement phase of the separation-individuation process.

Mrs. N., the patient who reported the thermostat dream, was clearly approaching termination in the following session.

I can see that I am many faceted—the angry or aggressive me, the soft me, the scared me. They can all coexist. I don't have to see from the viewpoint of one or the other in the general scheme of things. I'm finding that this coexistence is the main reason I feel at peace. I don't feel ripped apart—because first I feel this and then I feel that. I feel the whole kettle can be there. It's a mix, and I can accept it—that I can have thoughts of violence and hatred, and accepting these I can then have more peaceful and joyous feelings. Mainly I feel I can take care of myself. I feel very good about myself. I can cope with things as they come up. Something very different has happened. (You seem to feel a real shift in how you experience yourself.) I am very grateful to you for this. This working on the business with me and my mother I believe is the major factor in all this. I think about her with her strength and her meanness, and I can separate her from me and don't think of her with rancor. I see her, and I see me. What I feel, think, experience, and interpret is *me*! What's from nature and what's from nurture doesn't matter. The fact that what I have is an identification with her doesn't make me her. It has nothing to do with good or bad, but if it works for me. The choices are mine. No one can maneuver me into anything I don't want. The way I have worked with you and with myself has given me a lot of self-esteem. It was my courage and my good sense in sticking with you.

Having resolved the conflict around identifying with the ambivalently experienced mother, she can complete the process of internalization of maternal functions, and she can fully differentiate what is her from what is her mother so that she does not have to ward off the identifications from this point of view.

Giovacchini (1978) emphasizes the importance of separating the "functional modality" from the person who had performed that function (p. 70).

> The self-representation, secure in its autonomy, feels enhanced as it is capable of successfully adapting to the needs of the internal world and the exigencies of the outer world. [p. 71]

At the same time, the patient can differentiate her contribution from the contribution of the therapist, resolving any residual idealization of the therapist. In so doing, her self-esteem becomes solidified around the real and separate individual she now experiences herself to be. She is no longer dependent upon a strong other (a man) to provide that self-esteem and to provide security. She has taken the final step in the separation-individuation process and has reached the point of object constancy, of a well-grounded identity, and a healthy self-esteem.

The waxing and waning of object constancy and a less than fully consolidated identity make the child vulnerable to the stresses of the oedipal situation, and the stresses of the oedipal situation contribute to the waning. Regressive flight aimed at protecting the dependent bond with the needed object may also activate other preoedipal manifestations. The regression may necessitate mobilization of more primitive narcissistic defenses against the anxiety and shame that goes with the regression, as in the case of Mr. B. This sometimes makes the diagnosis hazy, but even in the context of grandiose fantasies, the higher levels of organization and integration are maintained. That is, the grandiosity in this instance will constitute a defense rather than a central component of the character structure. As Giovacchini (1979) comments: "We have to examine many character traits in terms of their defensive potential as well as manifesting ego defects" (p. 270). As I commented earlier, the child does not have to invent its defenses; rather are

they drawn from earlier states that occur normally or spontaneously in the course of development.

Mr. B., a successful executive in his mid-thirties, could not
establish an ongoing relationship with a woman, his presenting
complaint. In this setting he behaved dependently with a pseudo-
incompetence aimed at mobilizing the woman's caretaking response.
He was murderously competitive at sports. He had friends, a well-
developed conscience, a firm sense of identity and boundaries of
the self, satisfaction in work, and ego interests and activities. There
was no object splitting, and he clearly could recognize and tolerate
ambivalence. However, from time to time his self-esteem would be
devastated by humiliation that went with the regression vis-à-vis
the object, and he recovered through the use of grandiose fantasies
that were fed by his real-life success. There was an observing ego, a
reliable working alliance, and a minimum of acting out, although
in the early stage of treatment his need to maintain iron control of
the treatment process constituted a formidable problem. The need
to control and the grandiosity were reminiscent of some narcissistic
patients, but the other aspects of ego integration mitigated against
this diagnosis.

The mother's habitual nudity both excited and frightened him as
a child. Passivity, inadequacy, and denial of sexuality protected
him from the danger of being suffocated by his "custodial" mother,
and the female genital became the concretized focus of the threat of
suffocation and symbolized both oedipal and preoedipal dangers.
Aware of the sexual conflict in the transference and its relevance to
his relationship with his "residual mother," he commented:

> I can't be comfortably abandoned with someone when I still
> have these conflicts unresolved. I have to be able to resolve
> them to be able to view separation not as abandonment. The
> unresolved conflict binds me to that person.

At this point the interpretation was made that he could not take
his mother's love and affection inside him as long as it was sexualized and those feelings were taboo. In other words, the oedipal

strivings constituted a barrier to the achievement of object constancy. He commented further:

> The love I wanted from my mother I got. But the price was anxiety. So I can't move in and move out of that love because I'm suspended by the anxiety.

Mr. B.'s remarks recall Freud's observation (1923) that "identification is the sole condition under which the id can give up its objects" (p. 29). And as Schecter (1968) adds, identification is "required for the gradual relinquishing of the more primitive object ties" (p. 63).

Object relations development—the development of self- and object-representations—is essentially hierarchical in nature. Each successive stage is colored by the preexisting character structure, and the character structure is modified with the achievement of each new developmental task. Clearly there can be no object constancy and no consolidation of individuality if there is any significant preexisting pathology of the developmental process and a corresponding defect in structure. With repair of the damaged ego in treatment, ideally the patient progresses to the point where the issues of the final step of the separation-individuation process are confronted and worked through.

The developmental timetable introduces the Oedipus complex at the point at which the child is emerging as a separate entity vis-à-vis the now separate object. What happens to the Oedipus complex when issues of separation-individuation are still unresolved? The interaction of oedipal and preoedipal issues needs to be evaluated in each patient.

Chapter 8

INTERACTION OF OEDIPAL AND PREOEDIPAL ISSUES

THEORETICAL CONSIDERATIONS

What about the Oedipus complex? Where does it fit in theoretically and clinically with a developmental, object relations point of view?

If we keep in mind that any new developmental phase or event takes place within the context of a preexisting character structure, we can expect that the form and expression of oedipal issues will vary from child to child and later from patient to patient. At the emergence of oedipal strivings one child may still be struggling with the task of differentiation from an engulfing mother; another may be consumed with rage at an abandoning mother; and a more evolved child may have negotiated the tasks of separation and individuation, attaining a modicum of object constancy. The impact of those oedipal strivings will be different for each of these children, and the impact of the preexisting character will contribute to the shape of the Oedipus complex for each of them as well. The impact of oedipal striving will also be different for the little boy and little girl. While the little boy is drawn regressively toward the preoedipal mother, the little girl may be propelled precipitously away from her in a manner that interferes with the final steps in the achievement of object constancy.

Shapiro (1977) writes: "The oedipus complex is presented as a universal, developmentally determined mental organization that incorporates pregenital factors in a new hierarchic structure" (p. 559). He says further: "With maturation there is a discontinuous hierarchic organization such that structuralization at each stage reorganizes the mnemic traces of the prior stages. Thus, the oedipal constellation may supersede earlier experiences rendering them less 'toxic' than their previous level might suggest" (p. 565). Here Shapiro represents a view that minimizes the impact of the pre-existing psychic structure, concluding "that severe character pathologies show a variation in oedipal themes cannot be denied. That they are different from oedipal themes in neurotics, except in their intensity, rigidity, and external instability, is questionable" (p. 575).

Shapiro says, in effect, that the pregenital character is asssimilated into and transformed by the Oedipus complex. It is my view that later stages of hierarchical development are equally—at the very least—assimilated into and transformed by earlier ones; that oedipal themes in character disorders are indeed different from those observed in neurosis and that, in some instances, the deficits of structure abort the development of the Oedipus complex.

The oedipal situation is, by definition, triangular. The preoedipal situation is dyadic, at least in its earlier stages. Without some degree of differentiation from the mother of symbiosis there cannot be a triangle. Furthermore, there is a requirement not only of a differentiated self but also of two differentiated (from each other) others. A third person (father) may represent predominantly a threat to the symbiotic tie in which instance the danger is not that of castration but of object loss and consequent annihilation of the self. The impact of oedipal instinctive strivings on the little girl in this instance can only be traumatic, as in the case of Miss R. described below. They do not, as Shapiro suggests, supersede the earlier experiences, rendering them less toxic. They are toxic in and of themselves! The impact on the little boy, on the other hand, may be to reinforce the sense of merger and threaten not only psychic differentiation but physical differentiation and gender identity as well. In this situation we may see the defense of schizoid detachment and reliance on the grandiose self.

In cases of pathological narcissism with self and object splitting, the triangular arrangement may be between the self and externalized good and bad objects. This may be acted out within the oedipal triangle itself or in any triangle in which the good-object image is projected onto one individual and the bad-object image is projected onto another. In this instance we have not so much rivalry and the fear of punishment—although that may also occur—as a masochistic relationship with a bad, persecuting, frustrating object alongside an idealizing relationship with a good, rescuing object. Despite oedipal overtones, the early preoedipal object relations situation still obtains and is acted out with a cast of three. The onset of the oedipal period brings about a sexualization of this object relations theme, but it is still essentially one of narcissistic investment of the object(s) and has little to do with a true triangle consisting of well-differentiated individuals. This situation lends itself readily to acting out, and the therapist and therapy are often assimilated into the script. The case of Miss T. is an example of this kind of clinical problem.

In a more evolved character, we may see the impact of residual, unresolved narcissistic issues that color the oedipal situation and that must be tended to before there can be a resolution of the Oedipus complex. Miss F. is an example of this kind of patient.

Assuming that preoedipal and oedipal factors affect one another in a reciprocal fashion and that character structure in terms of self-representation and the quality of object relations is the more fundamental issue, a developmental diagnosis of every patient will include a formulation of this interaction.

OEDIPAL ISSUES IN THE BORDERLINE PATIENT

Miss R., a young, highly intelligent, professional woman, used detachment as a defense against loss of self through merger. This detachment left her feeling empty and dead. She seemed almost oblivious of her father. Despite repressed yearnings for emotional contact with him, he had little valence for her. Her relationship with her boyfriend, like that with her mother, was colored by the

struggle for separateness, her detachment, and the defensive grandiosity that protected her from the sense of object loss that accompanied the detachment. The nascent Oedipus complex as revealed
once early in treatment by an expression of these yearnings, was
aborted as an outcome of the combination of maternal demands for
symbiotic mirroring and the consequent structural deficit in
differentiation, the father's emotional detachment and unavailability, and the trauma of oedipal stirrings. She recalled, ". . . the
feeling I have of my head being in a vise and not allowed to look
around, of being forced to keep my eyes and concentration in one
place. I think of when I was very little, I got up early. In the living
room where my father was putting his socks on, I saw his penis. He
realized it and covered up and told me not to look." For this
little girl, preexisting structural pathology—the failure of
differentiation—also interfered with the development of a set of
differentiated objects vis-à-vis the self, while the oedipal anxiety
reinforced the clinging to the symbiotic mother. The following is
from the eightieth session.

Recently when I've called my parents I didn't make any effort
to chat any more. I'm taking the offensive of what my father
does. He always says, "Talk to Mother." Now I just say, "Hi,
where's Mommy?" I have a sense that my struggles are with
my mother. I feel they exclude my father. In my mind I'm saying, "Wait your turn. I want to work all this out with my
mother." In a way, thinking of them separately seems a big
change. To separate them and think of them in relation to me
is very different. In the past I've been conscious of my
mother's relationship with me. My father was lumped onto the
side. Now the picture I get is one of an equilateral triangle but
the focus is on my mother. I don't consider the other. It didn't
used to be like that. I guess I feel that as I pull away from
mother, I also pull away from him. Mother—defining each of
us—with my father I have a feeling of pushing him into the
background, and am feeling a lot of hostility to him right now.
I think of him as having skewed my mother's reactions to me.
It's easier to resolve my relationship to her without him

around. I also think of my father as very delicate. I'm aware of the detachment, but I get the image of a brick turret. Whatever is inside is a vacuum. What is not a vacuum is very delicate—very fragile.

Perception of the father seemed to relate primarily to his impact on the mother and her mothering behavior. About a month and a half before the session recounted above, Miss R.'s therapist's husband died suddenly. A dream reported upon resumption of sessions after a two-week absence was very short. "I dreamed about a kitchen. That's all I remember." Her associations were as follows.

I think of my childhood in terms of the kitchen. I hung around the kitchen where my mother was. I guess it would be the testing ground of whether I could live up to her, to match what she was in the kitchen. I also associate the kitchen in the dream with family dinners. There was a round table there. What stands out for me is that my father wasn't home on Monday or Wednesday because he was working. I guess I think of the kitchen more in terms of those dinners. My mother would have plainer dinners, scrambled eggs, when he wasn't coming home. (I wonder if there is some connection with my husband's not coming home. Maybe you will be wondering what kind of dinner you will be having here.) Possibly. I was pretty sure he was your husband, even with different names. I wanted to believe it was somebody I didn't know. (Crying.) It upsets me that it wasn't. I guess thinking about what else the dinner without my father meant was that there was a relaxing of tension. I didn't have to perform as much. I don't know why the scrambled eggs were so vivid. (Did you like them?) Yes, [laughs] but it wasn't appropriate for dinner. It was a declaration that things were not going on as they should. My father wasn't there.

Her father's historical failure was that of failing to provide the secondary attachment that would have facilitated Miss R.'s separation and individuation from mother—the earliest task of the father. Her failure to differentiate herself from mother was paralleled by her failure to differentiate mother from father. "My father was lumped onto the side." The Oedipus complex requires three separately perceived beings. As a result of her analytic work, which has focused on the issue of differentiation, she approaches the possibility of a true oedipal situation. "Now the picture I get is one of an equilateral triangle, but the focus is on my mother." She senses that there is business with father, but postpones this as it still has less salience for her than the issues with the engulfing mother. With the emergence of the triangle as boundaries between self and object become more clearly drawn, we catch a glimpse of the latent oedipal issues.

Miss R. related a dream in the seventy-nineth session that was clearly in this direction. This was the only dream she refused to associate to, saying it made her too anxious. She says in effect, "I cannot look at my feelings about my father until I have secured my separateness from my mother." Indeed, she gives good anterospective supervision on this point, recognizing that the oedipal pull would threaten the newly won and still tentative and fluctuating boundaries of the self. It is interesting that as she becomes aware of her father as an individual separate from mother, she projects onto his shadowy identity the image of her own buried and fragile self. Whereas the merger with mother entails an annihilation of self with the introjection of the maternal image, merger with father entails the projection of the schizoid self image onto him.

It is quite probable that there are many female patients who bring issues of incomplete differentiation to their oedipally charged relationships with men. Analysis of the blatant oedipal material will fail if the tasks of separation and individuation vis-à-vis the mother or, transferentially, the therapist, are not tended to first.

Pathological narcissism, whether in the context of a borderline character or a narcissistic personality, will distort the quality of the oedipal situation in a variety of ways. Miss L., a homosexual woman in her early thirties, also showed structural deficits with respect to differentiation. Narcissistic demands and the rage that went with their frustration were more central to her pathology than in the case of Miss R. Miss R.'s detachment and dependence upon the grandiose self precluded the emergence of the idealizing transference with its potential disappointments.

Miss L. played out, over and over, the scenario of seducing a woman away from her husband or boyfriend, acting out each time her need to regain omnipotent control over the needed, idealized object. Father was primarily a competitor for mother and must be defeated to protect her from the danger of object loss. The rage evoked when she lost omnipotent control threatened her connection with the good object. The borderline aspects of her object relationships were clear when she would experience annihilation and panic under the impact of object loss. She was unable to tolerate the male physically because he was "alien" and did not permit the total mirroring that she needed to feel connected with the object—the developmental basis for her homosexuality.

Miss L. had previously been in treatment with a male analyst for several years. He regarded her homosexuality as a neurotic symptom, a flight from oedipal dangers, and this was the focus of her treatment. During this time she had rage outbursts and was hospitalized several times for depression.

The oedipal dangers in this situation, however, were specifically colored by the preoedipal, developmental deficits. That is, the father with whom she did eventually develop a loving relationship might seduce her away from the mother with whom she was still symbiotically bound. Many women deny attachment to mother under the pull of the Oedipus complex and bring the dependency wishes of the rapprochement phase to the father and, as an adult, to men in general. But in the case of Miss L., this step could not be taken since the loss of mother and the connection with her would have meant the annihilation of the self. This was the same danger that confronted Miss R., but in this instance there was an emotional relationship with the father—although it was too little and too late to facilitate earlier differentiation and insufficient to counteract her mother's infantilizing seduction. She was still tying her daughter's shoes when the latter was fourteen years old. Steps toward autonomy were punished even as an adult with disapproval and withdrawal of love. Because of the structural deficit the Oedipus complex was not able to bring about the kind of hierarchical

reorganization suggested by Shapiro. Instead the instinctual strivings were assimilated into the undifferentiated self-object representation with a consequent picture of homosexuality in a borderline
character structure.

Much of the reparative work with Miss L. consisted of the
activation and reinforcement of the autonomous functions (interests and talents) and of her ambitions, all of which had been
renounced in the service of maintenance of the symbiotic bond.
Under the threat of object loss with the rapprochement crisis,
further differentiation was also compromised. The therapeutic relationship enabled her to develop her interests, talents, and ambitions within the context of object relatedness and to assimilate them
into her self-representation, promoting and supporting further
differentiation. She is now on an extended vacation from treatment
and relates to the therapist from afar as the good mother of
rapprochement. She makes contact once or twice a year, mean-
while developing a firmer sense of who she is and what she can do.
On another level the relationship from afar protects the relationship
from the extreme anger she experiences with too much wanting and
thus, too much frustration. The sexualization of the relationship
with mother sets the stage for an inherently greater potential for
frustration, both narcissistic and sexual. She thinks that she may
return to treatment at a later date, that there is still work to be
done. But by and large, the borderline issues are less debilitating
and structuralization seems to be continuing.

OBJECT SPLITTING AND THE OEDIPUS COMPLEX:
THE MASOCHISTIC TRIANGLE

In 1975, I wrote of object splitting:

Where self-object merger experiences are significantly discrep-
ant, usually reflecting maternal ambivalence, synthesizing
them is a task too monumental for the infantile ego, and both
kinds of experience will acquire a compelling salience. . . .
The origins of the split in the relationship with the object, and

thus in the self, arises from the disparity of experience which is too extensive for the child to form into an integrated, single, self-other experience. To separate out of the dual symbiosis would require two parallel processes, since integration at this stage of perceptual-cognitive development is impossible.

Should the differentiation of self from non-self be from the bad object only, the merger with the good object remains and will be the basis for later attempts to establish symbiotic relationships with idealized others, alongside a paranoid view of the now separated-out bad mother-world.

Should the differentiation of self be from the good object only, we might be likely to find an idealized view of the external world alongside a tendency to seek out a symbiotic relationship with a bad or hurtful other, a possible aetiological factor in masochism. [p. 100]

In her comprehensive review of the literature on masochism, Panken (1973) summarizes the important formulations of Berliner and Menaker.

Their contribution briefly lies in the following: emphasis on object relations, with particular stress on preoedipal experiences; view of masochism as a defense rather than as predominantly based on instinctual processes, i.e., as defense against awareness of the early deprivation and therefore, as a means of avoiding separation; perception that it is not one's own sadism but rather the sadism of the love object that is turned against the self; and the debunking of the accretion of thinking concerning the inherent guilt of the child for instinctual aggressions, placing responsibility on parents whose ambivalent attitudes initially set up the sadomasochistic interactions. [pp. 60–61]

These conclusions are consistent with a view of masochism as an acting out of the intrapsychic split between the good and bad object within the context of a triangle. This acting out requires a cast of three: the bad, persecutory, frustrating object, the good, rescuing object, and the good self.

The tenacity of the bond with the bad object contrasts sharply with the rather indiscriminate and interchangeable nature of the "designated" good object. The issue of designation versus attachment is highlighted by the easy interchangeability of such people. Relationships with sequential therapists may go through a predictable series of steps in which each fails to live up to the designated role and is discarded. This contrasts with the narcissistic personality described by Kohut (1971) who projects both bad object and idealized object-representations onto the single therapist—that is, within a dyadic set-up. Other than the manner in which the split becomes manifest and the kinds of defenses used against the anxieties inherent in the situation, the masochistic character and the narcissistic personality are very similar in character structure. Masochism may be indicative of a character disorder rather than a neurosis.

In the masochistic patient the good object serves the critical function of maintaining the existence of the good self. A significant aspect of being the designated good object is to function as proxy for the rage that the good self must not experience lest it become the bad self and therefore subject to the hate directed at the bad object with whom it is still symbiotically bound and identified. I have observed that very few (if any) masochistic individuals suffer in silence. They rather characteristically seek out support, comfort, or as they often refer to it, "validation" from others, often from their therapists. Tapping into the archaic, unconscious anger of the child-victim of the designated good object, the masochistic individual is often quite successful in mobilizing the listener's anger toward the bad object. This has two important defensive functions: one is to make the anger acceptable to the superego and the other is to avoid the anxiety of intrapsychic conflict.

The patient avoids having to face the depths of his or her own bad self anger with its destructive potential since, now "validated," it is experienced as morally justified and can therefore be assimilated into the good self. The individual can also avoid the conflict inherent in the experience of ambivalence toward the object. Externalizing the negative pole, the hate for the bad object, into the designated good object, who becomes the container for his rage (Langs 1976), he then experiences only the positive, loving feelings toward the early object. Thus, the internal conflict is converted into an external one. The listener (therapist) may actively urge the individual to break off the relationship with this obviously destructive person. The bond is then defended on the basis of its importance and the love that can now be felt for the object.

In frustration at the failure of the patient to make any progress and with a growing sense of impotence, the anger of the therapist, which has been mobilized toward the bad object, may now be turned on the frustrating patient. This may set a new cycle in motion in which the therapist becomes identified with the bad, persecutory object. The masochistic patient is likely to deal with the disappointment in the therapist by complaining about his insensitivity to friends, enlisting their support, and again, validation—even their advice to change therapists. One can identify a chain of triangles in which the same theme is endlessly played out.

The continuing acting out of the split in a manner that enmeshes therapy and the therapist within this structure renders treatment useless. The split must be confronted quite directly, and the way it is externalized and acted out must be analyzed. If the therapist gets caught up with "supporting the patient's self-assertion" against the bad object or even actively supporting his anger he is no longer a therapist. He is the designated rescuing object participating in the acting out. To the extent that the therapist departs at any time from a stance of neutrality, he or she is likely to get caught up in this scenario.

I have noted that all such patients present a history of a ready-designated good object who gave the child support against the bad mother. It has been grandmothers, neighbor ladies, and, more difficult to disentangle, good oedipal daddies. In the latter situation the playing out of the split gets caught up in oedipal issues and becomes highly sexualized. Yet in the analytic work one must not become enamored of the ready oedipal material. The acting out and the sexualization of the split in the object-representation, as well as the split in the self, is fundamental and must be the focus of the earlier analytic work.

We can see that the developmental set-up itself, the fact that oedipal strivings pull the little girl away from mother toward father, makes this defense more readily available to her than to the little boy. She can more readily triangulate the intrapsychic structure in external reality. The little boy, in contrast, is drawn regressively toward the preoedipal mother by his oedipal strivings. The fact that moral masochism is found more in females can be understood from this point of view.

For the first two years of life, Miss T. lived with her mother, aunts, and grandmother. Mother was a chronically depressed and narcissistic woman. Father returned to the home when the patient was two years old at which time her parents formed a separate household. He related to her in a loving and teasing manner. Tickling was one of their favorite games. She was described as a difficult child subject to tantrums and anxious, clinging behavior.

Problems of integration because of the early multiple mothering were the focus in the first major phase of treatment. Structuralization was achieved through the relationship with the therapist. At one time Miss T. referred to her therapist in a dream as "her glue."

The pattern of her becoming enmeshed with emotionally unavailable men, coupled with her endless, querulous complaining about them became evident. With the progress in integration, eventually this pattern could be confronted. It is my firm belief that when there are problems at many developmental levels, attention must be paid first to the earlier ones if the individual is to have the structural equipment, as it were, to deal with the more complex issues of later stages of development.

In a way Miss T. needed the bad object to allow her unintegrated bad self a cohesive existence, since they were still symbiotically bound. With no bad object, the bad self as a structure was annihilated and the rage that had been assimilated into it would be experienced as disorganizing. Thus she would not be able to give up the bad object until she could let herself experience her bad self and begin to integrate it with the good self-representation. This would also facilitate the overall integration of the anger toward the frustrating object and subject it to the ameliorating influences of the positive feelings. The structuring of affect and impulse is essential to the development of ego controls. The split within the triangle, between mother and father, between the persecutory and frustrating relationship and the comforting, validating relationship, paralleled the intrapsychic split between good self and the undifferentiated bad self-object. It helped her repress the anger of the bad self, substituting for it the righteous indignation of the validated good self, satisfying the primitive, idealizing superego and affording some discharge of tension.

Historically and developmentally the object splitting paralleled the earlier splits in self- and object-representations that were the outcome of the pattern of multiple mothering during the first two years of her life. In effect, acting out allowed for more reality relatedness. Otherwise the split would be experienced intra-psychically and as fragmenting. Both acting out and projection "cured" the fragmentation, making her feel less "crazy." This is why the early integrative work was needed before the good/bad split could be confronted effectively.

Miss T.'s initial involvement with men was interesting in that she made a teasing game out of their unreliability and unavailability in addition to instituting direct, playful teasing in the earlier inter-actions. With this, the relationship took on intense sexual over-tones. That is, she thought she had found the playful, teasing oedipal father but instead found herself before long with the narcis-sistic, frustrating, preoedipal mother. The shifts in transference both with the present-day, real-life love object and with her therapist were independent of the genders of those involved. Ini-tially the real love object was transferentially the good oedipal daddy, soon to shift to bad, preoedipal mother. With the female therapist the initial transference was that of the jealous mother who did not want her to care about anyone but her (a situation intensi-fied by the little girl's oedipal strivings) and who did not want her to be sexual. Miss T. recalled believing that her vagina was called a "don't" because that was what mother said when she touched her genitals. This, of course, suggests a more classical oedipal dynamic. But very quickly there would be a shift to the earlier structural issue, the externalized object split. With the transference shift from teasing father to frustrating mother vis-à-vis the present day, real-life love object, there was a corresponding shift from jealous mother to rescuing father vis-à-vis the therapist. But this was the father postpuberty, at which time the intense physical relationship between father and daughter stopped and they developed an equally intense intellectual relationship. Not only did she want validation, but she wanted answers. She assumed the posture of not being able to do the cognitive work of therapy, insisting the therapist do it for her. Giving answers became the substitute for physical comfort, although it was unfortunately emotionally sterile and left her feeling "unnourished."

There was a crisis in therapy when Miss T. demanded an additional hour each week. She was deeply enmeshed in her relationship with a chronically depressed man who was unreliable and unpredictable in their day-to-day life planning and who actively came between her and her friends. She complained of lack of caring on the therapist's part when the additional session was denied. Rationale for the denial of the additional time was that she needed the extra time to balance the degree of frustration in her relationship with this man, to maintain the same homeostatic equilibrium as in the original mother-father situation. Her complaint about father was that although he agreed completely with her about mother, he never did anything about it, urging her to be patient with mother. The pattern was unsatisfactory but stable. With the highly sexualized oedipal phase, which continued on up to puberty, there was a coming together of the acting out of the split between good and bad object and the oedipal triangle.

With the denial of the additional session, that equilibrium was upset, setting the stage for further analytic work. Although the crisis threatened the therapeutic alliance at one point and she managed to get advice once again to change therapists, the alliance was solid enough to weather the storm.

Strongly repressed and still not dealt with is her terror of mother's potential rage and her belief that her mother really hated her. This, of course, was readily assimilated into the oedipal situation. However, far more devastating to her development was the fact that mother was enraged if she went beyond the maternal orbit to anyone, including girlfriends or boyfriends. It was not so much her mother's competitive response to her oedipal strivings as mother's narcissistic rage and need for omnipotent control that was at issue. The underlying fear of her mother constituted one factor in her inability to move out of bad relationships in her adult life. She says of her therapist, "You're not as available as I want, but you don't tie me up so that I can't do other things." Of her boyfriend she says—speaking of the transferential mother as well—"In order to get rid of him I have to fight with him to push him away. I'd have to kill him."

Exploration of what binds the patient symbiotically to the bad object takes us far beyond the notion of pleasure in pain. Miss T.'s own rage must be feared as potentially destructive of the symbiotic partner and thus, equally dangerous. In this case the impact of the Oedipus complex was to exacerbate the already intense struggle vis-à-vis the preoedipal mother. It also provided the vehicle for the externalization and acting out of the inner split.

The lack of differentiation of the bad self from the bad object and the feelings of "craziness" that went with evocation of the enraged bad self came into analytic focus in her fourth year of treatment with me. The following is from a single session.

> With Paul I'm like a bad child in a rage at my mother. . . . I'm in a mistrusting, angry state. There's an inside part of me that wants to scream that keeps coming out with him. I had the fantasy of going into his office and screaming that I was in a rage with him and that I wanted to kill him. When he didn't call back I thought it was because I sounded so crazy on the phone. (Are you feeling crazy?) Yes, when I want to let out the rage. (The rage makes you feel crazy?) Sometimes . . . when I get in a reasonable state I forget that I get so angry that I do feel crazy. (Tell me about the experience of feeling crazy.) Maybe it's the wrong word. The feeling of being crazy is around my sense of not being able to contain my anger. I'm not fragmented. My reality testing is okay. I'm just in a constant rage. I feel that I am a bad person. (Does it feel like you are back with your mother?) Yes. That is a little bit of what it feels like.

Note that the bad self vis-à-vis the bad object is structured. She notes "I'm not fragmented."

Then I'm afraid of his anger and start my appeasing behavior. I've been so mean and I want to leave, but somehow I can't. I'm feeling caught in an old bind. . . . We had a big fight Friday night. I can't even remember what it was about. I had a sense of my temper tantrums. . . . Then there are the good times. . . . (It sounds like when you feel good about him, you can experience your separateness, but when you're in a rage, you lose that separateness.) That's absolutely right! It is true that when I'm angry I have a great deal of trouble being separate. I could call one of my friends and spend the evening with her, but I feel locked in the rage. I want to go away for a week but I need him to say it's okay, that I should go and have a good time. When I feel positive and more separate I can forget about him. (With the craziness you feel the loss of your own boundaries.) The way I experience it is I am immobilized by my badness and anger and will sit around the house. One way out which I've stopped is to go to someone to make me feel better by saying how terrible they think he is. That's one way to stay separate. (That is, when you can get someone to function as a proxy for your anger and so hold on to the sense of your good and separate self.)

This is the acting out of the masochistic triangle.

And it makes me feel better to say I am good and he is bad. (Your good self is well differentiated. It has its own boundaries. Your bad self does not.) That's very fascinating! I do know how to take care of myself, to feed myself, but my relationship with Paul has cut me off from the ways in which I can nourish my good self. I wish to be rid of him, to go back to my life of being individuated, my good self with good relationships. If I could define my boundaries when I'm angry, I could go off and do something else and my anger wouldn't be so devastating. I'm tied up with guilt and being locked in. . . . I have a sense with him a lot of the time that I'm into a false self to cover up the bad self. It's different from the good self. (In what way?) I'm compliant. I avoid conflict from him and from me. A lot of the time I'm suspended. I prevent anger on both sides. I feel lethargic. I'm not ranting and raving, but I am very angry. When I'm in the false-self state I can't create my own separate space. (That's because the false self is in a reactive situation. How you are is contingent on how he is. You operate as a unit.) A lot of the time I'm being reactive to him—not only to keep him from being angry—at the same time so as not to get my own anger going. (Your anger is tied to his either way.)

Exploring the difficulty in accepting the separation of self from the bad object brought out the following material in a later session.

It's my fault. If I were affectionate, he'd be good. (So if he's bad, it's contingent upon you?) No, but I try to convince myself of that and I somehow believe it. (What might be the consequences of giving up that belief?) I'd get angry. If I dealt with my anxiety about conflict, maybe I could work things out. This week I feel there is a bad, angry, stubborn core there. (Tell me more about your getting angry if you give up the belief.) I don't know. It just popped into my head. It just feels if I didn't blame myself I would be in a rage at him. (You keep shifting the focus from yourself to him, as though if you could understand him you could control him.) I can't make him good. I feel despair about that. [Sighs.] I got in a rage at something this weekend. I felt guilty because I couldn't make him good. . . . (The fact that you can't control him confronts you with your separateness, that he's not an extension of you.) I tried to say that to myself today. I experienced his anger, his passive-aggressive, controlling anger. But I tell myself that he's not trying to be malevolent. (When you find you can't control him, you deny that he might wish to hurt you, so you won't be anxious.) That feels right, but I can't hold on to it.

She then reports three dreams in which the person in control goes out of control and is a danger to her, so she must control them.

With you I hope if I'm just good, if I come and pay my bill,
you won't be a danger. I get very anxious when I'm bad. I
think you'll be bad. I do feel I have to feed you to keep you
from being bad.

The maintenance of the symbiotic tie between the bad self and
the bad object, we see, allows the omnipotent illusion that she controls the dangerous bad object. To let herself perceive the separateness, to fully differentiate, is to put herself in jeopardy vis-à-vis the
object who is intrinsically bad rather than bad simply because she is
not good. The need for omnipotent control in the interest of survival prevents differentiation.

NARCISSISTIC FEATURES
IN THE OEDIPAL TRIANGLE

Narcissistic issues were apparent in Miss E., a young woman
who was an administrative assistant in a large corporation. Miss E.
was well differentiated and there were no borderline indicators in
spite of prominent narcissistic features. Almost all interpersonal
situations took on a triangular cast. The general theme was that the
individual who was left out would be hurt, enraged, and vindictive.
These, of course, were her own reactions, and they were projected
in situations where she was one who was included. She recalled
deliberately tormenting her mother with her seductive interaction
with her cooperative father.

She was sexually involved with her first boyfriend when her
father died suddenly of a heart attack. She connected his death
with her "infidelity." Thrown back into a dependent relationship
with her mother, she experienced guilt over her wishes for an affectionate and sexual relationship with a man and dealt with these
wishes by periodically "getting them out of my system" with men
who meant nothing to her. She felt that any real interest in anyone
other than her mother was essentially an act of unfaithfulness, and
she anticipated her mother's retaliatory abandonment.

Feelings of being excluded were magnified by her being told as soon as she could talk that she had been adopted. The awareness of having been given away along with the recognition that she was and always would be, at some level, an outsider in her adoptive family constituted a narcissistic insult that colored all future developmental steps. Analytic work revealed her hurt and rage at this felt exclusion from the family in general and the marital relationship in particular. The narcissistic injury resulting from this exclusion, along with the abandonment experienced vis-à-vis the sometimes overinvolved and domineering mother, generated the rage and the expectation of punishment—not castration, but rejection and frustration of her rapprochement needs. "She won't be there to console me when I need it."

Miss E.'s analyst died suddenly of a heart attack, recapitulating the trauma of her father's death. She was accepted for treatment by her analyst's wife because of a previous therapeutic alliance in group and because it was felt that referring her to someone else would also recapitulate the earlier trauma of the adoption. As the early stages of work proceeded with her new therapist, she decided to use the couch again. She apologized for lying down, saying as she did, "Good-bye." She proceeded to talk about a man she had spent the weekend with and anticipated that her therapist would be enraged at her focusing on this man instead of on her.

The attempt to resolve the envy of mother by identifying with her also interfered because of the issue of adoption. This came out transferentially as well.

> I built up a story in my mind about you. It seems outrageous, what I'm thinking. [Laughs.] Even before David died, maybe because I was so jealous of you. I wanted to be like you. You must have something, and if I have it he would love me like he loved you. But I could never get to you, except in group. I wanted to be friends with you. I was ashamed to watch you. After David died I was doing the same thing, though there was no purpose to it. . . . I felt so jealous of your family. I was glad for you but felt bad for me. It was a reminder that I wasn't like your family. I felt like taking revenge. I must sound awful.

When I called the group I felt, damn it, I would make my own family. . . . I didn't want everyone to go away at once.

And in the same session associating to a dream about her mother's heart-shaped locket:

This feeling when I talk about the necklace, the feeling that I had certain restrictions because I wasn't really her daughter.

That this restriction was sexual was revealed in the dream in which inside the necklace was the name Irving Stone. She immediately recalled that he wrote *Lust for Life*.

In the dream I had this shirt on, open low. My breasts looked swollen, bustier than I am. I was thinking how nice it looked on my soft breast, this necklace.

Although the idiosyncratic aspects of Miss E.'s history—the adoption—played a significant role in her dynamics, such residual narcissistic features, whatever their origin, can be expected to affect the Oedipus complex and its resolution profoundly. Miss E. will have to come to terms with the narcissistic issues before she can come to such a resolution. The issues of envy of the idealized object and the fear of being envied in the position of the idealized self would continue for some time to interfere with the transmuting internalizations essential to the achievement of libidinal object constancy. Unlike the situation with Miss R., both levels—preoedipal and oedipal—are prominent in the material and are analyzed concomitantly. If we listen carefully, the patient will provide the best supervision with respect to the direction and focus of our interventions.

CLINICAL CONSIDERATIONS

When presented with material that has both oedipal and preoedipal issues, how do we respond? The admixture of both levels seems to produce a sexualized preoedipal picture, whatever its nature. I find it most productive to extricate the two levels, essentially to desexualize the earlier developmental issues and focus upon them.

It is my opinion that considerations of structure take precedence over considerations of psychodynamics. Psychodynamics must be understood relevant to the structure in which they occur—that is, the dynamic interaction of various aspects of structure. I believe that in the treatment of character disorders, the major importance of the interpretation of psychodynamics is the clarification of structure, and the clarification of structure, in turn, is basic to the reconstructive work of treatment.

An example of the failure of intervention that, although probably correct, was inappropriate vis-à-vis the core developmental issue, is the case of Miss A.

A woman of thirty, she had been a patient in a clinic for over a year. There had been a change of therapist with the turnover of trainees. The presenting problem was a phobia that made it difficult for her to leave the house. Previously she had held a job and been married, and she had a six-year-old child. Her husband's leaving her precipitated the symptoms.

Focus of her treatment had been on her abusive father and the sexual aspects of his abuse. From childhood on he would come home drunk, berate her for being a slut, and throw her out of the house. Her relationship with her mother was rarely discussed. Her husband had been an older man and was understood as a "father figure."

Her new therapist (a middle-aged man) felt that oedipal issues were central. When the patient gave the therapist some perfume for Christmas, he confronted her with sexual fantasies about him. When he did this, she angrily informed him that this perfume was not the kind her husband had used, but the kind her mother used. She shortly got into her anger at the mother for her failure to protect her from her father. Her mother would hide or run to her own mother when her husband went into one of his tirades.

With the focus on the repressed anger toward the abandoning mother and toward the younger siblings whom she blamed for this abandonment, the symptoms as defense against the destructive potential of her rage were clarified. Previously they had been conceptualized as a defense against the forbidden sexual impulses. For a long time therapy went nowhere, and the patient continued to be phobic and to somatize.

Generally whether our focus is on the oedipal or preoedipal issues will depend upon the patient's material and associations. But even when the approach is oedipal in its emphasis, it is important, as this is being analyzed, to expose and work with the preexisting character pathology. For only with the repair of the structural deficits can there be a healthy resolution of the oedipal conflict. And in some instances, as in the situation with Mr. B., the repair of the structural deficit will go hand in hand with the resolution of the oedipal conflict. The achievement of object constancy depends upon the resolution of the oedipal conflict, and the resolution of the oedipal conflict depends upon the achievement of object constancy. With both issues in the foreground at the same time, the therapeutic goal can be achieved.

As Shapiro writes, the Oedipus complex "provides a vehicle to demonstrate to patients in a convincing manner how they continue to make their own future on the basis of the past reformulations of reality that they re-experience daily. The analyst shows them the anachronistic nature of their experience" (1977, p. 577).

Keeping in mind the principle that the preoedipal object-relations set-up—that is, the quality of self- and object-representations and their relationship with one another—interacts with oedipal strivings, we can expect to find a wide variety of clinical manifestations in this interaction. Another example would be the sexualized narcissistic rage of the sadist who must hurt or humiliate the sexual partner. In each instance the therapeutic tack would be to disentangle the interlocking threads, to essentially desexualize the structural issues, and to focus on the latter with the goal of structural repair. Oedipal interpretations, if indicated, should be made toward the end of illuminating the structural deficits and how they are played out in all situations.

Chapter 9

SEPARATION-INDIVIDUATION AND THE FALSE SELF

A central theme or concept in the developmental object relations approach to understanding the person and to formulating a rationale for treatment is that of the "self." Historically philosophers have been more comfortable with this concept than have behavioral or social scientists. Existential and humanistic psychologists have focused on the self in general and on the "authentic self" and the "experiencing self" in particular (Rogers 1967). This concern is the basis for their emphasis in treatment on the "here and now." Missing in their work, however, is a theory of how the self develops in the first place. Its existence is taken for granted. As a result, their approaches to treatment at times make naive assumptions about the availability of that self to the individual and to the treatment process.

It is not unusual to meet in practice a patient who in no way appears psychotic but who complains of feeling that he or she does not really exist. There are feelings of not being real, of fraudulence, and of futility. The individual in question may present a picture of an apparently well-integrated person who has achieved a fair degree of success in life. Yet for some reason he or she has not been able to experience these achievements as real. Whatever the intrinsic or extrinsic rewards that have come to the individual by virtue of these accomplishments, they cannot be used to nourish the self-esteem because they are "undeserved." This is not an issue of guilt, but one of a real belief that they do not belong to the self.

This kind of patient may present with a history of previous psychotherapy that, on the surface, appeared to be highly successful. Treatment was terminated when the individual's functioning and sense of well-being were significantly improved.

This person may come to you now feeling that none of it had any real substance or made any real difference. There are even deeper feelings of futility and despair with respect to the possibility for help or change. He or she may be ashamed to return to the original therapist because of the failure to continue to improve or to sustain the gains of previous treatment. Responsibility for the failure is taken on the self, and there is no awareness of negative feelings toward the former therapist.

Winnicott (1965), in his analysis of this kind of patient, came to be aware of a disturbance in identity that he referred to as the false self. With this kind of patient, the working alliance may be with the false self and, as a result, the work of therapy is not experienced as real and cannot be integrated or sustained.

Winnicott sees this issue as relevant to the interminable analysis. What needs to be recognized before any real work can be done is the patient's problem of nonexistence, the problem of the hidden, true self. Winnicott writes:

A principle might be enunciated, that in the False Self area of our analytic practice we find we make more headway by recognition of the patient's non-existence than by a long-continued working with the patient on the basis of ego-defense mechanisms. [p. 152]

This kind of history and diagnostic formulation is an indication that the mobilization of the real self is crucial to the effectiveness of treatment. Unless this can be accomplished in this situation, therapy becomes another exercise in futility for the individual.

ETIOLOGICAL FACTORS:
THE IMPINGING MOTHER OF SYMBIOSIS

The original organization of the self-object schema of the stage of normal symbiosis encompasses sensorimotor experiences as well as the mother's responses to and interaction with these spontaneously occurring phenomena. To the extent that she can adapt to the child's spontaneous behavior so that the mutual cuing and interaction of mother and child is smooth and relatively free of disruptive tensions, the child's real, experiencing self becomes central to the evolving schema. The first of these is the symbiotic self-object schema that later differentiates into the separate self- and object-representations.

Winnicott links the idea of a true self with the spontaneous gesture. It appears as soon as there is any mental organization of the person at all. At first it is mainly the summation of sensorimotor aliveness. He points out that motility and erotic elements are fused at this point. Eventually affect also becomes an integral part of the developing schema. And most important—through the smooth interaction with the mother—the child's spontaneity becomes tied to external reality as represented by the mother. This concept of the mother as the bridge to reality becomes important in the treatment process, when contact with the true self permits the therapist to function as the bridge to reality. This is crucial to the evolution of the reality-related self.

In addition, the true self develops greater complexity and relates to external reality through the autonomously developing functions of the organism such as motor and cognitive development. In this instance the limits and demands of the socialization process can be tolerated and accepted without disturbance or disruption of the self because it is, by then, adequately defined and experienced and in rewarding interaction with the environment.

But what happens when the mother is insensitive to or unresponsive to the spontaneous behavior of her infant, or when for reasons of her own she needs to override it? In this instance the mother's intercessions are impingements—intrusions into or disruptions of the spontaneous experiencing of the child. His own self-directed flow of attention and movement becomes reactive instead. For such a person life may become a series of reactions to impingements. It is *not* experienced as originating from within the self or as being centered in the self. Identity becomes consolidated around the reactive stance vis-à-vis the impinging object. The characteristic mode of behavior, of reacting to the environment rather than generating and initiating his own spontaneous and goal-directed behavior, can be seen in such a patient's response to his therapist as well as to the world in general.

An example of this kind of mothering early on was Mrs. D., who found her infant son's spontaneous motility both an irritant and a threat to her feelings of competence as a mother. Her four-year-old son was referred for treatment because of his "hyperactivity." In the course of the history taking she described how she and his father used to have to slap the boy's legs and hold him down because he would not hold still for diapering as an infant.

When the false self based upon reactions to impingements is an integral part of the self-object schema of symbiosis and thus of the self schema or self-representation of differentiation, it should be kept in mind that without this organization we are likely to meet with the disorganization and unintegration of psychosis. Psychotherapeutic or analytic endeavors might, in fact, make the patient worse rather than better.

The critical question is: Is there an accessible, core true self that can form the nucleus for the organizing of a true-self identity within the therapeutic matrix? The following material is from the sessions of a thirty-year-old professional woman with anorexia nervosa. The identity issue emerged early on. The importance of the number representing her weight was that it was an exact identity and one that was rooted within her own physical being. She became upset at the possibility that someone might tamper with the scale, which would mean that once again her identity was determined by some outside force.

I'm trying to get up the courage to go to bed with Frank. It's more scary than if I were twelve years old. (Scary?) Scary and distasteful. I don't want anyone touching me—I don't want people to come inside my magic circle—my detachment. (So you're protecting yourself from something.) mhm—not from sex. It's distasteful *because* it's coming in. . . . I want to eat food I like, not food I have to eat because someone has invited me to dinner. . . . I'm really resentful if anyone impinges on me. Even magazines coming in—I feel I *have* to read them, from cover to cover. I'm beating back a tide of things encroaching on me. I guess it's a whole identity crisis. Is that what I'm having? (That's a good way to put it.) The identity crisis is making me behave in such an unpleasant, to me, way—the detachment, the anxiety about pressures. It's not fun. (Crises usually aren't.) What am I afraid of? You said I was overwhelmed. I was with Tom (her former lover). Maybe I just don't know about who I am, or I can't let myself leak out, or if someone sees me, they'll know there's nothing in there. I don't want people telling me what to do. Maybe I'm overreacting. (I have a hunch your defenses have important survival value for you.) Maybe I need them for all those reasons. I don't know how Tom managed to get inside and have an effect. I actually let him in. Maybe that innocent in here (points to her chest) did feel overwhelmed. It's not distinguished—like an oyster, unformed—like an oyster and any grain of sand is bad. He got in and twisted me all around inside. I let my defenses down.

The patient has a sense of a true self, but it is unformed, like an oyster, an innocent. The false-self identity is based upon values espoused by her family, especially her being smart.

Probably it was that I had to define myself as smart because that's how my parents defined worth. With that to cling to, I didn't look further.

The inability to ward off impingement, even the impingement of the inanimate object like the magazine, necessitates massive defenses. Appetite becomes an impinging force to be resisted as well. Bruch (1973) writes of the anorexic, "these patients experienced their bodies as not being truly their own, as being under the influence of others" (p. 102).

A critical issue in treatment, of course, is that the therapist not be an impinging object to be warded off. Failures of empathy will be experienced as impingements. Essentially the patient must be the initiator, the therapist the responder. Respect for the autonomy of the patient is of paramount importance. If the early buildup of self- and object-representations permits an organized, real self, regardless of how relatively unelaborated, there is likely to be a cohesive self to rely upon the treatment process. In this instance the false self is of later origin.

THE IMPINGING PARENTS OF INDIVIDUATION

Mrs. P. was a twenty-nine-year-old professional woman who complained of a frequent feeling of not being real—often in her therapy sessions as well. Her view of herself reflected that of her parents: she was cold and selfish. They had called her a "touch-me-not" as a small child. They were not grossly bad parents and probably would be described by others as loving and concerned.

Fundamentally lacking, however, was a quality of empathy for and responsiveness to the felt needs of the little girl. They would pick her up and show her affection in response to their own feelings rather than in sensitive response to her need. When she needed affection, it was not available. When she was otherwise involved, affection came *at* her. Her real, needful self felt unresponded to. Affection had become an impingement to be warded off. When she attempted to withdraw physically to her room, this was unacceptable to her parents and with chiding, scolding, and demands, she was denied this retreat from the impinging environment.

Mrs. P. learned early that to relate with any semblance of harmony with the other meant subordinating her own state of being to that of the other. The false self, the responder-to-others, protected her real self from disappointment and hurt, but at the same time it isolated her from genuine human interaction.

Winnicott makes the point that maternal failure of the sort described here does not necessarily lead to a general failure of child care. The false self deriving from the child's adaptation to patterns of the existing failures may achieve a deceptive false integrity and a false ego strength, which results from an otherwise good and reliable environment. However, the false self in this instance cannot experience life or feel real.

To the extent that the individual must operate from the base of the false self, feelings, impulses, and wishes that are not consistent with that self must be split off and repressed. Just as the defense mechanisms may be used to defend against the anxiety inherent in intrapsychic conflict in more classical psychoanalytic terms, so they can be used to maintain the false self, which in turn protects the true self and maintains contact with the object world. Interpretation of the defenses in terms of id-superego conflict fails to address the core issue of nonexistence.

In the treatment situation the therapist's empathic awareness of, responsiveness to, and support of the real self, no matter what its manifestations, enables the patient to take further risks toward experiencing and living through the real self. Winnicott points out that this is a time of great dependence and considerable risk, but that the "good-enough adaptation" by the therapist allows the patient to shift his base of operations from the false self to the true self. Impulses, wishes, and feelings long split off and repressed can come into awareness and be integrated into the real self with the resulting feelings of realness and aliveness.

THE ROLE OF THE NARCISSISTIC MOTHER

I have been struck by the prevalence of narcissistic mothers in the history of those patients who are themselves therapists and have concluded that learning to sense and meet the needs of the narcissistic parent constitutes an effective training ground for the future psychotherapist. The adapting child develops a heightened sensitivity to the psychological status of the parent in question—more commonly the mother—and learns how to extract positive responses from the parent by catering to his or her narcissistic needs. This in effect is a surrender of self to the narcissistic needs of the object. The situation is especially relevant to the development of the false self, which seeks out situations in which the true self can feel safe.

The consequence of this mode of relating are varied but ultimately negative. If the object responds favorably and the behavior is rewarded, the real self still feels ungiven to since the reward has gone to the false self. There may be a temporary sense of well-being, but this is usually followed by the inability to hold on to or to internalize the positive responses. Feelings of depression or futility often ensue.

If the positive response is not forthcoming, there is frequently a sense of outrage at having been exploited. Behind the outrage are feelings of hurt and abandonment of the real self.

This stance vis-à-vis the object is a subtle but powerful source of interference in the therapeutic process. The patient who is exquisitely sensitive to cues from the other with respect to real or imagined, narcissistic needs and vulnerabilities automatically shifts to being and producing that which is perceived as needed by the therapist for the maintenance of his or her narcissistic or self-esteem needs. The patient does his best to make the therapist look good. It is not uncommon for an entire course of therapy to proceed along these lines right up to the point of termination. This is the kind of patient who later relapses and consults a different therapist. He does not return to the original therapist because he feels guilty and anxious at the prospect of making him or her "look bad."

A careful history taking should provide adequate warning that this situation might prevail. Making the potential hazard explicit at the outset enlists the patient in a valid alliance and communicates the therapist's readiness to accept the patient on grounds other than seduction.

The use of the couch with this kind of person is especially helpful—so long as it is not otherwise contraindicated—in that it reduces the automatic adjustment to subtle, visual cues. An attitude of neutrality on the part of the therapist reduces the potential for adjustment to verbal cues as well. The anxiety generated in this event becomes available for analysis.

Miss T. was a thirty-year-old woman, well-educated and well-functioning. There had been many years of previous treatment with some improvement socially, described by her as being "less crazy" in her relationships. Despite these changes she still experienced depression, despair, and a sense of futility.

She first presented herself to me with an air of rather brittle cheerfulness. She had learned that her depression simply alienated others, including her therapists, and was sure that I would become impatient with her as well.

At the start of treatment I saw Miss T. three times a week, and when her readiness to adapt to verbal and nonverbal cues became evident, I suggested the use of the couch. She resisted the idea at first because of her anticipation of the emergence of the depression.

There were sessions when she would turn her back to me to sleep. For a time I did not understand the meaning of the behavior, but thought to myself that she was demonstrating to me her experience with her depressed mother.

At the start of her second year with me she said, "Sometimes I think that being happy and relating to others is something I do for them. You have to do it if you're going to go on." She recalled a photograph of herself at the age of six in which she had a "plastic smile."

Miss T. realized that she rarely felt alive, and when I wondered when she did feel so she replied, "When I'm sleeping." She laughed and observed that this was a silly answer. I said I felt it was a most important answer—that this was a time when she did not have to react and adapt to others and thus was most in touch with her real self. This real self was detached and not object related, a fact that interfered with the final steps of the separation-individuation process, the achievement of object constancy.

Her mother had been a depressed and narcissistic woman, and Miss T. tried to placate her mother in order to make her more emotionally available, a process that contributed to the buildup of the false self. She was now left with the dilemma that to be alive (real) was to be isolated. She related either through the false self or with splitting and the acting out of the externalized split. She used schizoid defenses against both situations.

Miss T. demonstrates two principles: the power and persistence of attachment-seeking behavior and the fact that when the attachment is achieved and maintained through the false self, the process of internalization of the good-enough mother with the outcome of object constancy cannot take place. The real self does not participate in the attachment but is split off and in isolation. To be the real self is to experience object loss and consequently the depression that goes with it. Miss T.'s initial resistance to the use of the couch was due to the fear of object loss. Later in treatment it became apparent that this resistance was also a defense against the emergence of the bad symbiotic object in the transference. It became clear that there were three states: the false self; the detached, real, schizoid self; and the real, object-related self, which was split and only partially differentiated.

An early goal of treatment would be for me to be with her while she was alive (depressed, not relating, even asleep)—paradoxically, to be with her while she was alone so that I could eventually become the link between her real, schizoid self and external reality, just as the mother is the link between the spontaneous sensorimotor activity of the infant and external reality.

Eventually I would be the agent that would connect this real self with the other sectors of her personality. Her accomplishments would come to be felt as those of a cohesive, object-related self and would be available to her in the service of her self-esteem. Her real self-being-with-me would come to include positive affect as well as the initial depression. She was able to express real gratitude toward me for staying with her at these difficult times. This went on in a parallel fashion with the analysis of the third situation of object relatedness and its splitting and acting out in the masochistic triangle.

Miss T. also demonstrates how the preservation of the real self through isolation maintains its potential for a genuine relationship and for the therapeutic process.

FAMILY DYNAMICS
AND PROJECTIVE IDENTIFICATION

Slipp (1973) has described the role of family dynamics in severely disturbed identity formation and an object relations approach to understand the phenomenon of family homeostasis. He notes that although secondary-process cognition does develop in some areas, primary-process thinking persists in interpersonal relationships and personal identity.

In certain kinds of families the child does not "learn to experience a total sense of self or self-sameness apart from the family" (p. 378). Because he has not achieved self-esteem and ego identity, "the identified patient is unable to be spontaneous and assertive, but remains constantly *reactive* to others." He points out that what he calls the "symbiotic survival pattern" appears to "prevent the differentiation in the child of mental images of self and others."

Slipp's observations are of families in which object splitting is a major factor in parental character structure. Good and bad object images have not been coalesced into a single, ambivalently experienced other, and there is a corresponding split in the self-image or identity. Any one of these four images (good parent, bad parent, good self, bad self) may be projected (projective identification) onto another family member as a way to preserve the parental homeostasis. Because of the failure to differentiate self from other, perception of the other remains egocentric. Under these circumstances the other person's behavior "is not seen as separately motivated but as a reflection of one's own self-esteem and personal identity" (p. 386).

Slipp observes further that "the child unconsciously senses that his parent(s) are dependent upon him to act out their introject in order for them to gain magical control over past and present relationships." The child, in turn, incorporates the parental projection into his identity.

Commonly seen examples of this arrangement are children who accept the identity of the inadequate self of the parent, which then allows the parent to feel superadequate and so maintain his or her own self-esteem. In these instances one can see a stunting in many areas of what should be autonomous ego functioning, particularly the intellect.

Another child may be assigned the role of good parent and accepts the responsibility for the emotional well-being of the parent in question. When failing to meet the demands of the infantile mother or father, this child will be the recipient of the rage felt toward the disappointing parent.

The child who is expected to succeed in the interest of providing self-esteem for the parent is in the paradoxical position of also having to fail for the same reason. That is, the child's success in reality will highlight parental inadequacy and thus threaten parental self-esteem. The contradictory (double-binding) messages are "succeed for me, but fail for me" (Slipp 1976).

In these instances the child feels in magical control of the parent, but also feels controlled by the parent, and we find magical omnipotence alongside impotent rage.

The carrying out of the "irrational role assignment" (Framo 1970) maintains parental psychic equilibrium and with this the homeostasis of the family system. The consequences to the sense of self with the buildup of a false self on the basis of role assignment is a serious disturbance in identity. Here the primitive character structure of the parent(s) with object splitting as an integral aspect of that structure is the environmental stimulus to and reinforcement of an identity based on identification with the parental projection.

In this instance the false self based on identification is more pathological in that it requires the structure of the symbiotic arrangement to maintain it. With the false self based on parental reinforcement of defensive identificatory processes of early childhood (such as identification with the aggressor), the child spontaneously identifies with and integrates certain aspects of the parents. As Slipp points out, in the symbiotic survival pattern the child having the constellation of traits and characteristics that most closely fit the requirements of the parental dynamics is chosen by the parents to play out the role. Thus the identity in this instance is more alien to the real self than in the situation in which the child is the spontaneous chooser.

The child who spontaneously identifies with chosen aspects of the parents selects traits or characteristics of that parent and integrates these into the total character. The child who takes the identity of either half of the split object or the split self of the parent is taking as his total identity a split-off portion of the parental ego. It is in this arrangement that the extent of the symbiosis is understood as well as the potential for loss of identity and psychotic disorganization when the arrangement is disrupted.

The child who is chosen for the projective identification is chosen early, often on the basis of sex. A thirteen-year-old adopted girl was referred because of runaway behavior and school refusal. One night she phoned and asked to be put in the hospital to prevent her killing either herself or her parents. At this hospital the father took me aside and told me, "The day we got her (aged two weeks) I took one look at her and said to myself, 'She's going to be trouble!'"

The person who has been the recipient of the projective identifications and whose identity resides in that role is not simply passively compliant to the wishes and needs of the other. Because of the symbiotic basis for his identity, he attempts to actively coerce others, including the therapist, into the complementary role. The tenacity with which he clings to the role reflects the fear of loss of identity and self cohesion rather than fear of loss of the object per se.

Giovacchini (1979) writes of the need of the patient with a character disorder to re-create in the present environment, and especially in the transference, "an environment that he believes he can cope with. In the transference, he externalizes some aspects of his inner organization as well as projects affects, impulses, and attitudes" (p. 218). The false self attempts to maneuver or coerce behavior from the environment, which is reciprocal to the false-self identity organization and in which it can function in the familiar manner. It is critical that the therapist does not participate in this acting out. Depression and anxiety are likely to emerge in the benign and neutral analytic setting, and the work of analysis can proceed.

Although Winnicott places the false self based on identification further along the continuum of health, the individual whose false self is based on identification with parental projections clearly belongs to a "sicker" category. Mobilization of the real self may not be possible without loss of the brittle hold of his identity. As Slipp points out, this type of child is likely to decompensate when the structure of the symbiotic family situation is changed or lost. Those identifications that are part of the final steps of the separation-individuation process and that lead to object constancy do not yield a false-self identity. They are assimilated into a real self structure.

CLINICAL EXAMPLE

Mrs. S. was a talented and moderately successful woman who had been in treatment for five years with very little change in or outside of therapy. Her childlike coquettishness with her male therapist and her intensely hostile competitiveness with women, especially with the female cotherapist, suggested the oedipal struggle. She presented as supercompetent, but nevertheless experiencing vague anxieties and underlying depression.

Some work was done with her rage toward her arbitrary and tyrannical father, and she became better able to assert herself with authority figures. Other than this behavioral change the character and symptomatology remained unyielding to the efforts of the therapist. Furthermore, her defenses were entirely ego syntonic, and she was callously indifferent to her impact on others.

Mrs. S. never fully engaged with the members of her therapy group, and it was only after one of them left and she stopped interacting almost entirely that her relationship pattern became evident. When the other person aggressively acted out the power she coveted, she would become allied with that individual, showing interest in that person and even excitement in the interaction. Otherwise she sat in disdainful disinterest, stating she simply couldn't be bothered.

One could imagine the impact of this kind of mother on a developing child in viewing her alternate engagements and withdrawals depending upon the availability of others to participate in her projective identifications. The group members were asked to comment upon the impact of her mode of relating, and in general the responses were in the nature of, "I feel like I've been wiped out—like I don't exist."

It became increasingly clear that Mrs. S.'s identity resided in her mother's projective identifications. She needed her daughter to be powerful for her, since she herself was impotent in her own relationships, especially with her husband, the patient's father.

However, as described earlier, too much success or power on the part of the child highlights the parental impotence instead of acting as a defense against it. The child is given the messages, "win for me, but lose for me." Mrs. S. was caught in this bind, which both stirred up and prohibited her competitiveness. There was no overt conflict with the mother, and material having to do with their relationship was minimal in treatment where the father was seen as the major factor in her pathology.

The competitiveness with women who were both idealized and feared was suppressed, and her underlying pathological grandiosity and contempt for the women she could not compete with was evident in her attitude toward the female cotherapist in group, whom she refused to acknowledge as of importance and whom she openly hated.

What had been assumed to be problems that were oedipal in nature had to be reformulated as a more serious disorder of identity based upon her mother's projective identifications. Mrs. S. could not be a whole person and needed others to play out the unintegrated parts of herself so that she could feel alive and whole. She had to resist any analytic work directed at the defense mechanisms as they were essential to the maintenance of the false self, which in turn protected the mother's self-esteem and thus her own source of supplies. From the start her real self had to be denied, suppressed, and repressed, and as a result her identity could not evolve in an integrated fashion. The real self, cut off from object relatedness, evolved as a grandiose structure. At the same time, the whole object was not available to her for the process of developing object constancy. Her competitiveness and rage toward the powerful idealized object who must not be defeated stirred up intense early-separation-and-abandonment anxiety, and indeed she continued to be unable to move beyond the social orbit of her mother in her adult life, as they remained enmeshed in their symbiotic, mutual survival relationship.

Slipp (1973) writes:

Since intrapsychic conflicts are acted out in the interpersonal sphere, the parents continuously need the patient to stabilize their own personality. Thus, the identified patient cannot achieve his own separate identity and adequate ego controls. He requires a symbiotic relationship to sustain his *relational* ego identity and acts to perpetuate the system. To break from the symbiotic survival pattern is frought with the fear of being destroyed, of not surviving intact alone, as well as the fear of loss of control and destruction of the parents. [p. 395]

IMPLICATIONS FOR SEPARATION-INDIVIDUATION

The false self is without present or potential autonomy. It exists in relation to the corresponding object upon which it is contingent. Thus it cannot differentiate.

The isolated true self is in a chronic state of object deprivation or loss. Thus maternal functions are not available for the gradual assimilation or internalization that paves the way to object constancy. Because of the unavailability of environmental support, the true self may be thrown upon the pathological, grandiose self structure as a defense against anxiety. To the extent that the autonomous functions belonging to the true self are assimilated into this grandiose structure, they are not available for the evolution of a healthy self-esteem (chapter 10).

It is not always easy to detect the existence of the false self right away. I have come to trust my reactions to certain patients who do and say all the "right" things, who seem to emote appropriately, and who seem committed to treatment, but toward whom I have no sense of relatedness. These are not situations in which I am defended against something in the patient that elicits anxiety in me. There is a sociability but no sense of real relatedness with these patients. When this happens, I pay close attention for indicators of a false self and a corresponding false alliance. Until one can make contact with the real self, there is no treatment.

Chapter 10

CHARACTER DETACHMENT AND SELF-ESTEEM

As Tolpin (1971) notes, the achievement of object constancy constitutes a developmental leap that involves the gradual internalization of equilibrium-maintaining, maternal functions that leads to a separate, self-regulating self. Thus we can anticipate that the development of healthy narcissism, or self-esteem, will be closely related to the achievement of object constancy. Schecter (1978) defined character detachment as a "network of defenses and coping dynamisms that become relatively stable and structuralized, that is, chronic in the personality." Since character detachment will interfere with the achievement of object constancy, it will also interfere with the development of healthy self-esteem.

In this chapter I will consider a specific instance of impairment of object relatedness and its consequences for the development of healthy narcissism. I am referring in particular to those individuals whose autonomous functions matured outside the orbit of human relatedness. The unfolding autonomous functions are part of what is to be organized and integrated into the self-representation.

DEVELOPMENTAL ISSUES

For the purpose of this chapter I will review briefly certain relevant developmental issues. From about ten to sixteen or eighteen months of age the child is in the practicing subphase of the separation-individuation process. During this stage the child is heavily invested in the autonomous apparatuses of the self—locomotion, perception, and learning. He still shares to a considerable extent in the magic powers of the mother of symbiosis, and his mood is generally one of elation and what Karl Buhler (1927) referred to as function pleasure. As the child becomes increasingly aware of his separateness and realistic helplessness, which heralds the rapprochement phase of development, he turns back to the powerful mother for support. The practicing period and the rapprochement phase that follows is a critical switch point for the child. How successfully he negotiates it will depend upon the response of his environment at this time, as well as on the adequacy of earlier organization and integration. Maternal failure during this critical period may take the form of emotional abandonment or inappropriate and insensitive response to the child's behavior and communication. Either kind of failure may lead to developmental detachment on the part of the child. She may be overly pleased with his growing self-sufficiency insofar as it relieves her of chores or responsibility, or she may feel rejected on the basis of the same developmental strides. A clash of wills may develop and power struggles ensue.

When the mother interferes with the child's exercise of his autonomous functions, he may withdraw as a way of coping with her disruptive behavior. This may be part of an overall detachment that protects the child from the disruptive effects of an intrusive, impinging, interpersonal environment. In this instance the detachment might be considered to be adaptive insofar as it enables the child to continue to function at its optimum cognitive level. Nonetheless, it is also pathological insofar as it inhibits or aborts the capacity for human relatedness and with it the ultimate achievement of object constancy and healthy narcissism. In other cases, the child may not be able to defend against the disruptive environmental input and will react instead with frustration and rage. This is maladaptive insofar as the autonomous functions then become caught up in conflict, aggression becomes fused with rage, and there is a failure to develop a conflict-free sphere of functioning.

Healthy aggression is not available for competence and achievement, and the development of self-esteem is also blocked.

A second kind of maternal failure is the failure to be emotionally available to the child when needed. In some cases a child is prematurely cut off from maternal response to dependency needs due to the birth of a sibling at this critical point of recognition of separateness and well before the achievement of object constancy. Blanck and Blanck (1974) write of the general situation in which the mother welcomes too wholeheartedly her toddler's increasing independence as freeing her as well. The child experiences her attitude as an abandonment and is burdened with the fear of the loss of the object. The child then comes to rely upon its own maturing, autonomous apparatuses in lieu of the suddenly unavailable mother. Blanck and Blanck describe such premature ego development as "an unevenness in development characterized by pseudo-self-sufficiency in which part of the ego replaces the symbiotic partner," and in which there is a "concomitant absence of object cathexis" (p. 340). In this situation detachment becomes an essential aspect of the character structure.

Kohut (1971, p. 116) speaks of the importance of mother's self-confirming joy in response to the child's healthy narcissistic displays of his new developments and discoveries for the evolution of self-esteem. Whatever the reason for the failure of such mirroring responses—the mother's own narcissism, depression, preoccupation with other demands, or indifference—the unfolding capabilities of the child will have to develop outside the realm of human relatedness.

Some children persist in the pursuit of these capabilities in spite of the mother's failure to respond. Such persistence speaks for a degree of ego strength not evident in the child who relinquishes them in order to coerce maternal involvement and thus to preserve the mental connection with her. Under the threat of object loss, the healthier child is able to maintain a higher level of functioning of the autonomous apparatuses. Because there is a cohesive self, the object loss does not disorganize the self. On the other hand, when the threat of object loss is a threat to that cohesion, the autonomous functions may be renounced or seriously compromised with a concomitant loss of sense of self, and there is a regression to reconstitutive merger with the symbiotic object. A false-self identity consolidated around helplessness vis-à-vis a supercompetent mother may develop. The evolution of a false-self identity that is consolidated around a stance of helplessness vis-à-vis the powerful object is exemplified by a ten-year-old boy who wanted me to teach him to play the piano. I began by teaching him how to find middle C and all other Cs on the keyboard. Weeks would go by and first he would play all the Bs, then all the Ds, professing inability to remember where the Cs were. When I finally lost my temper, he was clearly delighted.

It was clear that he was interested, first, in involving me in a helping relationship with him, and then, in thwarting my efforts to help him. His defeat of parental objects gratified his need for power, reinforcing the secret grandiose self and making sure that authority figures had no power over him. Most importantly he protects the boundaries of his real but inadequately defined and frightened self. At school he defeats his teachers in the same manner, and although at one level shamed by his failure, at another he feels a sense of secret power at having defeated the powerful object. The kind of rage that lurked behind the façade of the helpless self was manifest in his wish to be an airplane pilot when he grew up, "So I can drop bombs and kill lots of people."

As I mentioned earlier, the rapprochement phase with the dawning recognition of separateness is the point at which covert pathology of an earlier organization process becomes manifest. In this situation it is not the abandonment of the object per se which causes the pathology, although it may be the precipitating factor.

However, in some children the simple recognition of separateness will have the same effect, even with available mothering. The failure to establish cohesion in the earlier buildup of the self- and object-representations of symbiosis is the critical factor. The object continues to be needed as a kind of prosthesis to avert fragmentation. The child who can deal with maternal failure at this point by detachment with continued high levels of functioning in the autonomous sphere has the cohesive self to turn to, replacing the lost symbiotic partner with part of the ego, as described by Blanck and Blanck. This child will become the adult patient who presents with the kind of disorder of self-esteem that is my focus here. Although this patient is clearly not borderline, it is often difficult to make a definitive diagnosis: is this a narcissistic personality with neurotic features or a neurotic character with prominent narcissistic features? One gets the sense of a person who seems to straddle both positions, although I believe that such a patient fits the criterion for a preneurotic personality insofar as there has been a failure to achieve object constancy. Whether renunciation of the defensive detachment reveals a borderline structure or a better integrated and differentiated, albeit preneurotic, character structure will be clarified in the quality of transference reactions.

THE GRANDIOSE SELF
AS A DEFENSIVE STRUCTURE
AND PATHOLOGY OF SELF-ESTEEM

At this point the question may be raised, Why should this particular adult have any significant problem with respect to self-esteem, since the high level of functioning itself, as in the business, artistic, or professional life should be a source of good feeling about the self? However, we often find, quite to the contrary, that the talents and abilities of the self are not a reliable source of such good feeling because of the object loss associated with their exercise. This loss, originally experienced during the separation-individuation process and interfering with the achievement of object constancy, leads to feelings of emptiness and depression. For an adult, there often is not sufficient motivation to sustain work or productivity and with it, self-esteem. Furthermore, the depression and inability to work are experienced as narcissistic wounds, which worsens the situation.

Most important is the defense that the child turns to in order to protect himself further from the anxiety and depression of object loss and loss of self-esteem. In addition to relating to part of the ego in lieu of the object, there is a concomitant regression to the more primitive, grandiose self-structure that existed before the recognition of separateness, which ushered the rapprochement period. When this is the case, achievements and accomplishments are assimilated into this primitive structure, preventing the development of a sense of realistic competence. In the adult patient, professional, artistic, or intellectual successes are experienced through the grandiose self and reinforce it.

We will see this same situation in the case of the individual who has used character detachment as a defense against the borderline dangers of loss of differentiation or disorganization. In the case of Miss R., who has been described earlier, the issue of the assimilation of the autonomous function, the intellect, into the defensive and compensatory, grandiose self-structure was manifest in what she referred to as being "in a state of grace" when the intellectual problems that confronted her could be managed with little or no effort. The understanding seemed to come magically. She had gotten through much of her schooling without any major confrontation of this state. However, when the tasks of her advanced schooling and professional life were not so readily managed, the unreality of the magical, mental omnipotence was exposed and she "fell from grace," suffering from feelings of helplessness, shame, and impotence. She avoided doing the work, and the inevitable failures of omission were then felt as further humiliations.

We see that the illusory omnipotence and perfection alternate with feelings of helplessness and shame, recapitulating the original developmental trauma of awareness of separateness and the experience of object loss, and the defensive regression to an earlier developmental stage. The individual is exquisitely vulnerable to the loss of self-esteem when reality intrudes and makes it impossible to live up to the fantasy idealization of the self. Rejection of an idea, criticism, or even as in the case of the young woman mentioned a moment ago, the experience of slight difficulty and the need for effort in a given task, can have devastating consequences, particularly with the borderline patient, where the grandiose self defends against the dangers of loss of self. With the humiliation of real or fantasied failure comes the depression of lost self-esteem as well as the sense of object loss that is reevoked by the failure of the grandiose self defense.

Very often the grandiose self is kept quite secret, but we can suspect its existence in persistent problems of shame and loss of self-esteem in the highly competent and able patient. Eventually the grandiosity must be explored and subjected to reality testing. Real ability must be extricated from fantasy to become available as a basis for healthy self-esteem. This is a delicate operation, however, as potential humiliation is always near at hand. I tend to suspect the existence of the secret grandiose self when a patient persists in maintaining an idealization of me as the source of all wisdom and strength. In one such instance (Mrs. W., chapter 5) the patient's predominating complaint was the inability to achieve or learn although she was highly skilled and intelligent in her field. She essentially castrated herself intellectually in order to prevent the other person from experiencing the same kind of envy and rage that she felt toward them since the competitive wishes of her grandiose self were to turn the tables, as it were. Despite the oedipal cast to her dynamics, the underlying developmental failure was due to the failure of the mother to mirror adequately and to relate to her unfolding mental abilities during the rapprochement period, as well as the mother's abandonment with the arrival of a new baby who was colicky and sickly from the start. Angry at the abandonment, the patient hid her ability, taking it into the compensatory, secret grandiose self-structure and, at the same time, coerced maternal help and care with an attitude of helplessness and deferentiality. This was played out with her supervisor and therapists. Low self-esteem plagued her, the potential for humiliation was high, and the grandiose self was kept secret from everyone. I began to suspect what was going on when I realized that I was unusually active and talkative with interpretations and explanations in her sessions, as though she were really incapable of doing the work herself. I believe that therapists are often deterred from exploration of hints about the existence of a primitive grandiose structure because of their own countertransferential concern—often unconscious— about the hidden contempt and envious rage that could spill on them at any moment—not to mention the narcissistic gratification inherent in being looked up to in this manner. There is pleasure in playing the "mentor" to the adoring student.

I'm talking here, of course, about the narcissistic transference described by Kohut (1971). However, I want to emphasize the point that the grandiose self is sometimes secret and difficult to reach. The patient may tend to look more neurotic and the core issue is often overlooked, leading to years of treatment with no essential change. Sometimes when the therapist is actively encouraging and supportive, the patient makes life changes and appears to be doing better, but these achievements "belong" to the idealized object, as it were, and not to the self. In this instance the therapist is participating in a *folie à deux* and is not available for the more difficult analytic work. Withholding his or her illusory powers from the patient evokes frustration and anger, under which circumstances the contempt of the grandiose self may be revealed. Withholding does not mean withholding of appropriate concern and empathy and skill; it means withholding the inappropriate help that the patient tells us he or she needs and that is often subtly coerced by means of inducing guilt or sympathy in the therapist.

Just as the autonomous functions may be assimilated into a pathological, grandiose self-structure, so may standards of right and wrong and the more sophisticated social values and ethical judgments. These identifications with parental and family values and standards learned in the process of socialization may give the appearance of a mature, well-developed superego. This is theoretically puzzling in the context of a character structure in which the pathological, grandiose self is a manifestation of a defect in the organization of the ego in general and of the self-representation in particular.

But in such individuals we are often struck by the rigidity of these attitudes as well as an attitude of moral superiority. Only as we come to see how they function to reinforce the grandiosity and to participate in the defensive functions of the pathological structure can we understand the significance of the grandiose superego.

Interpretations based upon the presumption of a mature superego that is in conflict with id impulses go nowhere. Indeed, when the grandiose self plays such an important role in the psychic economy of the individual, even questioning the superego severity is tantamount to an assault on the grandiose self and a threat to its defensive reliability.

This pathological development represents the later manifestation and reinforcement of the earlier condensation of idealized object images with the self-concept described by Kernberg (1975, p. 283), in his conceptualization of the genesis of the grandiose self.

Thus the grandiose self-structure, which has its cognitive roots in symbiosis and the earlier stages of the separation-individuation process, directs later development in pathological directions that augment and reinforce this structure, making it even more difficult of resolution. Whatever functions become part of it are unavailable for the achievement of reality-based self-esteem.

Kernberg notes that because the forerunners of the ego ideal and the mature superego—the idealized object images—are thus taken into the self-image and made part of it in this manner, there is a failure to develop ideals and the superego as a mature structure. In such a patient, expressed ideals serve to uphold the grandiose self and are not easily amenable to modification.

DETACHMENT IN THE TREATMENT SITUATION

I want to make some specific comments now about the issue of detachment and its relevance not only to self-esteem but also to the treatment process. Schecter (1978) notes that the therapeutic goal for the patient who manifests developmental detachment is to reestablish "human attachment in those areas where relatedness has been 'frozen' or cut off." The final therapeutic goal, he added, is "to bring back from disassociation the fractured disassociated parts of the self which can be re-structured or reintegrated . . . under the roof of the total self and under control of the ego." This is the situation in which the analyst functions as mediator of organization, as did the early mother.

The evolution of healthy narcissism, like other aspects of the self, must also "come under one roof": that is, it must take place within the sphere of object relatedness. The treatment of such disorders of narcissism, from this point of view, requires a building of stable relatedness with the analyst. As the exercising of the autonomous functions of the ego—that is, achievements both inside and outside the treatment hour—come within the orbit of human relatedness, the defensive, grandiose fantasies can be relinquished and a healthy self-esteem built upon realistic competence can evolve. Although Kohut (1971, 1977) appears to disagree with this, I believe that the attachment to him brings this about. He does not give adequate weight to the relational matrix per se.

The establishment of relatedness in the treatment situation is very difficult with many of these patients, however. If detachment originally protected the child from the disorganizing impact of an impinging mother, such disorganization will once again be feared. The individual who was forced to repress dependency needs because of maternal unavailability will be fearful of the potential helplessness and vulnerability associated with reawakened dependency wishes. And when self-esteem is tied to pseudo–self-sufficiency and defensive grandiosity, the potential for humiliation and shame is enormous.

Analysis of the resistance to attachment constitutes a major phase of the treatment process. Schecter notes further that "it is crucial to observe whether the detachment is of early origin, deep and almost total (that is, schizoid) or whether detachment is occurring in selective areas in a character disorder or neurotic personality. The prognosis and therapy are obviously quite different depending upon these criteria." It is important in each case to conceptualize not only the psychodynamic implications of the detachment but also the developmental, structural implications as well. Close attention to attaching and detaching vis-à-vis the therapist from hour to hour or from moment to moment is both instructive and productive for the treatment process. Dr. Frank Crewdson (1978) presented the case of a young man who had been in analysis for four years when Dr. Crewdson began to work quite specifically with the detachment he had observed in the sessions from time to time. Over a span of fourteen sessions the treatment came together most productively as the patient dealt with the frightening, fantasy, bad-object representation. He had defended against the emergence of this image and its concomitant projection onto his analyst by detaching when this projection threatened the alliance with the good object.

With patients in whom I believe there is potential for a psychotic transference, I don't touch the detachment for a long time until there is a stable, dependable, reality-oriented alliance. In some cases I don't believe it can be touched without precipitating a psychotic reaction. If I feel that there is a cohesive self that can be relied on, I will comment upon the detachment earlier and explore it with the patient quite directly. I have come to trust my own feelings as an indicator of the patient's detaching in the course of a session. Feelings of boredom or sleepiness are, for me, fairly reliable indicators.

I want to go into the more detailed clinical example of Miss D., who was a twenty-seven-year-old psychiatric nurse. The presenting complaint was chronic depression. My initial impression was that she had a schizoid personality. Despite this impression, however, the patient reacted with strong emotion to the empathic recognition of her dilemma: that she was caught between the wish to be taken care of and her need to maintain self-respect by her denial of that wish. Her emotional response to this suggested that there had not been a failure to develop relatedness so much as repression of it at a later developmental stage. Although she used schizoidlike defenses, she did not have a schizoid character structure.

Miss D. was the oldest of four children, the second sibling being eighteen months her junior. The self-sufficiency of the "big girl" brought her a certain amount of recognition, which reinforced the defensive premature ego development. Her relationship with her family had been rather abruptly aborted when she left home to go to college. She seldom had contact with them although there seemed to have been close involvement up to that time.

Her intermittent relationships with men tended to be masochistic in quality, characterized by her clinging behavior vis-à-vis a characteristically narcissistic and emotionally unavailable partner, and she despised herself for her dependency. She interpreted their unavailability as strength, inasmuch as if they wanted her it would imply that they were dependent and thus devalued. When she could remain cold and aloof, on the other hand, her self-esteem would be restored, but then she would feel emotionally dead. She vacillated between the dependency derived from the rapprochement phase of the separation-individuation process and the grandiose self that protected her from helplessness and shame.

In treatment she struggled against shame and resisted the regressive pull of the treatment situation. This she did with the aid of her defensive detachment. The sessions took on a deadness that mirrored her internal state, and I found myself struggling to stay awake during her hours. Finally we confronted the issue of the deadness itself, the defensive detachment, and its many ramifications. Most critical during this time was the need to be acutely sensitive to the self-esteem issue. An attitude of respect for her autonomy in particular affected her most profoundly and enabled her to relinquish the detachment. With this step she was able to renounce the pseudo–self-sufficiency and accompanying covert grandiosity. The preservation of autonomy was critical insofar as she could feel safe from being coerced or, more precisely, seduced, into a more regressed state of dependency with its attendant feelings of helplessness and shame. The autonomy issue came up around the ten-minute silences that began almost every hour. I waited patiently, sensing the importance of leaving the initiative to her. I did not interpret this as resistance, but after some time simply wondered about the silences. She was able to interpret her own need to be in charge and was grateful that I did not interfere with this or imply that it was bad by interpreting it. Issues of power are often closely tied in with self-esteem—that is, to be powerless is to be shamed.

Developmentally the first detachment in Miss D.'s life took place after there had been a satisfactory symbiotic phase with its expected ego organization. At the age of eighteen months she was forced into premature ego development because of the unavailability of her mother with the arrival of a second baby. With the need to turn to her own ego to replace the lost symbiotic partner, the stage was set for character detachment. It protected her from fear of abandonment and from the rage that would have been destructive to the now-repressed connection with the good mother of symbiosis. This aspect of her pathology was not reached in her treatment. The premature ego development was also a source of pride and the basis for the later self-esteem that reinforced the detachment as a central aspect of her personality. Detachment was also used selectively later on to protect her autonomy, which was always in danger from the seductive pull of a fantasied promise of the mothering for which she still yearned. This was exacerbated toward late adolescence when developmental pressures intensified the conflict. She dealt with this by cutting off contact with her family. Despite the pride she took in her pseudo–self-sufficiency, the deadness and depression overwhelmed any such good feelings about herself, and the depression itself was a source of shame.

After two and a half years of once-weekly analytic psychotherapy, Miss D. left treatment improved, but realizing that her work was incomplete. She felt there would still be problems in intimate relationships. Her leaving was not interpreted as resistance since this would have been experienced as an abrogation of her autonomy and a narcissistic wound. In spite of the unfinished work, she had come to be able to experience and express her feelings of love and gratitude to her therapist and experience the sadness of ending without recourse to defensive detachment. She had effected a rapprochement with her family in an age-appropriate way and was making plans to go back to school so that she could leave psychiatric nursing and enter the business world. She was giving up the caretaker role through which she had symbolically realized her own denied dependency needs and was turning to the unconflicted use of her healthy aggression and competence.

Miss D. had reacted as a child to the experience of emotional abandonment, which coincided with the rapprochement crisis. She reacted with precocious ego development and pseudo–self-sufficiency. This was in the context of a cohesive organized and reality-related self. The continuing dependency and shame issues were also related to the failure to achieve libidinal object constancy, which comes with the final stages of assimilation of maternal functions into the self. The grandiose self, to which she regressed, protected her from the anxiety of helplessness and the shame of dependency and needing.

Miss R. had reacted as a child not to abandonment but to the impingement of a narcissistic, nonempathic mother who failed to support differentiation. For her, the grandiose self served as a defense against loss of the object, which accompanied her defenses against loss of differentiation and annihilation of the self—the detachment.

It is interesting to note that in spite of the differences in history and in etiological factors in the environment—one dealing with abandonment and the other with impingement—and the differences in diagnosis, both young women as little girls took recourse to a defensive detachment with a consequent failure to achieve libidinal object constancy. Both entered treatment with complaints of emptiness and depression. Both had problems around self-esteem in spite of professional accomplishments, and both had a secret grandiose self into which their real competence had been assimilated. In the treatment of both, a combination of empathy and the analytic neutrality that protected their autonomy was critical, and in both the issue of detachment in the session became increasingly important to their work.

I have observed that the need to protect the self-esteem may be acted out in the treatment situation in many ways, some most subtle. If this acting out is not detected, it constitutes a powerful deterrent to change. I have in mind the situation with Mr. B., who seemed to be able to talk very casually about things that one might expect to cause him some embarrassment. When I wondered about his apparent good spirits as he went on, he revealed that he felt very good about himself for being such a good patient as to bring out this potentially painful material. In other words, he acted out the grandiose defense in the session, assimilating whatever he did as "good patient" into that defensive image. Only by noting the discrepancy between the material and affect could the self-esteem issue be made manifest and worked with. Despite his tremendous professional successes, shame and humiliation were his greatest fears. He noted that whatever his professional achievements, his fantasies would go them one better. The reality success did not diminish his need for the defensive grandiosity but were simply assimilated into it, feeding it, as it were. When this kind of defense is acted out in treatment, confrontation and interpretation are indicated. However, in view of the vulnerability to humiliation, one must use the utmost skill and tact in order not to provoke intensified defensiveness or premature termination. Countertransference reactions to subtle grandiosity have to be watched for. That is, the therapist's competitiveness may be mobilized and acted out.

Greenson (1967) writes: "I try to protect the patient's self-esteem, but if I feel it necessary to say something that I know he will feel as demeaning, I will do so knowingly, though I may express my regrets in some way" (p. 393). He also comments that "the compliant patient will often bury his feelings of humiliation and anger out of fear of losing love or incurring hostility. This the analyst may not always be able to prevent, but he should be alert to the possibility of it."

Working directly with the self-esteem issue as well as with the detachment that protects it will usually prevent flight from the treatment process or the institution of grandiose self-defenses as resistance to the treatment process. Ultimately the analytic work will facilitate the integration of both disowned and valued aspects of the self within the orbit of human relatedness, ameliorating the grandiosity that defends against the anxiety and depression of object loss and paving the way to a healthy narcissism.

Chapter 11

TREATMENT
OF THE NARCISSISTIC
PERSONALITY DISORDER

by David R. Doroff, Ed.D.

PRELIMINARY CONSIDERATIONS

The basic difficulty in treating the narcissistic personality disorder is that we must deal with an individual whose ego is most immature in the quality of its object relations. There may be other areas of deficient ego functioning, but the infantile quality of the object relations is central and absolutely crucial to the difficulties in living that such a person experiences and, of course, to the treatment process as well.

In the simplest way, the therapeutic task is that of enlisting the aid of an infantile individual in order that he may make use of the enabling situation of therapy to help himself to mature. In order to do this, we ask of this infantile person that he do what he has heretofore been unable to do—to fulfill such monumental tasks as tolerating frustration, bearing great amounts of anxiety without the usually employed unguents (e.g., alcoholism, drug abuse, taking flight, abusive behavior toward others, or other of the many and varied forms of acting out) and instead that he discipline himself to the task of talking about his ideas and feelings. Further, we ask of him that he learn to acknowledge others as persons in their own right—something else that he has been incapable of doing.

Whether the goals have been reconstructive or have been focused upon helping the individual introduce some element of order into a chaotic life, the treatment of the narcissistic personality has been difficult, with even modest success being far more often the exception than the rule. Part of the difficulty resides within the patient—in the limitations that are the inevitable consequences of his immature ego. The other part resides within the therapist—in the limits of his knowledge and in the suitability of his character for working with any particular patient. The past decade has seen an increased accumulation of clinical and theoretical material relevant to treating the narcissistic personality, and as a result the treatment is now more hopeful. Although the task remains formidable, we are better equipped in terms of what we understand.

At this time it is possible to find a number of definitions (or descriptions) as to exactly what is meant by "narcissistic personality disorder." The approach of this book has been developmental, focusing upon the nature and quality of the object relations in order to establish a character diagnosis. Although we do not ignore symptoms, we regard them as elaborative of the character structure, not definitive. Thus, narcissistic features in either an hysterical or borderline individual would not be sufficient to change the character diagnosis, however prominent they may be. If the essential quality of the object relations indicates a capacity to relate to others as persons in their own right, then we would consider the narcissistic elements to be elaborative in an otherwise more mature character structure. Similarly if the quality of the object relations reflects an incomplete differentiation of physical self (body ego), then we would consider the individual as borderline and once again include the narcissistic features as elaborative. This distinction is consistent with our own developmental approach based substantially upon the work of Mahler (1968, 1971) and is consistent with Kohut's delineation of the narcissistic personality disorder (1971).

Although the theoretical material relative to the narcissistic personality has been presented in some detail earlier in this book, for purposes of elucidating the relationship of treatment technique to theory, I would like to describe briefly some aspects of the narcissistic character structure.

DIFFERENTIAL CHARACTER DIAGNOSIS

Kohut (1971) has pointed out that despite the fact that he may appear rather strikingly like the borderline individual, the narcissistic personality differs in that he has the capacity to regress without either dedifferentiation or fragmentation. This is what Kohut describes as a "cohesive self." In consideration of the problem of differential diagnosis of character he comments:

> Disturbing as this psychopathology may be, it is important to realize that these patients have specific assets which differentiate them from the psychoses and borderline states. Unlike the patients who suffer from these latter disorders, patients with narcissistic personality disturbances have in essence attained a cohesive self and have constructed cohesive idealized archaic objects. And, unlike the conditions which prevail in the psychoses and borderline states, these patients are not seriously threatened by the possibility of an irreversible disintegration of the archaic self or of the narcissistically cathected archaic objects. [p. 4]

It may also be noted that the capacity to resist dedifferentiation and fragmentation is, as Kohut observes, a strong asset—one which gives the therapist a firmer ground on which to stand in the treatment process.

Of central importance is the differential character diagnosis, particularly in relation to making the differentiation between the narcissistic personality disorder and the borderline personality, since a clustering of narcissistic features is not at all uncommon in the borderline. There are two purposes in making this particular distinction. The first is that the core problems are not the same for the two groups, and hence the treatment aims in each are not the same (and, of course, treatment techniques and tactics will also differ). The second has to do with the borderline's capacity to experience a dissolution of the self. Given this possibility, the consequences of therapeutic error are even more potentially hazardous for the borderline.

The establishment of a character diagnosis through the evaluation of symptoms is an approach of long-standing tradition, but which we feel is inappropriate to the concept that character and development are fundamentally involved with each other. Kohut's approach to the diagnosis of character through the trial analysis (1971) is clearly the single most effective means, provided one has the opportunity for the study of character through the trial analysis. However, there are many situations where such a trial analysis is not an option at the therapist's disposal. Many patients seek relief but are not in a position to undergo the rigors of an analysis; many seek help through the psychological clinic, where such approaches are out of the question for a variety of reasons. However, a psychotherapy that is derived from psychoanalytically based considerations is by no means inappropriate. In such a framework the therapist must take an active approach to eliciting the data that will help to establish the character diagnosis. Bearing in mind the severe ego weaknesses of the borderline, it is important to establish whether such clear lapses in reality testing are part of the patient's experiences. Further, the core problem of the borderline and the attendant oscillatory patterns must be looked for (Horner 1976). The following vignette is an example of a character diagnosis arrived at via the assessment of the object relations.

Dr. C., a member of a professional group, turned to me during a workshop group and announced his discomfort in my presence. He felt a distinct unease with me. There was something "mushy" about me that bothered him. I asked him if he could describe the mushiness. He indicated that it involved a sense that if he got too close he would in some way "sink in" to the mushiness and be lost. He was clearly describing his fantasy of merger with its concomitant loss of boundaries. Further inquiry indicated that the boundaries were somatic. For him there would be a loss of body ego. Since I had not, until that point, been otherwise involved with Dr. C., his focus on me indicated the underlying wish that, in turn, triggered the anxious response.

In this situation Dr. C. very clearly indicated his conflict and, in so doing, allowed a character diagnosis to be made. That particular conflict is a signal of the borderline personality. In order to rule out such a possible character diagnosis in an apparently narcissistic personality, the therapist must make an inquiry into the quality of the object relations. Both the borderline and the narcissistic individual share anxiety over the possibility of abandonment, but the narcissistic personality does not experience anxiety over the possibility of dissolution of the self. For the narcissistic personality the anxiety will not go further back than relating to the loss of autonomy or to the potential shame attendant in relinquishing the grandiosity.

DEVELOPMENTAL LEVEL AND TRANSFERENCES

The narcissistic patient is fixated at a point in development of the self and object world when the first aspect of self has been differentiated with a corresponding differentiation of object. However, it is important to remember that the level of differentiation clearly includes only the separation of the somatic self from the mothering person. It does not include any awareness of psychic differentiation. It is this fact, and this fact alone, that is so critical in the development of the peculiar quality of the object relations of the narcissistic personality and the chaotic aspects of those relationships. The failure of development to proceed to the point of enabling the individual to understand that others are persons in their own right, each with his own psychology and his own needs, leaves the narcissistic individual able to respond only to his own needs and with the expectation that others exist only for the gratification of those same needs.

The development of a specific treatment plan depends upon a determination of where, in the narcissistic spectrum, the individual is fixated. Kohut has delineated the transferences, and reference to them provides a set of indispensable criteria.

There are two main transferences, the idealizing transference and the mirror transference. It is the quality of the mirror transference, with its three subtransferences, that is most helpful in assessing the major point of fixation. The three mirror transferences are:

1. Merger through extension of the grandiose self.

This represents the most primitive stage of narcissism. Here, although the therapist is experienced as separate physically, he is not psychologically separate. The patient has no sense of the therapist as a person with separate psychological boundaries from his. Thus he "expects unquestioning dominance over him" (Kohut 1971, p. 115). In short, just as the mother was experienced as part of the psychic self, so is the therapist. The patient's psychological boundaries are fluid and are extended by him to include the therapist (see Doroff 1976).

An example of this kind of transference is given by the patient who expresses indignation over the therapist's seeing other patients, voicing outrage over any and all limits of the therapist's availability to him. Such persons, for example, regard it as a fundamental right to telephone the therapist whenever and as often as they wish. Typically they feel "entitled." They have a strong tendency to react with rage at any attempt on the part of the therapist to assert his own boundaries or to impose limits.

2. The alter-ego transferences (twinship).

At this point in development, differentiation has proceeded a bit further. Although a separateness is acknowledged, it is assumed by the patient that he and the therapist have essentially identical psychologies. The extent to which the patient is able to maintain a projective identification of the good self or good object with a lover, close friend, spouse, or child, often determines the longevity of the positive aspect (for the patient) of the relationship. Such individuals tend to be impulsive in establishing and disestablishing relationships. Life seems to be a quest to find a perfect twin—one that will experience things in exactly the same way. One young woman described the disillusionment with her lover over his failure to appreciate the films of Bergman. She felt the loss of a kindred spirit and experienced a sense of emptiness as a result.

3. **The mirror transference in the narrower sense.**

Kohut describes this as "the most mature" form of the mirror transference. Although separateness is clearly acknowledged, the therapist is asked to participate in the patient's narcissistic pleasure and thus confirm it. The therapist is important only for the purpose of his capacity to mirror the patient's narcissistic cathexis (see Doroff 1976). Failure on the part of the therapist to confirm the patient in his narcissism is experienced as a blow, one that endangers the relationship. Failure to take notice of or respond as desired to a patient's new shoes or new dress may be experienced as evidence of the therapist's inability to care.

THE IDEALIZING TRANSFERENCE

Gratification, for the narcissistic personality, means having a mother with the capacity to *know* what is wanted (so that it will not have to be asked for), to supply it with no time lag, and to make no demands in turn. The fantasy that the therapist will turn out to be just such an ideal, wished-for mother serves as the basis for the idealizing transference. It relates, of course, to that point in development when mother was experienced as powerful, knowing, providing an encompassing sense of well-being, and existing for the purpose of just such providing. In the treatment situation the therapist is often experienced as such by the narcissistic personality, particularly at or near the beginning of therapy.

Because of the intensity of the patient's idealization of the therapist, it is often possible to use this transference to begin the development of a therapeutic alliance. In fact, failure to take advantage of the idealization may quickly lead to a deteriorating situation. Essentially, the patient experiences the therapist as the source of his sense of well-being. That sense of well-being is dependent upon maintaining continuous contact. The patient feels empty if the relationship is disrupted. The key to the proper therapeutic exploitation of the idealizing transference is the combination of the patient's expectations that the therapist will provide everything he wants and the patient's need to maintain continuous contact. Thus the therapist has at his disposal the motivation for cooperation. It should be noted and emphasized that unselective and premature attempts to disabuse the patient of his unrealistic expectations can lead to an irreparable disruption of this very fragile alliance.

Careful attention to the nature and quality of the patient's expectations as they are articulated within the scope of the idealizing transference will yield valuable information as to the particular level of development in the narcissistic spectrum that constitutes the patient's main point of fixation. The expectations will correspond to the stages of the mirror transferences. An example of this is provided by the man who in the first moments of his inital consultation with me announced that he "knew" that I was the right therapist for him because I was so well able to understand "everything" about him. He felt certain that there would be no problem in communication with me, as there had been with others all his life. Inquiry served to clarify that in particular he wanted a completely accepting, wholly uncritical source of support. This was to include an open-handed endorsement of his business schemes, some of which had apparently produced disastrous results. Mr. H., incidentally, had come to me as one of a long line of therapists. All the others had failed to understand him. At critical points, according to him, they had betrayed his trust. Trustworthiness encompassed not merely endorsement of his ideas for the purpose of confirming his narcissism (the mirror transference in the narrower sense) but a willingness to be totally available to accepting his phone calls, whatever the circumstances. He could not accept limits on the therapist's availability, contending that the therapist had a responsibility to be totally available (merger through extension of the grandiose self). Though Mr. H. had a sufficiently intact ego so as to be able to realize the impossibility of his demands, he reacted with such rage to the merest frustration, keeping all his relationships in a continuous state of chaos. This included his attempts at getting the treatment he badly needed, but which he would precipitously break off.

Though part of the idealizing transference was focused at a level of the mirror transference in the narrower sense, Mr. H.'s main fixation point was earlier, at the level of merger through extension of the grandiose self. This was reflected through his wish for complete understanding and in the highly arbitrary manner of his "knowing" that I was the person to understand him. It was further reflected in his wishes for total domination of his object.

EGO RESOURCES

Whether we address ourselves to the problems of treating the neurotic, the character disorder, or the psychotic, we ultimately are involved in attempts to mobilize whatever ego resources the patient has available to him. When we are confronted with the formidable problems that the narcissistic personality presents, it is most important to begin an assessment of the available ego resources almost at once. The degree to which the individual exhibits ego strengths determines the capacity to accept and utilize some of the early demands and limitations imposed by the treatment situation. It also serves to indicate the extent to which the narcissism will impose severe restrictions upon the patient's availability for the work of therapy or, in those instances where the ego strengths are greater and more diverse, where there is a greater capacity to realistically accept the demands of the situation. In the instance where the ego strength is underestimated, there is likely to be a failure to engage the patient on a work basis and act overprotectively.

Mr. N., in his middle twenties, called for an appointment. He was extremely guarded over the phone and became quite anxious when I asked for his phone number. He did not wish his parents to know he was seeing me. He arrived on time for his appointment, but was visibly nervous and asked me if it was all right for him not to look at me when he talked. He seemed somewhat at a loss as to how to proceed but was responsive to my questions about the nature of the difficulty for which he sought help. He described himself as a person who was very "nervous" and suffered from a lack of "self-confidence." He was the only child, and his parents both overvalued and overprotected him. He was hovered over anxiously by both mother and father. He felt that his difficulties began when he was about six or seven years old and his father interfered with his fighting with other children. However, he developed an active interest and participated in athletics. Interestingly, the three sports he mentioned first as those in which he participated were football, boxing, and rugby. There is no question that these sports in particular served as vehicles for the discharge of aggression, but more importantly, from the standpoint of the assessment of ego strength, they indicated an urge for mastery over his feelings of weakness and a willingness to challenge his restrictive and over-protective parents on the issue of his needs for autonomy.

Mrs. N. also described having seen a therapist for a few months the previous year. However, he terminated because, "All he did was talk with me about sports. After a while I thought to myself, 'If that's therapy, the hell with it.'"

Mr. N.'s description of the overprotective behavior of the previous therapist is an example of the failure to evaluate effectively the ego resources and to use them to engage the patient in the treatment process.

In the treatment of those patients who suffer from preneurotic disorders, the therapeutic errors are often made in the opposite direction. There is often a failure to recognize some of the limits of the ego resources, and as a result the patient simply cannot meet the demands that the therapist imposes. Elsewhere (Doroff 1976) I described a man who had asked me during our first session if I "liked" him. My concern with limiting his narcissistic demands led me to attempt to impose what I thought was a reasonable structure of expectation. I responded that I was aware of his suffering, felt compassion, but otherwise didn't really know him as yet. I had essentially asked of this man who was desperate for reassurance that he live for a while with the threat of rejection hanging over his head. He never returned.

SUPEREGO RESOURCES

Just as some ego resources may be fairly mature, certain superego aspects may be relatively well developed. Even though we cannot infer a superego in the mature sense, we often find in the narcissistic person that some qualities of the superego have developed rather precociously. Such aspects as a well-articulated value system are by no means rarely found. An ego ideal (as an outgrowth of the ideal self) is likewise part of the personality of the narcissistic character. It is sometimes striking to find a strongly humanitarian set of ideals in an individual with no awareness of the needs or rights of others. The college student who may on the one hand be deeply devoted to a lofty cause and who on the other hand has no hesitation over stealing from a bookstore is an example of just such a coexistence of both self-serving and altruistic attitudes and behavior.

The superego (however immature it may be) has importance in the treatment of the narcissistic personality in two ways. The first is that it may be appealed to and mobilized in order to prevent or lessen the degree of acting out that is so destructive to the treatment process. However, in so doing, there is a risk involved. When he makes the appeal, there is a chance that the therapist will become identified by the patient with those aspects of his superego that he experiences as hostile or depriving. This is most likely to occur early in the treatment. Great care and consideration should be given before attempting to mobilize the superego in this way. Generally the safest approach to the appeal to the superego is through those superego aspects that the patient himself loves. These are usually the patient's ideals and values. Although the patient may evidence attitudes of self-entitled indulgence coexisting with these ideals of generosity and altruistic self-denial, the appeal to the ideals (if skillfully made) may serve the therapeutic purposes well.

Many narcissistic patients suffer from those superego aspects that are harsh and even persecutory. The therapist is often motivated out of compassion to attempt to alleviate the patient's sufferings. However, great care must be exercised in this matter from two points of view. In the first instance the superego, however harsh it may be, is often the only barrier between the patient and the acting out of asocial or even antisocial impulses.

Mr. G., a rather paranoid and narcissistic man in his middle twenties, was often depressed and expressed suicidal thoughts. He was often paralyzed by anxiety in social situations. His life was rather barren of gratification, partly due to his anxiety and depression and partly due to the paucity of ego interests in his life. He felt persecuted by his own superego for a variety of perverse sexual acts in which he had indulged. He described having attempted sex with his mother on one occasion while she slept. On a number of occasions he engaged in sex with his dog. These perverse behaviors, however much he felt guilty over them, also indicated severe lapses in superego functioning. Thus it was relatively easy, with the therapist's help, to free himself from whatever restraints remained. As a result he became a dealer in illegal drugs and soon after left treatment.

The second potentially serious and undesirable consequence of effecting a separation of superego and patient is that the patient now experiences an increased sense of alienation. However much the patient may feel at odds with his superego, it is a manifestation of an internal object, and a continuing connection with it is profoundly important to his continued functioning. For the borderline patient such a separation may precipitate a psychosis; for the narcissistic patient it may touch off severe anxiety states or depression as a consequence of the object loss. Here again, considerable care must be exercised in the modification attempts of the superego. I find it most helpful to make a preliminary statement to the patient of my awareness of his need for a conscience and of my respect for that need. I also make it clear that it is my impression that there is a lack of effective communication to the conscience, though much communication from it. This opens the way for some modification without a loss of those superego functions that are both socially and psychologically necessary. I will both reinforce those useful and healthy superego aspects while appealing to it to be less blatantly hostile, as one parent might protectively intercede with another on the child's behalf.

Mr. C., a salesman, suffered severe anxiety attacks that were almost totally incapacitating. He was able to describe his inner dialogue with himself in which he shouted and railed against himself exactly as his father did. After some preliminary work indicating my awareness of his need for a conscience, I addressed myself directly to the superego. "I know that you love him and are concerned for him, but I think that sometimes you lose sight of the fact that he really is a decent person. Yes, he does mess up sometimes, but he isn't a cruel or indifferent person. He has the capacity to care, and he has worthwhile values. I think he needs you to remind him, firmly, when he gets tempted to do something that you both know is wrong. But he needs your guidance and your love and your friendship."

THE EARLY STAGES OF TREATMENT

The very fact of the patient's narcissism with its developmental and transferential implications makes it clear, as Corwin (1974) has observed, "There is thus a problem of structuring therapy: it involves the development of a therapeutic strategy at all times and this *strategy is subservient to the patient's narcissism*" (italics mine).

Whether it seems therapeutically advisable to take the position that treatment will confine itself to an essentially supportive role or whether character reconstruction is seen as the goal, the narcissistic fixation and its attendant needs, as well as the narcissistic transferences, will be paramount in dictating the therapeutic strategy. Translated into more specific terms, this means that it is through rather than against the narcissism that change is accomplished. The narcissism sets the conditions under which a working alliance may be developed. The therapist who does not accept the limiting framework of the narcissism tends to commit the basic error against which Blanck and Blanck (1974) have advised: "The therapeutic climate must not repeat the pathogenic one" (p. 104).

In an earlier paper (1976) I described the approach to developing a working alliance with the narcissistic patient as "exploiting the transference." I would like to describe this approach further.

EXPLOITING THE TRANSFERENCE

The basis upon which even a minimally positive regard for the therapist exists is usually, with the narcissistic patient, based upon a mixture of desperation and hope. Almost always the narcissistic patient seeks therapy because he is in crisis. The crisis is likely to involve either a severe wound to the self-esteem or the loss of an attachment. The patient who arrives at the therapist's office for the first session is likely to be completely absorbed with his own needs to the point that he appears to be taking no notice of the therapist, except as the therapist's responses (or other aspects of behavior) are synchronous with the distress so as to reduce it. One is struck by the extent to which a highly personalized, essentially egocentric process often governs the selection of a therapist. One narcissistic patient remarked that he had decided to work with his therapist because the therapist was black and that meant he was oppressed—thus the patient felt he could readily identify his oppressed self with the therapist. A woman decided to enter treatment with me on the basis of the plants in my office—to her they meant an attitude of sympathy for her needs "to flower."

What basically governs the initial positive regard for the therapist by the narcissistic patient is, in short, certainly based on narcissistic needs and likely to be in some way idiosyncratic. Dickes (1975) has described such essentially peculiar behavior as it forms the basis of a therapeutic alliance. His position (which is very close to the position advocated here) is that the therapist must use caution in working with these distortions since they are the basis of the alliance and the alliance itself is fragile.

> The affectionate feelings based on transference and inspiring trust in the analyst are particularly beneficial in the early stages of treatment, during which the working alliance is developing. They help create the wish to please the analyst as representative of the good parent, a wish which is not based upon rational consideration but upon libidinous expectations of many types, including irrational hopes for parental approval and reward. Once again, it can be noted that the irrational elements may help to develop a good therapeutic climate. [p. 21]

It falls to the therapist that the task is to build this initially positive reaction into a working alliance and that the most likely means of doing so is to avoid premature efforts to disabuse the patient of his unrealistic notions, allowing instead for the gradual diminution of them via the therapeutic process. The fragility of the early relationship may not be able to withstand such a disruption.

The relationship of the idealizing transference to the development of a working alliance must be considered as the central area that governs the tactics of therapy. The idealizing transference forms the basis of the initial positive reactions toward the therapist. These reactions are the minimal necessity for the commencement of treatment. The idealizing transference, as it further develops, encompasses the profound belief that the therapist is the source of all the patient yearns for—love, security, esteem, power, and an overall sense of well-being. It is important to consider the idealizing transference within the context of the period of life from which it stems—when the infant has achieved somatic separation but has not yet achieved psychic autonomy. Progress in that direction depends upon two things from the maternal environment—a combination of phase-appropriate support of the infant's narcissistic demands and a phase-appropriate set of demands that are made upon the infant. Growth is achieved by maternal responses that neither overestimate the capacities of the developing child to tolerate frustration nor underestimate them. Sensitive, phase-appropriate responses are primarily a facet of the mother's maturity. Development through the narcissistic period can be retarded by the depriving mother who cannot respond effectively to the needs of the emerging child and thus fails to understand the legitimacy of such needs as her availability. We hear this echoed in the demands of our patients for our constant and total availability for them, as well as through their sense of having screamed endlessly for a mother who did not respond. On the other side of the scale is the individual whose psychological growth is retarded by the failure of the overly gratifying mother to make the minimally necessary demands. Mothers of this sort pride themselves on never frustrating their children and on being able to "sense" what the child needs without its having even to ask. Some years ago a cover appeared on *New York Magazine* that succinctly makes the point. Three persons are shown. An elderly matron, obviously of wealth, a liveried chauffeur, and, carried in the arms of the chaffeur, a young man. The woman is saying, "Of course he can walk. But thank God he doesn't have to!"

In the treatment situation the idealizing transference is likely to develop once the patient elects to see the therapist and treatment begins. Inevitably, as long as the therapist is essentially reasonable in his manner, there will be frustration for the patient. One need not specifically build in frustrating measures, nor need one go to extremes to avoid them. What becomes crucial is maintaining a posture of reasonableness, avoiding acting out one's counter-transference reactions, and helping the patient to observe his reactions to frustration. Normal development presents the young child with frustrations and expectations, but also with an essentially secure environment that supplies the help in meeting the demands. Fixation at this level involves a refusal to endure frustration and a demand for limitless gratification.

Another important aspect of narcissistic pathology is the lack of cathexis for one's own ego. There is often, in the narcissistic personality, an inability to take pleasure in one's own abilities and accomplishments. The total focus of energies is toward being gratified by another. Blanck and Blanck (1974) make the point that ego enhancement (and hence an increased cathexis of the ego's capabilities) is often promoted by the therapist's allowing the patient to become an increasingly active partner in the therapeutic effort.

This is certainly true of the narcissistic person. I try to make the point at the very beginning of my work with the narcissistic patient that I believe in his intelligence and in his capacity to become an equal partner in the therapeutic process. I don't emphasize his unrealistic expectations. They can be given up only as growth proceeds. Rather, I consider the patient's narcissism and support the healthier aspects of it. Instead of saying something like, "It must be difficult for you to endure having to wait for things, and this must make some problems for you," (which, by virtue of pointing out the ego deficiency, may assault the needed image of narcissistic perfection), I am more likely to remark, "When someone of your abilities and intelligence encounters difficulties like these, there is something going on that isn't as visible as it needs to be. I think that if you and I can form a working partnership we may begin making sense of it and help you to get a better handle on it." Here I support that aspect of the narcissism that is needed for the therapeutic alliance. It is the only basis of self-esteem that the patient has, and unrealistic or not, he will not (and should not) yield it until he has something better with which to replace it.

To phrase it a bit differently, the treatment situation allows for a regression during which the patient reexperiences the disabling circumstances. In the case of the narcissistic personality, the patient will reenact his feelings of endless frustration, reinstitute his demands for endless gratification, and experience the therapist alternately as the source of all he values and as an indifferent or sadistic person. The extent to which the patient has previously experienced the therapist as helpful plays a central role in determining his capacity to endure his feelings of a negative sort— whether they are frustrations, deprivation, persecution, rage, or humiliation—and to continue treatment rather than precipitously breaking it off. Many of those experiences of the therapist's helpfulness will be based upon the patient's estimate of what is helpful. And that estimate is likely to involve the patient's pathology as it is his health. It may well be based upon an experience of having his narcissism gratified as well as the development of insight. In fact, in the earlier stages of treatment it is more likely to be based upon narcissistic gratifications. What is crucial, once again, is the development of an enabling atmosphere. Just as surely as it is therapeutically necessary to enlist the most mature parts of the patient's ego at the beginning of treatment, it is equally important to avoid banishment of the more infantile aspects. Failure to allow for the infantile side of the patient's personality frequently results in the development of a false-self patient.

FURTHER CONSIDERATIONS
FOR THE EARLY STAGES OF TREATMENT

Preserving the Observing Ego

Apart from the unhappiness that drives the patient to seek treatment, the chief ally of the therapeutic process is the patient's capacity to observe his own reactions. The degree to which the patient can observe and reflect upon his experience determines, to a great extent, the progress he is able to make in therapy. The relatively healthy and mature ego of the neurotic is able to maintain a virtually uninterrupted capacity for self-observation. The more disturbed patient may periodically lose this capacity. For the borderline it may signal the onset of a psychotic episode. For the narcissistic personality it frequently signals the disruption of the working alliance and even of the therapeutic alliance. Although even a very brief excursion into psychosis is not likely to result (though it does occasionally occur), there will be a loss of perspective, and the patient will be temporarily overwhelmed by anxiety or rage. The consequences of such reactions often involve the patient acting out in a precipitous manner. A narcissistic individual may leave treatment, quit a job, divorce his spouse, etc. Into a life that may already be unstable, more chaos is introduced. In order to minimize the likelihood of such disruption, it is helpful to take steps to preserve the availability of the observing ego. Toward this end I believe that there is a great deal that the therapist can do from the very beginning of treatment.

It has been my observation that those experiences of disturbances in psychic equilibrium that can be anticipated are more easily managed by the patient than are those which are entirely unanticipated. While disturbances of equilibrium are managed with relative ease and with a minimal acting out by the neurotic patient, this is not the case for the more severely disturbed individual. Hence it is desirable to keep anxiety and other altered ego states within narrower limits. To this end I feel it is most appropriate to spend time with the patient (as early in therapy as possible) describing for him what he can reasonably anticipate in the course of treatment. This includes unanticipated anxiety states, changes in his perception of the therapist, impulses to precipitously break off treatment, and other impulses toward acting out in a manner that is likely to prove detrimental to his interests. In particular I emphasize sudden changes in his perception of the therapeutic relationship, for I place primary emphasis upon the importance of keeping the therapeutic alliance viable.

As another means of enlarging the ego's sphere of influence, I also devote some time to helping the patient understand what the treatment process needs of him. This is of course not necessary for every patient. Some persons are fairly sophisticated. Others have had prior treatment and are well acquainted with the process. However, many patients, particularly young adults, are often at a loss how to be a patient. The presumption that all that is necessary is to tell the patient once that he is to say whatever comes to his mind may be sufficient for a well-evolved, psychologically minded neurotic, but it is often frightening and confusing to the less mature character. Rather than adopting a purely passive role, I devote some time to teaching the patient how he can more ably become a fuller partner in the therapeutic process, emphasizing the fact that in this way he is able to enlist his more mature characteristics in helping to promote the growth of the less mature aspects of his personality.

Another helpful involvement of the patient's ego is through the use of the patient as consultant on his own case. This is a technique that I have found useful during times of impasse when, for whatever reason, the patient seems unable to sustain optimal distance from himself. Either there is too little distance, resulting in a diminution of the observing ego, or there is so great a distance that the patient feels too uninvolved to participate in the therapeutic work. Though he may not be greatly astute at the time, the act of becoming a consultant offers an opportunity to arrive at a more workable distance.

Mr. D., an unsuccessful actor in his mid-thirties, had a manner of recounting the events of his work-a-day experience with an almost identical sameness from session to session. He invariably presented himself as the victim of a callous and exploitative "system," complaining that his inability to be more successful in his career had to do with never getting a "decent break." When I was able to elicit more detail from him as to what actually took place, as contrasted with the conclusions that he normally presented, it became apparent that his attitude of entitlement had much to do with the unending round of rejections that he experienced. He had described an audition in which he had been clearly provocative, resulting in his being dismissed before being able to complete his reading. I asked him at that point to assume that he was a therapist and indicated that I would describe to him the events of a particular case in order to get a second opinion. I then described in detail the scene he had just related to me. As the "consultant" he was distant enough to recognize, for the first time, his own role in the creation of his difficulties.

One additional technique is worth mentioning. It is also an adjunct, again useful for creating distance when the observing ego is unavailable. Elsewhere (1975, pp. 117–118) I have described this technique, which asks the patient to describe his behavior as though it were a dream:

> Behavior . . . is not always observed, and often the observing itself is so selective that critical aspects are entirely omitted. . . . The ego will select that which . . . . is syntonic, and ignore that which may be expressive of forbidden aspects of the self, or (even more subtly) disinclude that which may well be all too syntonic, but which expresses particular aspects of character defect. The narcissistic personality, for example, experiences no dystonia over his attitude of entitlement, and may never report his own contributions to his difficulties simply because it does not even remotely occur to him that he does so contribute. . . .
>
> When it has become clear that the patient is unable to understand the point of the therapist's interventions, it may be a propitious time to ask the patient to pretend that what took place did not really take place, but rather was a dream that he had. As . . . [he] does so, he must first place himself (as observer and reporter) outside the dream. Insofar as the dream functions as a metaphor, the placing of the events within the framework of dreaming allows the patient to begin the interpretations of his behavior.

Setting Limits

Kernberg (1975) has commented upon the necessity of setting clear limits in the treatment of the borderline personality to prevent the kind of acting out that can be detrimental to the therapeutic effort, particularly the kind of acting out of the transference that occurs during the treatment session. Although the context is a discussion of the borderline patient, Kernberg's remarks here are equally appropriate for the narcissistic personality.

> In the typical analytic treatment of neurotic patients such act-ing out during the hours only occurs at points of severe regres-sion after many months of build-up, and can usually be resolved by interpretations alone. This is not so in the case of patients with borderline personality organization, and the therapist's efforts to deal with acting out within the therapeutic relation-ship by interpretation alone, especially when it is linked with a transference psychosis, frequently appears to fail. [p. 85]

Kernberg goes on to make the following points: first, that the resistance to interpretation reflects a loss of the observing ego; sec-ond, that the resistance to interpretation reflects the degree of gratification that the acting out provides for the patient; and third, that the setting of limits on the acting out will provoke anxiety of the sort that helps to clarify the underlying meaning of the acting out.

The propensity of the narcissistic patient to act out in service of defending himself against intense anxiety makes setting limits a fre-quently necessary therapeutic measure. Although the patient may be resentful of it and will frequently accuse the therapist of sadism, deprivation, incompetence, lack of understanding, etc., limit set-ting is an act on the part of the therapist in response to the patient's ego deficiency. By being the one who sets the limits, the therapist provides for the patient what his own ego is unable to provide. In an unpublished paper on the borderline patient, Greenson (1970) has remarked, "My task is to strengthen those weak ego functions which are responsible for the patient's psychotic reactions. I must become the bearer of reality, the emissary between fantasy and reality, for the patient. I try to supply those ego functions he is lacking at the moment."

Similarly, with the narcissistic patient, limit setting utilizes the therapist's ego in order to promote growth of the patient's ego.

Translated in specific instances, this may involve informing a patient that he does not have the right to scream abusively at the therapist; the therapist makes a distinction between the communication of one's feelings and acting them out. The patient has to accept the reality of the therapist's boundaries and forgo the gratification of acting out transference hate. I have similarly limited a woman who felt entitled to put her feet on the furniture.

Whether the patient suffers from a lack of limitations or from too-early imposition of too-severe limits, the therapist must communicate a respect for his own, as well as the patient's boundaries. This is best done early, rather than late, and in an absence of annoyance so as to avoid the possibility of limit setting being confused with acting out the countertransference.

Among the more infantile of the narcissistic personalities, limit setting may be crucial. The patient whose primary fixation point is at the level of the mirror transference in the narrower sense is less likely to experience severe or frequent losses of the observing ego than will a patient whose primary point of fixation is at a level of merger through extension of the grandiose self. The latter patient is more likely to need clear limits set on acting out within the therapeutic hour. Patients of this degree of immaturity may often be incapable of truly enlisting with the therapist in a working alliance and will attempt to control the therapist by controlling the therapeutic hour. While one may agree with Greenson's observation (1967) that the patient selects the material for the hour, this does not imply total passivity on the part of the therapist. Various kinds of activity are necessary, and when the patient's control of the hour embodies the major resistance, then the therapist must act to set limits—most specifically choosing to bring the fact of resistance to the fore as the primary material to be discussed.

Other forms of limit setting are at times necessary. The limiting of telephone calls is described by Dickes (1975) and provides a useful model.

> The telephone also posed a problem. . . . She was free to call me but only in a real emergency. During the entire treatment she only used the phone improperly once during the first

month of treatment when she called presumably because of an urgent matter. I listened briefly until I was certain that there was no really important emergency and firmly reminded her of our agreement and told her that the matter was not an emergency. I then hung up. [p. 16]

The narcissistic personality may use the telephone as a form of acting out and as a method of resistance. Clearly enough, the most frequent dynamic underlying its misuse is the wish to have the therapist completely under one's domination. Failure by the therapist to set limits can allow a serious threat to the treatment to develop. The acting out may continue, allowing an antitherapeutic equilibrium to be maintained; the therapist's patience may be soon exhausted, creating a resentment toward the patient and toward the therapy itself.

Evaluating the Alliance

The therapeutic alliance will be severely strained many times during the course of therapy, particularly with preneurotic personalities. Almost any sort of confrontation will place it under stress. The capacity of the patient to form an alliance and the capacity of the alliance to endure under stress determines the degree to which the therapist can make use of stress for the purposes of promoting growth.

Dickes (1975) has delineated two alliances that he has designated the *therapeutic* and the *working* alliances. The former is composed of many elements, some of them nonrational, comprising the "full-scale therapeutic rapport which includes all the elements favorable to the progress of therapy. This includes such factors as the patient's motivation for treatment based on ego-alien symptoms, positive transference, and the rational relationship between patient and therapist" (p. 1).

Dickes considers the working alliance as more limited in scope, based more upon rational or reality factors and derived from the maturer parts of the patient's ego. For the purposes considered here, it should be noted that the working alliance also addresses itself to the work requisites of therapy and that it is often absent during the early stages of therapy, though a therapeutic alliance may be present.

From the point of view of the role of the alliance in the treatment process, it may be considered that the less mature the ego, the greater must be the role of the therapeutic alliance. Further, it is often the nonrational aspects of the therapeutic alliance that serve to maintain the therapeutic bond during those times when the rational ego may be under greatest duress.

In order to assess the capability of the patient to deal with stressful material at any particular point in the treatment process, it is important to consider the quality of the therapeutic alliance. This is a particularly important consideration with the narcissistic personality since the aspect of interpersonal involvement is usually on a need-satisfying basis and cathexis may be withdrawn at any moment from the therapist or from the treatment itself. There are some criteria that I have found useful in evaluating the strength of the therapeutic alliance.

1. Has the patient demonstrated a degree of self-motivation for the work of therapy?

2. If not, to what extent is the patient willing to undertake it at the request of the therapist? And to what extent can he make use of what is thus experienced?

3. To what extent can the patient acknowledge a false-self involvement and begin being his real self?

4. What are the demonstrated capacities for an attachment to the therapist as a "real" (nontransferential) person?

5. What capacities for self-confrontation have been demonstrated?

6. What capacities for confrontation by the therapist have been demonstrated?

7. To what extent has the patient indicated the ability to endure disappointment or frustration by the therapist without severe acting out?

8. Can the patient experience his anger toward the therapist without a severe withdrawal of cathexis?

There are undoubtedly other criteria that can be employed for evaluating the strength of the alliance, and each patient should be considered with respect to his own levels of functioning. The above criteria are not presented as a definitive list, but rather in the hope of indicating how guidelines can be developed that relate the clinical picture to the theoretical material in the evaluative situation.

TREATMENT FURTHER IN PROCESS

Interpretation Versus Handling of the Transference

The neurotic patient has the capacity to respond almost at once to correct interpretation. This is essentially true, even for those times when acting out is being used to avoid painful transferential material. However, the preneurotic personality does not have at his disposal the same ego strength and often fails to react favorably to interpretation—at times becoming even more resistant. Hence, it falls to the therapist to consider how the transference can be handled. By *handling* I refer to any means other than interpretation used by the therapist to promote a therapeutically desirable stasis. Most often this translates into a restoration of an observing ego. The decision as to whether to interpret or to handle the transference rests upon a determination of the extent to which an observing ego is at the patient's disposal. Because of the essential immaturity of the ego of the narcissistic patient (and even more so the borderline patient), the observing ego is often not available. The patient frequently cannot distinguish the transferential from the realistic aspects of his reactions to the therapist. Often an attempt to interpret an aspect of negative transference will be experienced by the patient as a repetition of the parental failure to hear and respond to the needs of the young child. The patient will insist upon the correctness of his perception, though it may involve serious distortion. At such times attempts at interpretation are likely to have an opposite effect from the desired one and may even, if persisted, lead to iatrogenic pathology. Perhaps no other aspect of handling the transference is so basic as the simple practice of restraint from premature attempts at interpretation. This in itself is among the measures most likely to encourage a return to a therapeutically viable stasis. At other times a statement such as,

"Perhaps I misunderstood you," is helpful in restoring the therapeutic misalliance.

Another aspect of handling the transference is either to work emphatically within it, or when indicated to allow the patient to avoid it. An example of each is given below.

Ms. D., a woman in her late twenties, had been referred at her own request. Her father himself was a practicing therapist and had been much idealized by her. Ms. D.'s mother was described as very proper, very cold, very organized. "She's like a machine. She has no feelings. Only efficiency." Ms. D.'s life was one of a series of attempts to find a niche for herself by an attachment to a glamorous man. However, her choices were invariably narcissistic men who attempted to use her as a self-aggrandizing display. (Ms. D. was a woman whose appearance was certain to evoke notice. She was tall, red-haired, and carried and dressed herself rather flamboyantly.) The emotional nourishment she sought was invariably lacking due to the narcissistic nature of the men to whom she attached herself.

She had been raised by her mother, and despite her mother's ability to provide for her in terms of a stable and predictable world, she felt constrained and ill-nourished. Though she rarely saw her father (the parental divorce occurred during her mother's pregnancy), she idealized him. At the time she entered treatment it was clear to her that she needed to sort out the patterns of her relationships. She had fled the constraining life that her mother provided and suffered repetitious disappointments in a series of affairs with fatherlike men whose narcissism precluded their being able to give to her. It was clear that she was fairly well motivated, though unstable.

She avoided discussing any reactions toward me and most often talked nearly nonstop, apparently as a way of limiting my interventions. On those occasions when I raised the issue of her perceptions and expectations of me, she reassured me that she knew that I was a doctor and that it was perfectly all right for her to say anything at all. Though I had developed some hypotheses and quite a bit more curiosity regarding her avoidance of any ideas of feelings regarding our relationship, I felt it more appropriate to accept this clear delineation of her ego boundaries. A year and a half after having entered treatment she terminated it—not abruptly, but clearly with many issues unresolved. With the matter of the transference, I felt again that it was therapeutically advisable to allow her to be in charge. I accepted her termination and the reasons she provided, adding only that should she wish to see me again at some future time, I would be pleased to see her.

A year and a half later she returned. Almost at once she began addressing some of the transferential issues that she had avoided before. It became clear that my respect for her ego boundaries (see Horner 1973) had made it possible for her to return. (Incidentally, I have found this to be extremely important with the preneurotic personality—allowing the patient to terminate without excessive rumination over resistances often makes it possible for him to return.) At the core of some aspects of the negative transference had been her perceptions of me as being like her mother. My attitude of listening carefully had been experienced as a motherlike lack of emotion. She had been fearful that I wanted to "take over" and start managing and directing her life. It was interesting to note that during the course of our work she took a job as a "girl friday" and in a fairly short time succeeded in organizing and making more efficient a chaotic office. Clearly enough, these aspects of self, adaptive and useful though they were, were experienced by Ms. D. as ego-alien and as threatening to that self that sought to maintain its individuated aspects. To be like mother was to be not-self. She was able to experiment successfully to the extent that she could use her own capacities for efficiency and organization in an area of her life that was peripheral, less central to her sense of self, and thus maintain a feeling of her own identity while utilizing an aspect of self that represented mother. Only later was she able to describe the anxieties she had over my being like her mother. When she could first experience me as noninterfering, she was then able to discuss her fears.

Working within the transference is particularly useful when the patient has established an ability to maintain an observing ego and, at the same time, is besieged by transferential fantasies of the therapist that are disturbing to him.

Ms. I., a professional woman, had for years succeeded in keeping out of her awareness an underlying depression. She had been abruptly separated from her nursemaid at the age of three. Her life had been dominated by a fear-ridden struggle to survive the consequences of that loss. She had managed to develop a fairly wide range of diversions. She used trips, work, alcohol, friends, and two unsuccessful marriages to avoid reexperiencing the original depression that followed the loss of her nursemaid. She entered treatment with me on a somewhat impulsive basis, having unconsciously identified me with the lost nursemaid. It became evident rather early that the nature of her transferences to me was narcissistic and that she was capable of a great deal of acting out. It became a primary concern to help her to stabilize in the treatment situation to forestall the kind of acting out that would undermine the treatment effort, including the possibility that she would act out by precipitously leaving treatment.

In order to effect this hoped-for stabilization, I concentrated on exploring with her the two major transferences to me: the loved and lost nursemaid and the critical mother who replaced the nursemaid. For many months the sessions were almost monothematic, being variations of focusing upon the acting out and interpreting it in terms of the transferences and her defenses against remembering.

The results of this were that she developed a greater capacity to observe herself, reduced her acting out, became far more confrontable than she had been, and in general, accepted an increased share of the responsibility for the therapeutic work.

Pitfalls

There are some particular types of therapeutic errors that are commonly encountered when working with the narcissistic personality. Although these errors have their roots in the countertransference, I would like to briefly mention them apart from the problems of countertransference.

The first is essentially in response to the patient who presents himself as an adoring child and through the idealizing transference appeals to the maternal, protective feelings in the therapist. Such patients are usually masochistic without being obviously so. There is often little in the way of a wish for growth, and they enter treatment seeking alleviation of distressing symptoms such as chronic, unfocused anxiety, a lack of self-esteem, or loneliness. In life they have been adapters, given to determining what is prized by the authority figure and appearing to provide it. In therapy they seem to make excellent patients, a phenomenon that is more apparent than real. There is a focal inability to perceive one's own contributions to the unhappiness in one's life and a presentation of self in what might be termed a "Little Orphan Annie" symptom. These persons do appear to be genuine victims of a loveless and ungiving world and often succeed in evoking from the therapist a wish to nurture and restore them to health. Unwittingly the therapist enters into an alliance with a false self that acts the part of the good patient, giving the therapist what he wants in exchange for the unspoken agreement that the therapist will never say anything that will upset the patient. Thus deprived of any expectations, demands or frustrations, the patient has little motivation for growth and appears content to maintain this level of relationship indefinitely.

Another class of error is that of confrontation. The upsurge of various "psychotherapies" in recent years has led to a generalized misunderstanding and misuse of the concept of confrontation, and in the wake of it the narcissistic personalities have probably borne the brunt of confrontation. Why this should be so is understandable when one considers the capacity of the narcissistic person to see people only in terms of their need-fulfilling functions. The therapist who is unsure of his theoretical ground and may be vulnerable to the sort of existential annihilation that is implicit in such treatment is likely to respond with a confrontation more suited to his own needs than to the patient's needs. The justification of this on the basis that the patient "needs" confronting assumes that he hasn't yet had any—an assumption that is not very likely to be the case.

Some years ago a seventeen-year-old student was referred to me by his therapist with the explanation that he was "obnoxious" and needed confronting badly. Edwin, the student, arrived at my office and while still in the waiting room managed to live up to his reputation by turning the radio up to such a level of volume that it intruded into the office, disturbing a treatment session then in progress. What was quickly established, however, was that Edwin had a history of being a successful provocateur and had managed to have himself confronted in one manner or another wherever he went. What the referring therapist had expressed was not so much a prescription as a wish.

If the confrontation is with a provocative and masochistic patient, then the therapist has succeeded only in confirming the patient's worst suspicions and justifying some of the underlying paranoid attitudes. If the confrontation is with a narcissistic personality who has allowed an attachment to the therapist to develop or is in some other way feeling particularly vulnerable, the resulting wound to the narcissism may be so severe that it has the effect of rupturing the therapeutic alliance entirely beyond repair.

Two additional aspects of the narcissistic configuration deserve comment as they are sources of potentially serious therapeutic errors. These are the paranoid elements and the masochistic elements. With the former there is the problem of the patient's long-standing and focal inability to trust. Because the therapeutic effort so fundamentally needs trust as a basic ingredient in its hope for success, it is understandable that its absence should provoke anxiety in the therapist. Yet it needs special recognition and very careful handling. My basic approach to problems of trust is to communicate to the patient that I am aware of his anxiety about trust. Further, that I respect it and will not attempt to force, coerce, trick him, or employ any means to induce trust. Also, that I assume his lack of trust exists for a good reason and that I hope to understand why; and that he alone shall determine for himself the degree, at any given time, to which he is willing to trust or to withhold trust. Over the years I have found that this approach, based upon a genuine respect for the patient's defenses in light of his history, is most helpful in allowing the needed trust to develop as an integral part of the maturing, therapeutic relationship.

Regarding the masochistic element, there are difficulties that are, in some respects, even more formidable than the paranoid attitudes. Because of the masochistic wish to be reunited with the "bad" mother, the therapist often finds himself struggling to maintain a position of therapeutic equanimity in the face of some of the patient's provocations. Additionally, there is the hidden aspect of masochism—specifically, the wish for power. The need to keep it hidden (from self as well as others) often makes for a peculiar alliance—one that is with a false self. Here the situation calls for utmost tact in helping the patient to accept that hidden part of his self. It is only with a clarification of this and an acceptance by the patient of his own power wishes that an alliance can be established on a broader, more inclusive basis and with a more real self.

Special Stress Situation

Because of the rapid fluctuations in ego states and in various aspects of the transference as well, one must expect that there will be frequent periods of disruptions of the therapeutic and working alliances. The effect of such periods is often that of discouragement for both patient and therapist. One must anticipate periods of maniclike excitement, prolonged depression, withdrawal of cathexis from treatment (from the therapist, from the self), and often long periods of unrelenting hostility toward the therapist. It is often the case for the inexperienced therapist that a siege of a few weeks (to say nothing of a few months) is sufficient to convince him that the treatment is hopeless and that both patient and therapist are better served if treatment is discontinued. Occasionally this may be true—but more often than not, what is truly needed is a therapist whose tenacity matches the patient's despair and who is willing to continue to work with the patient and remain steadfast in the struggle. Mr. N., a patient of mine for several years, has had sieges of unremitting hostility toward me that have lasted for six or more months. He has expressed a profound sense of disbelief in his ever reaching the level of maturity and integration that he seeks. During these periods he feels no sense of connection with me, denigrates me and his therapy, and vows to abandon his career and make his living by driving a truck or taxi. However, when he has successfully weathered such a period, he remarks that it is my steadfastness and willingness to see him through that keeps him in treatment and helps him get through the period. Basically I would make the same suggestion in the face of any of the more stressful periods. The therapist's responsibility is to remain available and willing to be helpful even though the patient may declare that he does not wish such help or that he devalues it. To whatever extent interpretation may be helpful, it should be used. Similarly, exploration or some form of handling the transference can be used. It is important to expect such stress-filled and disruptive reactions when treating the narcissistic personality.

Healing the Split

In both the borderline and the narcissistic patient, object splitting is frequently encountered and involves self splitting as well as object splitting. What is of greatest importance, however, is that the patient cannot experience himself as a whole person as long as the split remains. Because of the very early stage of development during which the split-self, split-object experience arises, I shall refer to self-object splitting rather than to the more traditional designation of object splitting.

The individual needs an object of certain attributes who responds in such a manner that the good-self identity is maintained. This is the basis for the idealizing transference. The object (therapist) imparts to the patient a sense that he (the patient) is a "good" person. However, in order to maintain this good-object–good-self constellation, a state of object perfection must be maintained. Since this is manifestly impossible in reality, mechanisms of denial and displacement must be resorted to. The individual eventually is faced with either a psychotic denial of reality or a loss of object of (in the case of more successful treatment) ambivalence.

What we see clinically in our adult narcissistic patients are the varied aspects of the splitting at work, usually sequentially. Behavior that is often regarded as promiscuous, for example, may reflect the failure of idealization and the subsequent fleeing from the object to a new idealized object when it can no longer function in the need-satisfying way of helping to maintain the good-self–good-object constellation. In taking a history from a new patient, one may learn that there have been several previous therapists. This is likely to indicate successive failures of the idealizing transference with subsequent breaking off of treatment. The therapeutic goal becomes that of helping the patient to stay in treatment in order to develop an ambivalent relationship, to tolerate the ambivalence, to accept the reality of imperfection and, in short, to heal the split. Thus, promiscuity, for example, may have relatively little to do with sex or morals or mores, but with the endless, repetitive search for an ideal object in order that a good self can be maintained.

Ms. Q., whom I described in an earlier paper (1976) had been referred for group by her therapist. However, it came to light that Ms. Q. had in addition to Dr. L., her primary therapist, and the group, *two* other therapists whom she kept "in reserve," seeing them on an emergency basis. What was revealed was that the "emergencies" were all of a similar nature—they had to do with eruptions of rage. During these periods she would use one of her "reserve" therapists and by so doing, deflect the rage away from Dr. L., thus maintaining her in a state of perfection. The group was similarly used—as a depository for her anger. The use of multiple therapists created a stasis that avoided the issue of ambivalence and ensured that the split would be maintained.

The use of group as a primary or adjunctive form of therapy raises the serious question of whether it helps or impedes growth. Horner (1975) feels that it is contraindicated for the narcissistic personality. She notes:

> The group situation facilitates object splitting, which is characteristic of the narcissistic patient. In the one to one therapy setting, the inability to tolerate ambivalence and the extreme libidinal swings with respect to the therapist are clear and can be worked with. In a group, the group is often used to maintain the split, representing either the good or bad object, with the therapist defined as its counterpart. The work of integrating the good and bad single object representations is interfered with as a result. [p. 304]

If one does choose to include group as part of the treatment for the narcissistic personality, it is crucial to be alert to the object splitting that is certain to be facilitated. Dr. S., an experienced therapist, expressed surprise at the fact that he himself received very little hostility from his narcissistic patients, naively observing that they were very hostile in group.

Mr. D., the actor previously described, sought the perfect woman. He was a physically attractive man and did not have much difficulty in finding women. However, his affairs were serial and short lived. Each woman had some "defect" or other that quickly caused an erosion of feeling. In Mr. D.'s case, the locus of the imperfection was the woman's physical appearance. He sought a "playboy bunny," describing at length and in detail the physical attributes necessary for the state of perfection he sought in a woman. When he did finally meet his "perfect" woman and then abandoned her after a brief time, it became clear to him that it wasn't *physical* perfection that he sought. Shortly following this he became angry at me for the first time for my failure to act in a confirming manner to maintain his sense of good-self. Gradually the exploration of the splitting mechanisms and their consequences took over the center of our attention. At this writing Mr. D. is seriously involved with a woman he has been seeing for over a year, and though he complains that her breasts are too large, he manages to remain attached to her and to treat her with kindness and consideration.

Because of the frequency with which it appears in the narcissistic personality, splitting must be considered as always potentially present and a serious obstacle to therapeutic progress. The therapist should be alerted for it and in the early sessions direct inquiries to determine its manifestations and to help make the patient aware, particularly with regard to anticipating the appearance of splitting in the therapeutic relationship. The combination of alerting the patient to its existence and importance, preparing him for its appearance in the treatment relationship, and the focus upon it, as well as the protracted, working-through period constitutes a reasonable therapeutic plan for healing the split.

RESISTANCE

The concept of resistance in relation to the narcissistic personality has a peculiar aspect to it in that it isn't of the same quality as it is with the neurotic patient. With the latter, resistance can be easily described as something that is mainly particular to the treatment situation. With the narcissistic personality it is the very warp and woof of the individual's existence. The characteristics of unending demands, attempts at exercising control over the other, a belief in one's entitlement, extreme negativism, overriding fear of having one's boundaries violated (coupled with an inability to recognize the boundaries of others), poorly controlled hostility: these are the parts of the individual's personality that are dominant and that readily make their appearance in the treatment situation. As such they make for a highly unstable alliance—one that has little in the way of "healthy" motivation and can be ruptured quite easily, often at the merest frustration, often without the therapist being aware of what has taken place. Greenson's classification of resistances (1967), which is exemplary for its clarity, comprehensiveness and cohesiveness, suggests an approach that may be useful for considering the narcissistic personality but that may need some modification to be considered here.

Like Greenson, I would consider the transference resistance to be the most important kind, particularly so with the narcissistic personality. However, though the source of the major resistance may be the same in both the neurotic and the character disorder, the manifestations of the resistance are not in the same proportions for both these groups. With the narcissistic personality the major manifestation of resistance is acting out. The greatest problem that this presents is that the acting out, by virtue of the fact that it is so essentially ego syntonic, presents no particular conflict to the patient and thus will often not be brought up by him in the treatment situation. Thus the therapist is left with a situation in which a constant antitherapeutic drain exists and about which he is left in the dark.

Consistent with the approaches that I described earlier in this chapter is the technique that I find useful for dealing with the character resistance of the narcissistic personality. This involves a kind of informing, or teaching. I feel that however limited insight of a genuine nature may be, however shallow intellectual insight may be, it is a beginning and an important one. It is for many persons the only means of access that they have to themselves and to controlling behavior that would be detrimental to the treatment. With this in mind and with a further aim of enlisting the patient as a full partner in the treatment process, I begin at once to try to elicit information that will help me to understand his patterns of acting out. I will, for instance, inquire of the patient if he is aware of his usual methods of coping with distress. As I make the inquiries, I will also take pains to inform the patient that he will experience distress during treatment and will tend to use these same methods to alleviate it. I will also explain the fundamental concerns that we have about it and ask that he try to observe himself and report to me what he has observed. I will further appeal to the more mature part of his ego by indicating that observing and reporting are important steps along the road to securing the kind of autonomy that he seeks.

The final phase of the overall strategy for dealing with character resistance is to make the patient aware of his resistance as it is manifest during the treatment session. This has the additional value of bringing the focus still closer to the transference. As the patient develops the willingness and the capability to observe his own resistances, their manifestations, and the source of them, he moves closer and closer to becoming an essentially analytic patient—one who is able to mobilize a relatively high degree of ego strength for the purpose of fuller participation in his own treatment.

COUNTERTRANSFERENCE

The less mature the patient is, the less able he is to distinguish transference from reality. While we wish to encourage the development of transferential regression, we prefer that it occur in a carefully circumscribed place, time, and manner. The overwhelming of the reality ego poses a serious threat to the patient's well-being, to the therapeutic progress, and to the therapist's endeavors—as well as to various aspects of his self-regard. The neurotic patient is capable of saying, "I know it isn't so, but it feels right now as though you must be disgusted with me." The healthy ego of the neurotic allows for an easy coexistence of fantasy and reality. His ego strength allows him to maintain a reasonably accurate assessment of his own boundaries and the therapist's boundaries. By so doing, he acts in a manner that reassures the therapist. The reassurance takes the form of accepting that things are to be talked about, not acted upon. Thus the therapist can continue his work in comparative comfort. The countertransferences with which he must deal are not of the same proportions and intensities that arise from the work with the preneurotic personality.

In considering the countertransferences that are encountered in working with the narcissistic personality, one needs to consider the attributes of the character structure itself. The object relations that are characteristic are particularly revealing. For the narcissistic personality all others exist to fill his needs. Consequently they are not responded to as persons in their own right. This results in an onslaught against the therapist's own sense of self. It is approximately equivalent to being existentially annihilated. Kohut (1971) describes it as "the specifically frightening implication of feeling drawn into an anonymous existence in the narcissistic web of another person's psychological organization" (p. 276). The tenacious, unrelenting projections that often occur pose problems for the therapist not merely in the realm of self-control against acting out but due to the paranoid sensitivity of the patient, which can zero in on some vulnerable aspect of the therapist's personality, to his self-esteem as well. One colleague characterized the results as comprising the "battered therapist syndrome." Faced with the kind of intense hatred that such patients project onto him (and without the calming reassurance of the neurotic), the therapist is indeed sorely tried. Acting out by the therapist frequently takes the form of interpretations that may be retaliatory rather than clarifying, confrontations that have the effect of allowing the therapist the discharge of accumulated rage, referral of the patient out for group ("he needs confrontation"), referral to another therapist, or the termination of treatment entirely without referral.

Another aspect of the narcissistic personality that creates countertransferential difficulties is the profound sense of entitlement that such patients often manifest. It will almost certainly emerge at some point in treatment in the form of demands upon the therapist delivered by the patient, who believes in the absolute reasonableness of these demands, no matter how imposing they may be. When they are frustrated, the patient is likely to react with a combination of rage and guilt inducement. Refusal of a demand is likely to be categorized as evidence of the therapist's indifference, insensitivity, incompetence, and sadism. To whatever extent the therapist struggles with self-doubt, the accusations fall on fertile soil. In this instance there is a temptation to waver in the firmness of one's position. The therapist with his already obsessive penchant for considering all sides of any question may well begin to wonder if the patient isn't right in his accusations—especially when they begin to provoke reactive hostility. Thus emerges the therapist's discouragement and with it a wondering if both patient and therapist wouldn't be better off if the entire project were abandoned.

In another paper (1976) I described the reactions of the narcissistic patient to the frustrations that therapy imposes. I categorized them as object splitting, regression to grandiosity, hostile withdrawal, guilt inducement, and termination of treatment. In addition to these, I indicated that there were some clearly identifiable reactions to object loss. Insofar as these are the most typical reactions of the narcissistic patient to the frustrations of treatment and insofar as the patient's aggression will be chiefly directed toward the therapist's narcissism, the therapist is likely to have similar tendencies to react. Often the nature of the counter-transference provides invaluable information into an otherwise incomprehensible treatment difficulty. Kohut's description of the reaction of fear (1971) is an example of how the therapist's reaction may be a useful lead in determining the underlying nature of the interaction. Within the context of assuming some degree of paralleled processes, it is only appropriate to inquire whether the therapist who is feeling suddenly just a little depressed may be suffering from the loss of the patient's idealizing transference. Though this transference may be unrealistic, it appeals to the therapist's narcissism, supporting it by confirming the therapist as he wishes himself to be. Similarly one may pause to wonder if the sudden lateness of the normally punctual therapist for his hour with the narcissistic patient might not be a case of tit for tat. In this instance, is he treating the patient with the same indifference and/or contempt with which he has been treated?

Freud's recommendation to the therapist (1912) is most appropriate here: "he must turn his own unconscious like a receptive organ towards the transmitting unconscious of the patient. He must adjust himself to the patient as a telephone receiver is adjusted to the transmitting microphone" (pp. 115–116).

A final note in the treatment of the narcissistic personality concerns itself with the therapist's tendencies toward grandiosity. A realistic assessment of one's limitations is crucial. Both Kohut (1971) and Kernberg (1975) are in agreement that each therapist must not have too many narcissistic patients. I add my opinion in agreement with theirs. These are difficult patients to work with. Treatment is long and wearing at best. Progress is slow, and the demand for discipline is great. An exhausted therapist is of little value to his patients or to himself.

CASE STUDY

Mr. D., the actor previously mentioned, had been referred by a therapist with whom he had been working. Though some important work had been accomplished over a period of about three years, particularly in the area of introducing a degree of stability into an otherwise chaotic life, there had been little progress in the last year. I was later able to clarify that the stalemate was due to acting out the transference during the hour.

Mr. D. was the youngest of four children. His father was a highly respected and much-beloved physician in the small town in which he practiced and in which the family lived. He died in Mr. D.'s early adolescence. Around his father grew a mystique to the effect that he was something of a saint. He was considered a wholly unselfish man, given to cheerfully sacrificing his time, his efforts, and his privacy for the sake of his patients. He was held up to Mr. D. in his childhood and adolescence as a model to which Mr. D. was to aspire.

Mr. D.'s mother was devoutly religious. She was intense in extolling the virtues of work, discipline, and self-sacrifice. She regarded Mr. D. as her baby and apparently struggled against her impulses to indulge in babying him.

Mr. D.'s brother and two sisters regarded him as a mixture of the family pet and the family foil. A good deal of sadistic teasing fell to him from them. Much of the teasing was instigated by the mother, with whom he seemed to be constantly and endlessly at war. She had a nickname for him, which was given in the spirit of ridicule. He was referred to as "Slaby," which was a contraction of "slow baby," referring to both his position at the bottom of the family totem pole and to his characteristic mode of passive-aggressive resistance to pressure by being chronically late.

Despite the evolution of a narcissistic and passive-aggressive character structure, Mr. D. was able to attend and successfully graduate from the drama school of a first-rate college. He was a man of high intelligence and sensitivity, quite gifted in both his profession and his avocation of photography. However, he was most unsuccessful professionally. His narcissistic attitudes of entitlement and belligerency offended and alienated those persons who were in a position to hire him. He would occasionally secure acting jobs that might have been springboards to the development of a successful career but would inevitably undermine his chances.

When he entered treatment originally he was a marginally functioning person. His therapist described him as nearly overwhelmed by panic. He appeared to respond almost immediately to his therapist (a woman) and became calmer. From what could be reconstructed, his therapy seems to have been largely experiential, with Mr. D. responding to his therapist with an idealizing transference and working very hard to please her. As he had in the family, he adopted a role in his first treatment. In his family his role had been that of "Slaby," who is infantile, incompetent, who messes. In treatment he initially became the "good patient" who does what his therapist (ideal mother) expects of him. In both situations a large part of his personality remained split off. In treatment it was also his more able, competent self that was split off, but additionally, in the early stages of treatment, it was also his hostile and passive-aggressive self. He had responded with a strongly idealizing transference to the warmth and concern of his therapist. But with the failure of the idealizing transference (as reality intervened to frustrate his infantile expectations of having a perfect and omnipotent mother who could function as an extension of himself to gratify *all* his wishes), he reverted to a hostile and negative transference. He did not invoke the grandiose self in order to separate from his therapist but rather attempted to coerce from her the submission to his will that he sought. He began to reenact the struggles he had with his mother. One of his earliest memories was of his mother trying to get him to the toilet and his defecating on her before she could get him there. This became reenacted in treatment and became the point at which he arrived at an impasse. He was locked into a transferential perception that his therapist was trying to dominate him and reacted by a refusal (disguised) to assume either control or responsibility for his behavior. Under the guise of being the good patient he dutifully reported his dreams, which were monothematic and, as his therapist characterized them, "shit" dreams. Session after session for many months was spent by him in recounting (with evident hostile pleasure) the intimate details of his dreams of defecation. It was at that point of impasse that he was referred to me.

As he had with his first therapist, he quickly developed an idealizing transference toward me. On one level I became the longed-for father who had been too busy to be available to him. On a deeper level the idealization was of mother, since I, too, was expected to provide him with whatever he wished for. Just as he had turned hopefully to his father in childhood, so he turned to me. And just as he experienced disappointment with his father's failure to fulfill all his expectations, so he experienced disappointment with me. With the failure of the idealizing transference he became angry with me, but in his characteristic manner not directly so. Instead he began (as he was later to characterize it) to whine. His whining was an attempt at coercion through guilt inducement. He presented himself to me as suffering from my failure to have helped him. His sessions were dominated for many months with an almost singsong complaining about my failures to help him. When I interpreted his behavior as resistance to assuming responsibility for himself just as he had refused to assume responsibility earlier in his life, he would respond by making feeble gestures at responsibility and then resume complaining, this time augmenting his complaints with the allegation that he had tried, but it was really beyond his capability.

His relationship to his social and working world were of a similar nature. He complained unendingly about the women that he was involved with. They failed to appreciate him, they failed to love him adequately, they were physically imperfect, they rejected him, except for those in whom he wasn't interested. As for finding employment, it was a similar situation. The agents were callous and indifferent, the casting directors wouldn't give him a decent break, it was all a matter of who you knew. In all his complaints about finding work in his profession there was some truth, but the truth was misused by him to obviate the issue of his own responsibility.

One of the means that he used to avoid a confrontation with the aspect of his contributions to his own misery was to present accounts of what happened in a manner that omitted the details, including only his conclusions. As this became apparent, I brought his attention to it and suggested that he give me a more detailed description of what had taken place, as though it were a script that he was reading. I asked for a line-by-line account of exactly who had said what. As he did this, he revealed his own sarcastic and provocative remarks that had resulted in his being summarily dismissed from an audition without his being able to complete the reading. Similarly I insisted on his giving me a line-by-line account of the social interchanges in which he was involved. This too led to a confrontation of the effect of his behavior. Both of these areas were then compared with his behavior in the treatment situation and further compared with the overall conduct of his life as they represented infantile attempts at forcing the world (mother) to give him what he wanted on his terms. Over and over I made the point that I would do my best to help him understand himself, but that the rest was up to him. His reactions to this were usually outbursts of rage. He accused me of being utterly unsympathetic to him and of trying to force him to do that which was beyond his means. He made the point repeatedly that if he were able to do for himself, he wouldn't be in treatment in the first place. I must acknowledge that for many months I felt as though I were under siege. In truth I was, for he had made it clear that he planned to extend his domain over me. Though I felt sure of my character diagnosis of him and though I felt sure that my steadfastness in neither being provoked nor coerced was what he needed most, many times I felt discouraged, tired, frustrated, bored, and annoyed.

Despite what seemed to be an endless and unremitting siege of thinly veiled hostility, the confrontations (which he could not deny) and my consistent interpretations of his character resistance (which were given within the context of a sympathetic appreciation of his family's inability to understand where he was developmentally during infancy and childhood) had the effect of allowing a gradual diminution of the resistance. He began to accept the role of observer and reporter of his own behavior. Some of the chronic aspects of resistance to change were in process of change.

His chronic lateness seemed to be on the wane, whether to an audition or to a treatment session. His whining was replaced by an almost enthusiastic wanting to know more about his own character and its functioning. He accepted greater responsibility for the progress (or lack of it) in treatment. His characteristic projection of blame onto others shifted to an attitude of wanting to explore how he might have undermined himself.

With regard to some of the internal structural changes, they appear to proceed more slowly than the behavioral changes. However, one example relates to the change in superego precursor. Mr. D. had narcissistically claimed the right to dirty others just as he had joyously defecated on his mother as an infant. However, near the end of his third year of treatment with me he reported a dream in which he sees a puppy in a toilet and instead of pulling it out, proceeds to urinate on it. This is followed by his becoming frightened. He understood the puppy in the toilet to represent a helpless person and his urinating on it as an act of unmitigated hostility. ("That's the way I really feel, like pissing on somebody.") It was the experience of becoming frightened that marked a change. Until then he would not have experienced the fear. Though in this instance we see little concern for the rights of others or of any sense that what he does is morally wrong, we do see the precursor of a superego, the sense that there are consequences. This marks a further advance in his quest to renounce his own grandiosity. It is a more realistic awareness that he lives in a world in which there are consequences.

In the past year he has become involved with a woman to whom he has formed a strong attachment. In this relationship he has been able to accept the idea that she too has needs. To some extent he has been able to achieve a higher level of narcissistic pleasure through his ability to think in terms of her needs and to minister to them. She is the first woman with whom he has been involved without the idea of perfection being in the forefront of his feelings about her. In the past he has been involved with many women and has always (with one exception) complained that each of them has some physical imperfection that limited his enjoyment. In the second year of his treatment this issue came to the fore. He had complained about each of the women with whom he had been involved that there was some physical anomaly that was "a turn-off." He was resistant to any interpretation of the meaning of the idea of perfection to him. It was only after he met a woman whom he described as being physically perfect and the most beautiful he had ever known that the issue could be considered more fruitfully. After having managed to have sex with her and then finding that her other characteristics were more of a disappointment than any physical imperfection might have been, he began to think about the meaning of perfection to him, equating it finally with his need to maintain his grandiose self. He felt that it was important to have a woman of such beauty that she would mirror him as he wished to be. To have an imperfect woman meant to have his sense of perfect self tarnished. I was able to then help him to relate this to his long-standing inability to trust. For him, to be less than perfect (grandiose) meant to be helpless. This in turn was connected to his sense of himself as having been truly helpless (during his infancy) to make his mother respond more appropriately to his needs. He had been, on one hand, pushed prematurely to be responsible far beyond his reasonable capacities. On the other hand there had been an expectation that he would fail. There were even certain rewards that fell to him in his role as "Slaby," the family clown. It was suggested that there might have been subtle reinforcement from his sisters for his behavior, which was so enraging to his mother. It seemed like an endless dilemma for him.

Many sessions were punctuated with his demanding of me that I tell him what to do. I would point out to him that he must decide for himself what to do. He would then beseech me for a solution, claiming that his career hinged upon it. I would indicate to him that there were two problems with telling him what to do. The first was that I would then be like mother, who told him what to do, which was likely to provoke him to act in the opposite direction. The second problem was that by telling him what to do I would be treating him with contempt, presupposing that he was utterly incapable of discovering for himself what to do. This theme dominated our sessions for many months.

At this point in his treatment he works analytically and fairly well. He has confronted the fact of my insistence on the maintenance of my own ego boundaries and responded first with rage and then with genuine depression, signifying a profound shift in the narcissistic position. The depression means a deep sense of loss. In this case the loss is the passing of the hope for narcissistic domination over me. It signifies his acceptance of the fact of my psychological separateness from him and a temporary fear and anguish over this loss. With this acceptance has come the increased capacity to assume responsibility and the wish for realistic effectiveness instead of grandiosity. Not long ago he visited his mother. For the first time he was able to maintain a sense of equanimity. He found the visit pleasant, but strange. The strangeness seems to be in his perception of her. He reported that she was "sort of a little old lady, getting on. It was funny, I felt sorry for her. She seemed so lonely."

Chapter 12

DIAGNOSIS: THE MEDICAL MODEL, EGO ASSESSMENT, AND THE DEVELOPMENTAL MODEL

The use of the medical model as an approach to diagnosis (and presumably treatment) is best exemplified by the Diagnostic and Statistical Manual of the American Psychiatric Association. DSM III, like its predecessors, take a clinical, descriptive approach to classification. What are broadly referred to in this book and by others—e.g., Giovacchini (1978, 1979)—as the character disorders, are classified in DSM III as the Personality Disorders. These, in turn, are subdivided into three clusters.

The first cluster includes Paranoid, Introverted, and Schizotypal Personality Disorders. Individuals with these disorders often appear "odd" or eccentric. The second cluster includes Histrionic, Narcissistic, Antisocial, and Borderline Personality Disorders. Individuals with these disorders appear dramatic, emotional, or erratic. The third cluster includes Avoidant, Dependent, Compulsive, and Passive-Aggressive Personality Disorders. Individuals with these disorders often appear anxious or fearful. Finally there is a residual category for Other or Mixed Personality Disorders that can be used for other specific personality disorders or for cases with mixed features that do not qualify for any of the specific Personality Disorders described in this manual, but are of sufficient severity to cause either significant impairment in adaptive functioning or subjective distress. [DSM III, 12/13/77, p. K:3]

In his recent review of concepts of the borderline personality, Meissner (1978) notes a recent shift "from a phenomenological or symptomatic evaluation to a greater attention to evaluating the organization and integration of structural aspects of the personality" (p. 562).

Although still using the standard diagnostic terms, Giovacchini (1979) defines each in terms of character structure rather than on the basis of clinical symptoms. He likes the term *character disorders* because the word *character* emphasizes the ego and its modalities and because the word *disorder* implies a disturbance at the structural level. This point of view minimizes the role of intra-psychic conflict and emphasizes the structural defects (p. 61).

Giovacchini breaks the character disorders down into five categories, pointing out that they are only general guidelines. He says that "to attempt further precision would be tantamount to measuring to a degree beyond the capacity of the measuring instrument. One cannot expect to find microscopic clarity when our investigations are conducted macroscopically" (p. 64).

The subcategories described by Giovacchini are: (1) the schizoid disorders ("The Hopeless Patient"); (2) borderline disorders ("The Helpless Patient"); (3) character neuroses—which include the narcissistic disorders ("The Alienated Patient"); the affective disorders ("The Miserable Patient"); and the psychotic disorders ("The Delusional Patient").

He describes the broad general category—the character disorders—as being unable to master the problems imposed upon them by the environment. "They find themselves perplexed, unable to get along with their fellow man, and plagued by existential questions and identity problems insofar as they do not know who they are, why they exist, or where they fit into the general scheme of things" (p. 62). Giovacchini notes that the general composite picture will vary according to whatever special defensive adaptations are used by the patient to cope with the world of reality. An example of this would be the schizoid defenses used by an individual with otherwise borderline characteristics.

Blanck and Blanck also address themselves to the limitations of the medical model and the importance of working on the developmental diagnosis for each patient. They comment that "standard psychiatric nomenclature suffers . . . from the attempt to squeeze psychological data, which are of a different order from the physical, into the medical mold" (p. 91). They choose to base their diagnosis on the structure of the ego in which a symptom is embedded.

Blanck and Blanck propose four groups of ego impairment. One is the *ego defect*, which is constitutional so far as is presently known, and which shows as an impairment of the autonomous functions. Children with learning disorders would fit into this group. Second there are the *ego deviations*, which are the outcome of early developmental departures from normality. An example of this is what Blanck and Blanck describe as premature ego development. "Quantitatively, a deviation may be so slight that development is not impaired substantially on the one extreme, or it may be so great that subsequent development is severely hampered on the other with, of course, many falling in between" (p. 93).

They use the term *ego distortion* to refer to faulty perceptions of self- and object-representations. It seems to me that these distinctions may often be less than clear-cut. Both ego defect and ego deviation can affect the course of development of self- and object-representations.

The fourth category of ego impairment described by Blanck and Blanck is that of *ego regression*. Ego regression is manifest in a loss or diminution of function as the result of backward movement from a higher level of development to a lower one. The general term *ego modification* applies to all four categories.

Blanck and Blanck emphasize that all sorts of symptoms, even those usually considered to be psychotic, may be found in normal and neurotic structures as well. They also note that these diagnoses change during treatment "because ego-building techniques have as their goal alteration of ego structure. In fact, one way of describing the purpose of treatment is to change the diagnosis" (p. 97).

BORDERLINE AND NARCISSISTIC DISORDERS

In recent years the literature has abounded with discussions about two particular diagnostic concepts—the borderline personality and the narcissistic personality disorder. Here more than anywhere else we see the attempt to order the data concerning character structure and its development in a manner that will yield clear diagnostic categories in the tradition of the medical model. But as Meissner (1978) notes, there is still theoretical disagreement regarding the basic pathology of the borderline personality. He wonders if theoretical formulations tend to mask an underlying diagnostic heterogeneity. He cites Kernberg's view (1975) of what Kernberg refers to as the borderline personality organization, which he applies to these patients

> who do have a specific, stable, pathological personality organization; their personality organization is not a transitory state fluctuating beyond neurosis and psychosis. [p. 3]

Meissner (1978) delineates the areas of deficit found in the borderline individual.

> 1) instinctual defects 2) defensive impairment 3) impairments or defects in other areas of ego functioning and integration 4) developmental defects 5) narcissistic defects 6) defects and impairments in object relations 7) the organization and pathology of the false self, and 8) forms of identity diffusion. [p. 564]

Difficulties in arriving at agreed-upon diagnostic categories relate to the lack of agreement on how to organize the data. Using the development of object relations, of self- and object-representations, as the organizing principle enables us to see more clearly the interrelationships of the ego functions overall as well as of the deficits described by Meissner.

In 1975 I wrote of the ego functions:

What is not taken into consideration here is the essentially hierarchical aspects of these functions. The synthetic function seems most closely related to the innate competency of the organism itself, its ability to assimilate, organize, and integrate its experience from the very start. Difference in the extent of this innate competency may well explain why one child can master, at least relatively successfully, unfavorable environmental factors, while another child cannot. . . . So far as the remaining functions are concerned, it seems equally clear that *object relations development is primary*, providing the matrix within which the other functions develop. [p. 95]

We can use this same perspective in examining the functional interrelationships of the deficits described by Meissner. For instance, my view, like that of Loewald (1971), is that we can see the development of the instinctual drives as part of the overall developmental process in which they are shaped and modified by the quality of interaction with significant others. For the character disorders in general, and more so for the more primitive patient, anger and hostile aggression result from the failure or the inability of the environment to respond to the infant with good-enough empathic caretaking to protect the child from excessive frustration and from overwhelming traumatic states. Such states interfere with or overcome the synthesizing capabilities of the infant and thus interfere with patterning and structuring. Insofar as anger and aggression remain unpatterned and unstructured, they are outside the realm of ego control. Despite the depths of rage in the narcissistic personality disorder, it is organized vis-à-vis the bad object and is under better control than in the borderline personality, for whom rage can be disorganizing or may be expressed in a less controlled and less specific object-directed manner.

One need not take recourse to a concept of excessive innate aggression, as is Kernberg's view (1975). Perhaps because of physiological vulnerabilities some babies may be difficult, if not impossible, to calm and comfort at times. Still, the anger and hostile aggression will have to be viewed as secondary to the failure of the environment, for whatever reason. The issue of innate, destructive aggression as opposed to aggression in response to environmental failure in the genesis of character disorders is one of the major points of disagreement between Kernberg and Kohut, with Kohut taking the latter view. I view all self-initiated, assertive and eventually goal-directed actions as a manifestation of innate aggression. They are neither hostile nor destructive in themselves, but only become so when fused with negative affect.

In his overview of current concepts of the borderline personality, Meissner also reviews the typical defenses used in borderline conditions. These are "splitting, projection, projective identification, primitive idealization, and denial." With respect to splitting, I do not agree with Kernberg that splitting comes about as the result of a defensive maneuver but share Atkin's view (1974).

> The "cleavage" in the cognitive, thought, and linguistic functions that will be demonstrated . . . can best be understood . . . as developmental arrest. No anxiety was produced in the analysis of the dysfunction, a proof that it is not a defense. (Where no knitting into a whole has taken place there can be no "split" in Kernberg's sense.) I found that only after some maturity of the ego occurred as a result of psychoanalysis did anxiety appear when the discrepancies were analyzed. Only then was the dysfunction used as a defense, with resistance to giving it up. [pp. 13–14]

Modell (1961) speaks of the denial of separation that creates the illusion that the object is somehow part of the self and therefore cannot be lost. I have also commented on the denial of separateness from the bad object in the masochistic character as a way to maintain the illusion of omnipotent control as a defense against the anxiety, or even terror, of the potentially destructive object (chapter 8).

The essential quality of the defenses of the damaged ego relates to what is being defended against. It is not so much anxiety per se, but what the anxiety portends—i.e., the dissolution of the self or object loss and its attendant separation anxiety. If a particular affect, thought, or impulse threatens to disrupt, disorganize, or impinge upon the organization of the self, then the defense against that which is toxic to the existence of the self must be rigid, bringing to bear denial of reality if that is what is needed. Projective identification, with the externalization of an aspect of the self or of an unassimilated introject, protects the individual from becoming lost in the intrapsychic world and maintains a link with external reality, distorted though it may be.

In short, the defenses found in the character disorders in general have the monumental task of maintaining the structure of the self and the avoidance of psychosis, the loss of touch with external reality. As such they require a greater distortion of reality, greater rigidity, and a more ferocious fighting off of any assault upon these defenses. The ego, which is itself damaged, is called upon to erect defenses aimed toward its own survival and the survival of the self in particular. Thus the nature of the defenses in the character disorders is determined by the status of object relations development and the quality of the self- and object-representations.

Pathological narcissism is also associated with the character disorders. Teicholz (1978) reviews current concepts of narcissism, commenting first on Stolorow's functional definition (1975), which dispenses with the concept of libido, as "a relationship or mental activity (which) is understood to be narcissistic to the extent that it serves the psychic function of providing structural cohesion, temporal stability, or positive affective coloring to the self-representation" (p. 836). She comments further that "whereas the mainstream definition holds that any libido is 'narcissistic' that is invested in the self, Kohut holds that any libido is narcissistic that has an idealizing or self-aggrandizing quality."

In her view of concepts of superego development, Teicholz comments that the "ego ideal is in one respect only a further development, chronologically and hierarchically—a further differentiation and integration of the experiences that originally contributed to the earliest self-representations" (p. 844). This is consistent with my comments that the superego, including the ego ideal, is the outcome of the transmuting internalizations of the functions of the maternal introject during the rapprochement phase of the separation-individuation process, a process that culminates in identity and object constancy. She cites Jacobson (1974), who wrote:

The maturation of the ego . . . [leads] to an acceptance of what is realistic and reasonable, it accomplishes at least a partial victory of the reality principle, not only over the pleasure principle, but also over exaggerated "idealism" and thus over the superego. Only then do the superego functions work with more neutralized energy. [p. 130]

In 1975 I wrote of the stages and processes in the development of early object relations and their associated pathologies, constructing a diagram which was misleading inasmuch as it suggested that the point of developmental fixation, the point beyond which further differentiation and integration of self- and object-representations could not evolve, is also the point of primary etiological import. With respect to the character disorders, it is important to look further back, beyond the developmental node at which the pathology became evident, to consider what went before, the nature of the character structure as it evolved up to that point. The revised diagram appears in chapter 2 of the present volume.

I view the narcissistic personality as emerging at the junction of the practicing period in which the developmental anlage of the grandiose self comes about and the very beginning of the rapprochement phase at which time the self is experienced as helpless and the object is viewed as all-powerful. As of this point there has been little, if anything, in the way of transmuting internalizations of maternal functions that pave the way to object constancy.

Mahler (1971) discriminates between individuation, which is the evolution of intrapsychic autonomy, and separation, which involves differentiation, distancing, boundary structuring and disengagement from the mother. She points out that the two processes run on two intertwined but not always synchronized developmental tracks (p. 407). Although the narcissistic personality has achieved secure boundary structuring with differentiation of self from nonself (the first differentiation, chapter 4), he has not yet achieved intrapsychic autonomy.

Kohut (1971) emphasizes the differences between the narcissistic personality and psychoses or borderline states. While patients with narcissistic personality disturbances have in essence attained a cohesive self, this is not true of the psychotic or borderline individual. The narcississtic personality has also constructed idealized, archaic objects that are, to some degree, differentiated from the self. Furthermore, "unlike the conditions which prevail in the psychoses and borderline states, these patients are not seriously threatened by the possibility of an irreversible disintegration of the archaic self or of the narcissistically cathected archaic objects" (p. 4).

Kohut sees the single most important discriminating feature between narcissistic personalities and borderline or psychotic patients as the failure of the latter to attain a cohesive self-object. Because of this failure that takes place during the symbiotic stage, they are unable to bring together cohesive narcissistic structures—either the grandiose self or the idealized object—so there are no analyzable transferences.

> The borderline has a less cohesive self that is easily subject to fragmentation so that he is unable to maintain the boundaries between self and object. The threat of disintegration is more central and critical in borderlines, whereas the disruption of the narcissistic relationship plays the more prominent role in narcissistic personalities. [Meissner 1978, pp. 584–585]

Meissner is critical of formulations drawn in terms of the cohesiveness of self as he does not see that they offer any ground for distinguishing between borderline pathology and psychotic levels of organization (p. 585). The issue of reality testing as the distinguishing feature between the borderline personality and the psychotic patient is relevant to this argument. Cohesiveness is a necessary but not sufficient discriminatory variable with respect to making these diagnostic formulations.

In the first chapter of this book I wrote that the mother functions as the mediator of organization and of reality relatedness, and her internalized image becomes the cornerstone for the capacity for human object relatedness. This overall configuration of events sets the stage for the evolution of a cohesive, reality-related, object-related, self.

Cohesiveness reflects the capacity of the synthetic function of the ego to organize experience—both inner and outer—into patterns, the essence of structuralization. This can take place either with or without reality relatedness, and indeed the well-organized delusional system is a tribute to the synthetic function in the face of gross environmental failure. Thus, while cohesiveness is the critical distinguishing feature between the narcissistic personality and the borderline character structure, reality relatedness and reality testing are the critical distinguishing features between the borderline character and the psychotic personality organization. Some of the difficulties in current theory building are due to the neglect of important interrelationships with, instead, a linear view of the various, developing constituents of the personality. When one looks at the functions of the ego in this manner, the reciprocal and interlocking developmental impact is lost. I believe that the concept of object relations development as the matrix within which the other functions of the ego unfold and the concept of self, per se, as an organizing principle clarify the process. We must construct a diagnostic diagram for a given patient on which he is located along the three axes of cohesiveness, object relatedness, and reality relatedness, and compare the individual structure, in this manner, with an "ideal" structure.

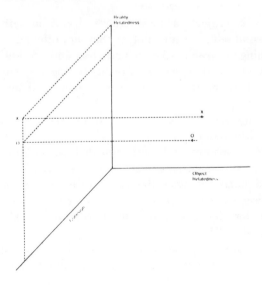

Hypothetical patient A, in this instance, is someone who has difficulties in the area of self-esteem because of a significant degree of emotional abandonment with the rapprochement period, so that the unfolding autonomous functions developed outside the realm of object relatedness. There is no impairment of cohesion, but there is an absence of internalized maternal functions and thus a failure to develop object constancy, with some dependence upon a grandiose self as a defense against the anxiety and depression of object loss. The lower rating on reality relatedness reflects the importance of the illusory, grandiose self.

I am making no attempt to construct a diagram characteristic for any given diagnostic grouping. Its purpose is to formulate a view of the patient's character structure that can be directly related to treatment. In the next chapter I address this problem directly. Suffice it to say here with respect to the hypothetical patient, the therapeutic task would be to promote reality relatedness and thus an overall integration of the self. Because of the reliable cohesiveness I do not have to be concerned that an intervention will be experienced as annihilating of the self, as in the example of a therapeutic error reported in the next chapter.

With respect to the development of both cohesiveness and reality relatedness, this would relate to the quality of very early maternal care—whether it was to a sufficient degree in harmony with that which came from the child to bring into some semblance of harmonious integration experiences of the real self vis-à-vis the object and external reality of which the mother is a representation and to which she is a bridge. The greater the failure of the mother to bridge internal with external reality, the greater the likelihood of psychosis. The patient with the delusion of being pregnant with the Messiah is an example of this kind of situation. Her mother was psychotic and failed in this respect. The cohesiveness and organization of her secret, delusional self is not what is at issue. It is the degree of reality relatedness. Of course we find defects in cohesiveness as well, particularly with respect to her rage. The early, excessive frustration and thus traumatic anger interfered with her synthesizing capabilities in the early, organizing phase of development. The extent to which failure of both cohesion and reality relatedness, whether partial or pervasive, will determine the severity of the psychosis.

Thus, I see a difference between the narcissistic personality and the borderline character structure in the same terms as does Kohut, with the additional comment that the borderline is then differentiated from the psychotic by the presence of reality relatedness as a characteristic of the self.

I view the narcissistic personality as emerging at the junction of the practicing period in which the developmental anlage of the grandiose self comes about and the very beginning of the rapprochement phase of the separation-individuation process at which time the self is experienced as helpless and the object is viewed as all-powerful. As of this point there has been little in the way of the transmuting internalizations of maternal functions that pave the way to object constancy and an autonomous self. Maternal ambivalence from the very start has led to the formation of two relatively cohesive self-object representations, one positive in quality and the other negative. Their practically equal salience reflects the mother's ambivalence. For this reason the integrating of the split images is not possible. Continued experiences vis-à-vis the maternal ambivalence continue to reinforce the split, overriding the cognitive development that originally enables the child to form an integrated image under the aegis of "I" and an integrated object image under the image of "Mama." Because the child cannot move forward toward object constancy and an autonomous self, he is either thrown into total dependence upon an unreliable object or back upon the grandiose self in the face of the failure of the object.

I view the borderline condition as emerging—but not beginning— with the recognition of separateness at the beginning of the rapprochement period. Because of the weaknesses inherent in the structure with respect to cohesion, the recognition of separateness evokes severe separation anxiety and restitutive defenses against the dangers of the breakup of the self for which the undifferentiated object has been a kind of "glue." One patient said, "You are the glue that holds me together."

Both the narcissistic personality and the borderline individual retreat from the impact of full differentiation that comes with the rapprochement period. The narcissistic personality retreats because the persisting split into good- and bad-object images, and the corresponding good- and bad-self images, predispose him to extreme reactions to environmental failure, reactions of humiliation and/or rage, and the anxiety of not being able to control the source of narcissistic supplies. He retreats to the grandiose self as a defense against the anxiety of object loss and as a defense against shame.

The borderline retreats from the full impact of the recognition of separateness because the structure of the self is threatened, insofar as the connection with the undifferentiated object constitutes a kind of prosthesis for his tenuously organized self. He may retreat only so far as the grandiose self, or he may move further to dedifferentiation through merger, which would constitute the break from reality to which the borderline is susceptible.

THE SCHIZOID CHARACTER
AND THE BORDERLINE SYNDROME

I see the schizoid character as a variant of the borderline syndrome. The characterological detachment is a defense against the anxieties of the borderline situation. In 1974 I wrote of schizoid withdrawal as

> a flight forward, a premature severing of the symbiotic bond, in a kind of pseudo-individuation. Since the separation process is, in this instance, so precipitous, it does not allow for the gradual internalization of the libidinal object which culminates in . . . object constancy. (Although) attachment has been achieved with the schizoid individual . . . it is later denied in the effort to escape the engulfment of symbiosis. [p. 103]

In chapter 3 I described Mr. A., whose schizoid flight was from the terrifying image of the bad object of symbiosis, the "harpy" who would tear him apart. The earlier the flight, the more pervasive the characterological detachment, as described by Schecter (1978). The use of schizoid defenses in a clearly borderline character was manifest in the material of Miss R. The reason I believe that the schizoid individual did form attachments that were later denied is in the contrast with those individuals in whom there were no attachments, individuals described by Bowlby (1946) and by Rutter (1974). The complete failure of attachment from the very start leads to the formation of the psychopathic individual who does not have the capacity to form relationships. I have found that the schizoid patient relates, when he does, with the same fears as borderlines in general. In other words, I see the schizoid personality disorder as a subgrouping of the borderline personality. As Giovacchini (1979) writes with respect to the character disorders, "This is a general composite picture which will vary according to particular characterological defenses—that is, special defensive adaptations employed to cope with what the patient experiences as inordinately complex surroundings and reality" (p. 62).

I stated earlier that I do not believe that the child has to invent its defenses, but instead he draws upon the memory of ego states that have been experienced previously in the course of development. I also wrote of the developmental, schizoid, core self that is organized early as the infant encounters the nonpersonal world around it and organizes these experiences vis-à-vis the perceiving self. The schizoid character regresses to this comparatively safer ego state from the anxieties of symbiosis with a dangerous object. One man reported early memories of crying in his crib. His retreat to a schizoid character defense was the final response to repeated abandonments, like the stage of detachment described by Bowlby (1973). At a later date, when the schizoid defenses were relinquished, he expressed fears of engulfment and had difficulty differentiating aspects of self from object. Once the schizoid defenses are put aside, the borderline issues emerge in full flower.

I mentioned earlier that the concept of self is useful as an organizing principle in theory building. Using that concept here, I would say that in the borderline individual the self is uncertain, amorphous, impossible to define. There are basic defects in the patterning of the self in the borderline situation. In the narcissistic personality the self is patterned, but the patterns are not integrated—they are split. Then there are those individuals in whom the self is well defined and experienced ambivalently but where there has been a failure to assimilate significant maternal functions into the self, resulting in a state of continued dependency upon the object. The final step toward an autonomous self and object constancy has not been accomplished. This was exemplified in the case of Mrs. N. described in chapter 6, whose mother still had the key to her internal "thermostat." I have had difficulty in assigning the latter type of situation to any diagnostic category. They are clearly not borderline, and they are not narcissistic personalities. Yet they still suffer from preneurotic issues. Using Giovacchini's distinction (1979) between character neurosis and the narcissistic personality, it seems to make sense to me to call this kind of character difficulty the character neurosis. I usually find that unresolved ambivalence toward the mother of separation is the critical factor. The resistance to identification with a hated object is a defense against potential self-hate.

THE DIAGNOSTIC PROCESS

Given the issues of character structure to be explored in the diagnostic process, what of that process itself? How do we go about getting the data we need to make our diagnostic formulation?

We cannot always come to a clear formulation without an extended period of evaluation that will go hand in hand with treatment. It may be unclear at the beginning, for instance, whether the patient has regressed under stress to what Zetzel (1971) calls a borderline state, or whether this is characterologically and structurally a borderline patient.

Blanck and Blanck (1974) remind us that all sorts of symptoms, even those usually considered to be psychotic, may be found in normal and neurotic structure as well.

I view the diagnosis as a working hypothesis, nevertheless, and generally feel that I should be able to formulate some kind of tentative hypothesis by the end of the first session. I probably tend to entertain the hypothesis of the greater possible pathology, with the view of avoiding serious therapeutic errors that may lead to the flight of the patient. As new data comes in, as in theory building, the diagnosis is modified as necessary. The diagnosis is, in effect, a theory about the personality of the individual patient, and as with any good theory, there should be an internal consistency, correspondence with the external facts, and predictive as well as explanatory validity. Blanck and Blanck speak of the "interweaving of diagnosis and treatment" (p. 113).

The diagnostic interview must be carried out with full clinical skill and sensitivity, recognizing that the treatment process is set in motion with the first phone call and even before, with referral and the decision to call.

Transference (and countertransference) elements may be strong at the outset, inasmuch as the absence of data allows for maximum projection. This is why I like to inquire about any dreams since the first appointment was made. Such initial dreams often lay out the core issues of the character structure and the manner in which they will be manifest in the treatment process, particularly resistance related to the transference.

A forty-year-old man with a history of many previous attempts at treatment, all ending after about two years with an intractable negative transference, reported the following dream in our first interview. Although it was a dream recalled from childhood, it was remembered at this time which, gave it the same import had he dreamed it anew.

> There was a mouse, and my mother got frightened and grabbed me up in her arms and jumped out the window with me.

In essence his dream reflected his early experience that being taken care of was based more on the needs and anxieties of the mother and endangered the survival of the self. Learning to tend to these needs and anxieties of the object, he developed a false, caretaker self, and the real self remained frightened and isolated. This was acted out in treatment, and everything he said or did, including his prevailing mood, was based on what he "read" as the needs of the therapist. He would then leave the session feeling isolated and depressed, as well as angry and exploited. He was afraid to expose the real self lest it be vulnerable to the defective judgment of the mother, as well as to her narcissistic rage if he failed to meet her needs. He did not stay in treatment with me, having brought with him many years of distrust built up vis-à-vis therapists, which quickly translated into contempt accompanied by the mobilization of his grandiose self. In retrospect, my too-early interpretation of the dream, which at first made him feel hopeful, frightened him. It was experienced as impinging, which then made me the bad object that would annihilate him.

I generally find that an early formulation of the core problem, empathically stated, facilitates the building of an alliance, of a sense of being understood. Such a statement may be something like, "It sounds like you really have to struggle to maintain the sense of your own boundaries," or "It sounds like you are afraid that if you exercise any degree of autonomy, you will surely be abandoned, and this seems to make you understandably anxious." Thinking back to the patient just mentioned, I would have to add that in stating the core problem in this manner, one must be sure that the statement of the problem does not in itself constitute an override of the defenses or an impingement upon the self.

When the patient hates his symptoms and therefore the self who has the symptoms, I may comment that in my experience such behavior at one time had important survival value and that it will be important for us to discover what this is together. I do not negate the negative judgment in a way that communicates unwillingness to relate to that hated self, however. In fact, the implied wish to understand the hated self also implies its acceptance in a way that promotes a working alliance. Perhaps my fundamental belief that "irrationality" is understandable and my clear alliance with the survival of the self make the empathic statement of the core, characterological defect and the attendant attempts at adaptation, a statement of hope as well.

I also find that my own initial "gut" reactions may tell me a great deal, depending as they do on the subtler cues of interaction. Liking the person too quickly alerts me to the patient's seductiveness or to a possible subtly idealizing attitude. Deadness in me alerts me to detachment. Dislike alerts me to covert contempt. Knowing and defining my own countertransference tendencies give me an additional resource for the formulation of the hypothesis. There are also those reactions not particularly idiosyncratic to me, such as a sense of confusion that reflects the inner confusion of the patient, which is also manifest in his manner of presenting. When I cannot get any sense of the person at all with respect to character structure or dynamics, I consider the possibility of a false self.

The data we need to make our diagnosis may or may not emerge at the beginning of treatment. Blanck and Blanck (1974) make the important point that it is not desirable to insist upon details before a trusting therapeutic alliance has been developed.

> We do not want diagnostic information for its own sake, at the expense of the patient and at the sacrifice of a therapeutic alliance. Therefore, we have to be content with less information at the outset and with a tentative rather than a firm diagnosis. [p. 106]

By and large, my approach to assessment is a way of evaluating the extent to which there is a cohesive, reality-related, object-related self-structure and to what degree and in what manner these may be compromised. In effect, my thinking follows the format of this book, an approach that clearly takes as central to the character the development of object relations and the current status of self- and object-representations. One should be able to answer the following questions as the diagnostic process moves along.

Attachment. What about the quality of attachment? Was there a failure of attachment from the start? We are not likely to encounter this situation with someone who has voluntarily sought out treatment. Was there a disruption of early attachment? Is this a schizoid character? Were there multiple, unintegrated attachments, resulting in a deficit in the cohesion of the self? Was there an attachment through a false self? Is there a true self available to the treatment process? Has there been a defensive detachment? If so, what purpose does it serve? How will the issues of attachment and detachment be manifest in the treatment process? Should the detachment be confronted and interpreted or not? If so, when and how?

Cohesion. Is there a cohesive self-representation or representations? We can have a relative degree of cohesion even in the presence of splits in the self. Are affects integrated and structured, bringing them under the aegis of ego controls, or are they unintegrated, split off, and potentially disorganizing? Which affects are integrated? Which are not? The same questions may be asked of impulse, motility, perception, thought, and somatic experience.

Object relatedness. Is there a cohesive object-representation or are objects related to only on the basis of their need-satisfying functions? Are good- and bad-object images still split or have they been integrated, and is there an awareness of and tolerance for ambivalence? How about object constancy? Which maternal functions have been assimilated into the self, and which aspects of the object remain as unassimilated introjects? How are the unassimilated introjects manifest in the transference? Are they an integral part of the character structure, emerging through projective identification vis-à-vis the analyst? Or do they emerge in fantasy, dreams, or free association, as remnants of earlier stages of development in the context of an otherwise more evolved character? Have the autonomous functions been organized and integrated within the realm of object relatedness, or is their expression associated with object loss?

Differentiation. Is there a differentiated self? Is there only partial differentiation, such as the differentiation from the good object but not from the bad object as in the masochistic character described in chapter 8? Under what circumstances is there a failure of differentiation? And how is it manifest—in more concrete terms with a dedifferentiation of body image or as a failure to be able to differentiate the feelings of the self from those of the object? Does the defect in differentiation reflect a developmental impasse, or does it emerge with regression as a defense, as when the borderline individual regresses to further dedifferentiation to protect himself from the disorganizing impact of recognition of separateness at the beginning of the rapprochement phase of the separation-individuation process?

False self. Is there a false-self identity that has been consolidated around reactions to an impinging environment rather than an identity that is consistent with that which is intrinsic to the core self? If so, at what point in development did this come about? Is the false self the whole of conscious identity, or is there a secret self that is conscious but that is vigilantly protected from a potentially hurtful environment? What is the nature of the true self? Is it amorphous? Is it organized but secret? Does the false self seek out conditions in which it is safe for the real self to emerge? Is the true self in contact with reality, or is it essentially delusional in nature?

Grandiose self. Is there a grandiose self? Is it a central aspect of the character structure, as in the narcissistic personality or the borderline patient, or is it a remnant of the archaic past and serves as an ego defense in a more evolved character? Is it used intrapsychically to defend against humiliation or shame, or is it acted out vis-à-vis the object as in the narcissistic personality? What of the autonomous functions that emerged during the era of development of the early anlage of the grandiose self? Do they still belong to the grandiose self, or are they organized and integrated with a more realistic self-concept? That is, is there a reality-based self-esteem?

Idealized object. Does an idealized object remain as the illusory source of needed supplies, keeping the individual in a continuing state of dependency, or have the functions of the maternal introject been assimilated into the self, enabling a higher level of autonomy? Has this process of internalization resulted in the development of a superego, which provides both ideals and conscience? Are there positive social values that are the outcome of identifications with positively cathected objects?

Superego. Is the superego now clearly an aspect of the self, or is it still essentially a foreign body to be warded off or complied with in the manner of a dependent child? Is the patient capable of mature guilt, or does the unassimilated, angry introject now direct that anger at the self, resulting instead in depression associated with the loss of love of the needed object? Is the superego even more primitive and based upon the grandiose self-image (in which case it is easily corrupted when the rage associated with narcissistic entitlement overrides social, moral, or ethical issues)? Does such "righteous indignation" masquerade as morality?

Oedipus complex. If there are oedipal issues, are they clearly within the framework of the family triangle or its derivatives, or have they been assimilated into a dyadic preoedipal structure that resulted in the sexualization of early object relationship issues and situations? Is this manifest in perversions? How is it manifest in the transference?

The other ego functions. In making my diagnostic assessment, I also want to evaluate the ego functions from the more traditional viewpoint of ego psychology. For instance, what about the synthetic function? Are there biological deficits, such as those that can be assumed on the basis of a history of learning disorder? If not, under what psychological conditions may it be overwhelmed?

And what about the defenses? Are there adequate defenses against anxiety, or does it constitute a traumatic state? Are the defenses important to the maintenance of the integrity of the self, or are they used in the context of intrapsychic conflict in a more evolved character?

Are the autonomous functions autonomous, or have they been caught up in conflict? Are they part of the grandiose self? Have they been compromised as a defense against the dangers of projected envy? Are they associated with object loss?

Are instinctual drives integrated into the self and thus under some measure of ego control? Are there also superego controls as the result of the assimilation into the self of maternal self-esteem regulating functions?

Are the thought processes under the dominance of the reality principle? Or are they subverted in the service of maintaining the integrity or esteem of the self?

And what about the sense of reality and reality testing? According to Mahler (1952), "the most important transitory step in the adaptation to reality is . . . that step . . . in which the mother is gradually left outside the omnipotent orbit of the self." Has this step been taken? And does a false-self identity contribute to feelings of not being real?

TAKING THE HISTORY

At the very start of the treatment process the therapist is generally more active and directive insofar as his immediate goal is to take a history and formulate the problem. A certain amount of structure is introduced as questions are asked, questions that are based on the therapist's wish to know rather than on the patient's wish to reveal. Immediate information is forthcoming with respect to how this process goes.

When narcissistic demands and the need to control are prominent, there may be annoyance or outright anger that the therapist's needs are taking precedence over those of the self. At this point it is important not to become involved in a power struggle, in the interest of establishing a therapeutic alliance—or at least finding if one is possible.

Passive compliance, on the other hand, with no attempt to elaborate beyond a minimal response or to interject any thoughts or reactions of the self, suggests a dependent character, although little more can be said of it without more information.

What I am saying is that the nonverbal, stylistic, acted-out aspects of the character structure are important data to be noted. One gets a sense rather quickly if the individual is psychologically minded, if he is able to observe his own psychological processes and to comment upon them, or if his perception is primarily directed outward toward the environment. In the first instance we may anticipate the ready establishment of the working alliance in the presence of an observing ego. In the second situation we can anticipate an acting out of characterological problems and defenses and that treatment will also be characterized by acting out vis-à-vis the therapist. In this case, mobilizing the observing ego and establishing a working alliance will be the first major task. From the very start the most important data will be derived from the patient's manner of relating to the therapist.

But what of the specific questions that must be asked somewhere along the way? Even if they cannot be asked at the beginning, opportunities do arise for such inquiries as the therapeutic alliance develops, times when an inquiry fits in with what the patient is talking about and thus will not be experienced as an intrusion but as an expression of interest.

For example, I will want to know about peer relationships in childhood and adolescence. The narcissistic child does poorly with peers. They tend to pick up the grandiosity and the need to be special, sometimes attacking it with ridicule. To the extent that the child is locked into a parent-child mode of relating with its attendant developmental and structural issues, peer relationships will be compromised. Excessive dependency may be exploited by other children, but the overly dependent child also does poorly in the peer situation. Sexual and gender identifications and conflict in this area may be reflected in the choice of friends and activities. The girl who wants to play only with boys or the boy who wants to play only with girls may have such problems.

When the patient can tolerate and cooperate with a straightforward history taking, questions about peer relationship should be explored at that time. Otherwise I may wait until the issue of friends is initiated by the patient, at which time I may ask something like, "How was it with friends when you were little? Did you play with other kids on the block?" And, "Did you have friends at school?" Or, "Did you have a best friend?" And I may also wonder how the friend situation was during the adolescent years.

By and large, the diagnostic interview will be somewhat sketchy, and I will allow time for the details to be filled in as therapy proceeds. However, an overall look at what I might cover in a direct, straightforward history taking would be as follows.

The presenting problem. Why has the patient come to see the therapist? To understand the context of the presenting problem, I will inquire about the patient's current life situation with respect to work and important relationships. I may or may not inquire about sexual involvements at this time, depending upon whether the inquiry seems to be readily identifiable as part of the problem.

I will want to know the history of the problem. When did it start? Did it ever happen before? What made it go away? Or is it chronic?

Is the presenting problem well defined and related to specific life circumstances, or is it vague, diffuse, and something that has apparently always been a problem?

Previous treatment. I will want to know if there has been previous treatment. If so, how did it go? Why didn't the patient return to the previous therapist? How did the last therapy end? What were the main problems in the working relationship? What were the main psychological issues that were worked with?

One can learn a great deal about the transference issues likely to come to the fore from such a history. Without having to make a judgment about the competency of the previous therapist, we can detect what issues the patient is sensitive to and how he will react if he perceives—rightly or wrongly—a certain kind of response or behavior on the part of the therapist. Forewarned is indeed forearmed in this situation.

Family. Then I may say something like, "Tell me how it was for you growing up—who was in your family?" I will want to know who lived in the house, and who was important even if they did not live there.

I will ask, "How was it between you and your mother?" "How is it now?" And, "What about your father?" I will also inquire about the marital relationship and how that affected the patient as a child.

We also need to know about brothers and sisters, their ages, and their interrelationships. Whom was the patient closest to? Was he a parent to his sibs, or was a sib parent to him?

I will point out that in some families the members are assigned different roles—the bad one, the good one, mother's helper, the family's pride and joy, and I will ask what role the patient played in his family. I will consider whether a false-self identity was consolidated around a parental projective identification played out in the assigned role. Slipp (1973) writes about the "symbiotic survival pattern" and the part this kind of situation plays in the genesis of schizophrenia.

I may also inquire about the family attitudes toward sex and the nature of the patient's sex education.

When I am presented with an idealized view of the parents and of the family—"they were perfect"—I know that there will be difficulty ahead since change through treatment may be experienced as disloyalty to the family. I make no attempt to undermine the idealized view, as it will be taken as an attack on the family and possibly on the psychological structure of the patient himself.

One of the things I will consider about the patient's relationship to his family is if he has been "bound" in any of the ways described by Stierlin (1977). I believe that the failure to keep the family dynamics in mind may sometimes lead to the failure of treatment, especially if the patient is still actively involved with the family. Stierlin writes of "ego binding," in which developmental defects make it impossible to leave the symbiotic network. With "id binding," the overgratification of narcissistic wishes undermines the motivation to leave. And with "superego binding," the young person feels guilty about leaving the family, much as an abandoning parent.

Some of the most difficult cases I have worked with are those in which the individual is responsible for maintaining the self-esteem of the parent. Slipp (1977) writes of the "succeed for me, fail for me" bind, in which the child must win or succeed to make the parent proud as an extension of the patient and must not shame the parent by being more successful than the parent. I have not found that any amount of analytic work has helped unless the family patterns were directly explored and their impact on the self-image of the patient understood in these kinds of situations. Generally these patients are still intensely involved with their families of origin.

Peer relationships. At this point I will probably ask some of the questions I discussed earlier in this chapter.

School and work history. My next line of inquiry will be how it went in school. I want to know about divergence between ability and performance, which may relate to the degree in which autonomous functions have been caught up in conflict. School performance and work performance are generally related—issues of success and failure, of competition, and of grandiosity.

I may also pick up some indication of an early learning disorder, in which case I will think about constitutional factors in the genesis of psychopathology. It is important that we do not forget about issues of organism and spend years trying to analyze that which is organically based. Only recently in my work with Miss R. did it come out that her vivid visual imagery, which I felt contributed so greatly to her analytic work, has always been a source of great anxiety, making her feel different and even fearful of being crazy, as well as feeling unable to communicate with her family. She is in a highly verbal line of work, and there is no verbal cognitive deficit that can be observed. Grigg (1977) wrote about the implications of left-right cerebral specialization for psychoanalytic data collection and evaluation. He pointed out that "in arriving at some of his most original ideas, Einstein rarely thought in words at all. Rather 'physical entities,' some of visual, some of muscular types, occurred first, with conventional words having to be sought for laboriously in the second stage" (p. 453). Sharing this information about cognitive styles with the patient led to sobs of relief that there was not something terribly wrong with her. We then had to look at the way in which her "defect" actually made her feel special. It also represented to her the fragile core self that must be protected lest it disappear and there be nothing inside her.

At one point, in my own need to know, I asked questions that were clearly threatening to that vulnerable self, eliciting a reaction of panic on the part of the patient. This therapeutic error and how I handled it is described in the next chapter.

Reaction to beginning therapy. I will then inquire about what feelings the patient had since our initial phone conversation and in coming in for the appointment. I will also ask if he recalls any dreams during that period of time. Some patients are able to articulate their concerns at that time. "I was afraid that I wouldn't know what to say." "I was afraid you would say I was crazy." "I was afraid you wouldn't be able to help me." "I was afraid that you would not want to work with me." "I was angry that you couldn't make it at a time more convenient for me." "I didn't have any reaction."

Issues of helplessness, idealization, narcissistic entitlement, and unavailability of an observing ego can be hypothesized from these opening reactions.

The formulation. At this point I may make a statement as to what I see as the core problem. I try to do this without going beyond what is close to the patient's conscious awareness—though not yet formulated by him—and in a way acceptable to his self-esteem. Generally there is a feeling of relief and hopefulness if the patient feels understood. This is no time for exhibition of one's brilliant insights, as they may be experienced as truly magical or as intrusive into the self. The statement of the core problem should stay close to the material that has emerged in the interview.

Reactions to the first session. Finally I will inquire about reactions to the session and what the patient thinks about going on with our work. Negative reactions to the process or to me personally may emerge at this point. A woman who never returned commented that she couldn't stand how much I looked and dressed like her mother. Extreme negative transference reactions will usually work against the establishment of a working alliance. Idealization has its own problems. One woman commented, "I feel like I've found the mother I've always wanted." She had a history of meeting what she fantasied as the therapist's needs, which were her own projected demands, with the fantasy of reestablishing the idealized, symbiotic union. She would leave treatment when her hopes failed and she began to feel exploited. Although this was interpreted in the hope of forestalling the acting out, she was angry at my failure to accommodate with a reciprocal acting out. Previous therapists had become "friends," going so far as to invite her to their home. The emergence of her own dependency when she could not act out the role of caretaker with me made her feel shamed and vulnerable. She left treatment as a denial of need, but at least this time not feeling exploited. The door was left open for her return.

In the course of the history taking I will be alert to developmental issues, such as problems in separation and loss. If I sense that separation anxiety is a significant factor, I will inquire further about early separations and what they were like for the patient. That is, if there is important material to be explored, I will follow that line and leave other aspects of the history taking for later, if necessary. A core-issue statement such as, "It sounds like separations have always been painful for you," moves the diagnostic process into therapy proper. This may happen in the first session. The therapist must be ready to relinquish his more directive history taking stance in the interests of the requirements of the treatment aspect of the situation. From the very beginning, the therapist's concern is to establish the therapeutic matrix within which deficits in the ego in general and in the self in particular, can be repaired.

Chapter 13

THE THERAPEUTIC MATRIX

The consistent and predictable presence of the primary mothering person throughout the early months of life serves to tie the infant's experience together in a particular way. It is through her that body, impulse, feeling, action, and eventually thought become organized as part of the self and integrated not only with each other but also with external reality of which she is a representative. She is a bridge between the child's inner world of experience and the outer world of reality. The mothering person not only mediates this process of organization and reality relatedness, but her image is part of what is organized and is the basis for the development of object relatedness as well. Thus, her role in the evolution of the self- and object-representations is critical. When early development within the maternal matrix goes well, the outcome is the achievement of a cohesive, reality-related, object-related self.

Character pathology results from failures of this process of organization and may take the form of deficits of cohesion or integration, deficits of reality relatedness, or deficits of object relatedness. With the interruption or distortion of the development of early object relations, the individual does not arrive at the healthy outcome of the end of the separation-individuation process—a well-secured identity, object constancy, and the structuring of the superego, which regulates self-esteem.

In his introduction to *A Study of Interpersonal Relations*, Mullahy (1949) wrote that "fixed biological needs and drives and their frustrations do not provide the locus of mental illness, that instead the social order itself is the ultimate matrix of functional mental disorder" (p. xxxi).

And Chrzanowski (1978) points out that "Sullivan's major contribution consists in viewing the self as rooted in a network of relatedness to one's fellow human beings" (p. 38). He goes on to state that the therapist "functions more in the role of instrument than as his particular interpersonal self" (p. 42).

A modern interpersonal view might be synthesized to read that the social order of the therapeutic relationship is the ultimate matrix for the treatment of mental disorders, but that this matrix is based more upon what the therapist does than who he is.

What the therapist does—or should do—in any given treatment situation must bear directly upon the developmental, structural diagnosis. This diagnosis will take into consideration the quality of cohesion and integration, of reality relatedness, and of object relatedness. When it has been determined that there has been a failure or deficit in the organization of the self, we can view the major function of the analyst or therapist as parallel to that of the primary mothering person or persons of infancy—that is, as the mediator of organization within the therapeutic matrix.

This therapeutic matrix, the analogue of the good-enough mother of infancy and of separation and individuation, sets the stage for the repair of the defects of the character structure. It facilitates organization and integration of the various aspects of the self, some of which may have been cut off, denied, or repressed, and some of which may have a disorganizing impact when experienced. The therapeutic matrix facilitates the attachment process, which will eventually provide the basis for the internalization of maternal-therapist functions, as well as for the further integration of the self within a context of human relatedness. The therapeutic matrix facilitates differentiation, the structuring of ego boundaries, the achievement of identity coupled with the achievement of object constancy, and the structuring of the superego.

There is still no general consensus as to what is curative in the therapeutic or analytic situation. Spitz (1959) suggests that "anaclitic factors operating within the transference relation are adequate to enable the patient to re-establish his object relations . . . at that level at which his development was deficient" (p. 101). He, like others, emphasizes the importance of not interfering with this process, of not intruding, of not interfering with the patient's autonomy.

No directive or educative measures in the commonly accepted sense of the terms are necessary. Indeed, they can only disturb the natural process, which is so highly individualistic as to make it impossible for the particular therapist to direct it in its minute details. Any direction required is provided actually by the transference situation. This insures a process of development unfolding free from the anxieties, perils, threats of the original situation. [p. 111]

THE INTERPERSONAL DIMENSION

Giovacchini (1975c) comments that

there has been a shift from looking exclusively at the patient to focusing upon the interaction between patient and analyst, bringing the analyst's participation to the fore. Psychoanalysis . . . has become a highly interpersonal affair. [p. x]

Langs (1976) refers to what he calls the "bipersonal field," noting that every communication from the patient is influenced to a greater or lesser degree by the analyst and vice versa.

Tolpin (1978) takes issue with the notion of a nonspecific, extra-analytic "corrective emotional experience" and with the notion that improved self-esteem and the acquisition of purpose and ideals are by-products of analysis.

These are intrapsychic achievements which depend on the acquisition of new psychic structure—and these are precisely the acquisitions and improvements which are "expectable" when self-object transferences are explicitly recognized, interpreted, and worked through. In other words, these specific changes go hand in hand with the filling in of structural deficits. These changes are not merely hoped-for beneficial by-products of analysis—they are the goal and the outcome of the analytic work and the successful resolution of this species of transferences. [p. 182]

Although at one point Giovacchini (1972b) says that he sees a general agreement that the essence of psychoanalytic technique is insight-promoting interpretations of the transference relationship, he also takes note of the organizing function of the therapist. The therapist is like the mother who comforts the child in a manner that his affective state does not become traumatically overwhelming. Giovacchini comments that "by introducing the observational frame of reference . . . the analyst brings organization to a situation that would otherwise be hopelessly muddled for the patient" (p. 713). Still, his emphasis is on interpretation as the specific and major contribution to the patient's improvement.

Friedman (1978) comments that understanding, attachment, and integration are factors in achieving benefit from therapy. He emphasizes the part played by the personal attachment of the patient to the analyst. He reminds us that understanding goes beyond the intellectual and the verbal and defines attachment as a binding emotional reaction to the analyst. In human relations, attachment is how learning proceeds.

Meissner (1975) writes of the relevance of theory to clinical practice and notes that "ultimately the theory must provide a framework and a context of notions through which we are able to formulate and understand what it is that we experience with our patients" (p. 182). He calls attention to the implications of the analytic situation as a form of repetition of the early mother-child relationship. Not only interpretations, but the manner and style of the process and other unspecified factors operating more broadly within the analytic process will affect its outcome. Meissner speaks of the importance of the analyst's experiencing self "as an instrument of understanding" and responsiveness "as an empathic receptive organ by which the analyst and the patient are in relationship" (p. 204).

Up to now, those "certain important unspecified factors" have been neglected in the attempt to understand what it is that "cures" the patient. Emphasis is on interpretation, particularly the interpretation of the transference. If we examine the many complexities of the therapeutic matrix, we must also admit to our consideration the importance of the very presence of the therapist as an organizer. The quality of that presence and its impact on a given individual may either facilitate or interfere with organization. I have observed that when I am particularly fatigued, or perhaps distracted, and thus do not interject the "hmms" that say, "I am here and listening," the patient tends to fade away.

Tolpin (1978) reexamines the concept of the "corrective emotional experience" in the light of the analyst as a new object, providing the interpersonal matrix that allows for structuralization.

Ornstein and Ornstein (1975) consider the "nonspecific" aspects of interpretations that affect the patient's progress in analysis. Rather than the exact content of the interpretation, the correctness of wording, timing, and depth, even more important—or certainly equally important—is the manner and tone in which the interpretation is conveyed. They note that "many writers have commented on the possibility that what the patient perceives and responds to in the analyst's communications is not *what* is said but *how* it is said" (p. 228).

They emphasize the interpersonal dimension of the central, intrapsychic phenomena and add that "as long as resistances are seen only as externalizations of the ego's defensive structure, their interpersonal dimension will often be overlooked" (p. 263). They do not call for the fostering of a "real" relationship but feel that it is imperative that impinging reality aspects must be attended to in the interpretive process.

Ornstein and Ornstein point out that our interventions, although falling within the traditional frame of interpretation, may have either organizing or fragmenting impact:

Reconstructions, by addressing themselves to the whole person of the patient and to his entire experience, rather than to a small detail of it, will enhance self-cohesiveness. In contrast, the interpretive focus upon a single drive derivative, or upon a particular defense mechanism, tends to fragment the self [p. 267]

STRUCTURAL REPAIR

I have found that addressing the issue of structure per se rather than interpreting the content in which they are embedded will often be most effective in achieving a greater degree of structuralization. An example of this would be in the treatment of Miss R. when I commented, "Perhaps you want a wall for me to come up against," referring to her use of a wall of detachment to protect the boundaries of her self. Structuring interpretations are particularly important in the treatment of characterological pathology.

Giovacchini (1978) conceptualizes the role of the therapist in the further development of the patient in a way that is analogous to the role of the parent in the development of object constancy. He emphasizes that what is internalized in the process of internalizations that lead to object constancy are the maternal "modalities."

First of all the ego has to be able to recognize, at least partially, that sources of gratification reside in the external world and are outside its control. That is, differentiation preceeds introjection. This is why the concept of introjection is different from that of symbiotic merger. "The ego is now able to internalize the nuturing modality and the various aspects of the mother associated with that modality" (p. 69). The process of introjection results in a structure referred to as an introject: "The introject is the outcome of the internalization of functional modalities and *other attributes of the external object associated with that function*" (p. 69). Because of the emphasis on function and modality, Giovacchini refers to these introjects as "functional introjects." The analytic introject is of this nature. "It initially becomes internalized as a unifying modality. In treatment, the analyst can almost feel that his presence is holding the patient together" (p. 83). Thus the analytic attitude, as part of the therapeutic matrix, has structuring import.

Giovacchini notes further that this cohesive intrapsychic presence of the analyst, which helps bring together unintegrated modes of satisfaction, ultimately leads to the formation of what is later experienced as an inner source of nurture (p. 84). Here, of course, he describes the outcome of object constancy.

Tolpin (1978) notes that the concept of the self-object as the precursors of psychic structure links the most important contributions of psychoanalytic developmental psychology to a theory of treatment "which actually fosters a needed process of further structural growth" (p. 181).

THE THERAPIST AS GUARDIAN OF THE SELF

I believe that the single most critical and powerful message that one can communicate to the borderline patient—or indeed to any patient with a character disorder—is one's concern for and dedication to the survival of the self. The therapeutic alliance depends ultimately upon this fundamental trust.

I had insisted that the young woman with anorexia nervosa be monitored by a physician. I said that it wouldn't be very useful if she were to die while we were busy tending to her psyche. Unfortunately the physician told her she must gain twenty pounds at once or there would be no point in continuing to see her.

They're making me do it. It's making me nervous. . . . I'm getting depressed again. I don't know if I'm screwed up because the food thing is worse or vice versa. (On one hand you're struggling to maintain the boundaries of your self, and in doing that your self-esteem goes down when you are scolded for it.) I wish I could find some nice rules to follow. I think I could live with one hundred pounds. (What seems to be important is that *you* make the rules, perhaps in stages that you feel okay about.) I'm thinking, "They can't make me gain weight if I don't want to!" They have no right! (You feel it as an impingement.) Absolutely! (It's such a paradox—with your understandable concern for protecting the survival of yourself, you could die.) It's so insidious. I dwell on it all the time. It's nice to talk about it. The worst is feeling the different compulsions. . . . When the doctor weighed me, I felt ashamed of myself, but proud too. (The oyster feels very powerful.) It controls my whole existence. It sits there like a king in the middle of the throne room pulling strings. It's more powerful than my rational self. (Your secret self is your powerful self.) It's coming out now, not repressed. It represses itself. The oyster being the real me is doing it. (The determination of that little core self to survive is to be admired!) [smiles.]

Khan (1974) tells us that we must negotiate some sort of alliance with the patient's practice of self-cure.

> To treat this *practice of self-cure* merely as resistance is to fail to acknowledge its true value for the person of the patient. . . . To cure a cure is the paradox that faces us in these patients. [p. 97]

Khan cautions us that we must not be omnipotently curative at the cost of the person of the patient (p. 128).

Giovacchini (1979) notes that patients with characterological problems are acutely sensitive to what goes on in their important interpersonal relationships. He sees this as due to the sensitivity to intrusion. "They may have to be overly perceptive and vigilant for the protection of their helpless and vulnerable self-representations" (p. 439). In this instance the observing ego is primarily a defensive ego and is not available for analytic work. Such patients have a stance of vigilance. If in therapy it becomes clear that here the self will not be impinged upon, humiliated, nor will autonomy be abrogated, the observing ego will be released from its defensive vigilance and will become available for the analytic work.

An intrusive interaction consists of someone imposing something of himself upon another individual. "This can be an attitude, a point of view, or a moral value, but in any case the recipient feels it to be a breach of his autonomy . . ." (p. 448). I might add that for some patients anything short of total mirroring constitutes an impingement. The reaction to impingement may, in the narcissistic personality, be anger at the therapist's failure to mirror and the threat to the patient's need for omnipotent control of the needed object. There may be a paranoid reaction, viewing the impingement as an assault by the bad object who wishes to destroy him. The reaction to impingement with a borderline patient where the self is more tenuously organized may be more traumatic and experienced as annihilating of the self. The reaction of the narcissistic personality can be interpreted. That of the borderline who reacts with acute anxiety, even bordering on panic, may have to be handled instead.

Doroff (see chapter 11) distinguishes interpretation of the transference from handling the transference, saying, "By handling I refer to any means other than interpretation used by the therapist to promote a therapeutically desirable stasis. Most often this translates into a restoration of an observing ego." Handling the transference in the situation with the character disorder is a manifestation of restoration of an appropriate therapeutic matrix—one that has as its goal the facilitation of the various processes subsumed under the general category of organization. The following case material is an example of impingement (a therapeutic error) and restoration of the therapeutic matrix, the observing ego, and the therapeutic alliance.

The following session with Miss R. explores further her experiences of visual imagery, which she is coming to understand as a function of cognitive style and not an aberration. With the mobilization of my intellectual curiosity and my need to know, I forgot for a moment that the visual images were equated with the very vulnerable, isolated core self. I asked her if she had ever put any of her images down in art form—a complete departure from my meticulous respect for her boundaries and autonomy.

They're very abstract. I'd be afraid they would disappear. (You mean, if you put them outside yourself?) *Cries.* They won't exist for me. I didn't want to tell Jerry any more about the images when he asked. I didn't want to go into it. Maybe I *don't* think in images. (Are you afraid that I'm going to take them away from you?) I'm afraid they're not there. I have a sense that talking about it is wrong.

At this point I have not yet become fully aware that she is reacting to my inquiry per se.

I would neutralize the importance to get control because spontaneity is so frightening. Today I have an image that I'm like the Pillsbury dough-boy, being pinched and poked—not letting me move forward, stifling me, taking my wind away. I feel like I'm treading water right now—thinking of a capsized rowboat. (Do you feel in danger right now?) I feel very frightened. (When did it start?) When you talked about painting. (You became frightened when I invaded your inner world with my question, when I broke through your boundary. It must have felt as if you would lose the sense of your very self as existing.) I think of my early image of no inner core. I'm aware of going from a cylinder and of a core with particles going through the core, to a more spherical shape. The idea of thinking in pictures gives substance to that sphere. (I am truly sorry that I said anything that you experienced as so hurtful. What I said must have stirred up the fear that if I were to break through the sphere, there would be nothing to contain the pictures.) Hmm.

At this point she was clearly no longer anxious and returned to her concerns about being different. Her visual images throughout treatment have reflected the changes in the self-images in a startlingly and stirringly graphic manner. Changes in her associations, affect, and way of relating were always in harmony with the changes in imagery. As spontaneous experiences of her mind, these images were the most directly experienced manifestation of her core, real self. When, in my own need to know, I violated the boundaries of that core self, she became very frightened of the potential for dissolution of the self. My apology was genuinely felt and I believe clinically indicated and necessary for the reestablishment of trust and the therapeutic alliance. It was a way of saying, "I am not perfect in my understanding of you, but my imperfection is not malevolent." Because of the solidity of both therapeutic and working alliances heretofore, she recovered quickly from the effects of my unfortunate error.

This is a good example of what I mean when I say that consideration of structure must always take precedence over other issues and concerns and that everything the therapist says or does will have an impact upon the structure in significant ways. As the therapist is the mediator of organization and as the facilitator of structuralization, anything that is disruptive of that process is contraindicated—even a *correct* interpretation! In this instance, the therapist's need to know—a countertransference error—took precedence over the requirements of structure and was experienced as a danger to the self. Fortunately this young woman was an unusually fine observer and reporter of her own mental processes. In another situation such therapeutic errors might instead lead to acting out or to a sudden breaking off of treatment.

THE ANALYTIC SETTING AND THE STRUCTURING OF PSYCHIC BOUNDARIES

Giovacchini (1979) emphasizes the importance of defining the analytic setting in our work with patients with primitive mental states. The aim of the definition is to clarify the function of the analyst and the motivation for his analytic behavior. The content of the definition will vary, depending upon the dominant material and affect. The analyst in some way makes it clear that he reacts to the patient's feelings as intrapsychic phenomena that are interesting and worthy of understanding. He has an observational frame of reference, "one in which he does not feel elated or despairing or, in other instances, seduced or threatened by what he observes. . . . He maintains an *analytic attitude*, and by *defining the analytic setting* he is conveying this attitude to the patient" (p. 451).

Patients with primitive mental states often attempt to create a setting where their projections need not be viewed as projections. They attempt to induce in the therapist feelings and behaviors that are consistent with their views of themselves and of the interpersonal environment. Because the analytic setting and the therapist's analytic attitude do not "blend" with these distortions of reality, the patient is helped to "consolidate his ego boundaries and to see himself as a separate, discrete individual" (p. 453).

The analytic setting is an instrument par excellence for the mediation of organization. The consistent, reliable, nonintrusive presence of the therapist is analogous to the presence of the primary mothering person, who serves to tie the infant's experience together in a reality-related, object-related mode.

Winnicott (1965) defines the "holding environment" as one that conveys to the patient that the therapist knows and understands "the deepest anxiety that is being experienced or that is waiting to be experienced" (p. 240). Of some patients he says, "This holding, like the task of the mother in infant-care, acknowledges tacitly the tendency of the patient to disintegrate, to cease to exist, to fall for ever."

Winnicott distinguishes "holding" from "living with," noting that the term "living with"

> implies object relationship, and the emergence of the infant from the state of being merged with the mother, or his perception of objects as external to the self. [p. 44]

As soon as the infant is able to perceive that he and mother are separate, the mother appropriately changes her attitude and will wait for the child to give a signal as to its needs.

Applying this concept to treatment, Winnicott says:

> It is very important, except when the patient is regressed to earliest infancy and to a state of merging, that the analyst shall *not* know the answers except insofar as the patient gives the clues. . . . This limitation of the analyst's power is important to the patient. [p. 44]

One young woman whose material tended to be very vague often referred to the fact that things were "understood" in interpersonal situations, especially in her family. I commented that she would probably have to deal here with my shortcoming that I am not a mind reader. She remarked:

> It's a part of me that's overdeveloped. I would get frustrated with my sister for having to say things that I thought were obvious. I'm too quick to understand what people try to say and finish it for them.

In effect, I defined the situation as one in which I would not merge with her on my part. It was a statement of boundaries. The definition of the setting is itself an interpretation that promotes structuralization.

Just as the holding environment provides the matrix within which organization can take place, so the "living with" environment provides the matrix within which differentiation of self from object can take place. The therapist must be attuned to the patient as is the mother to the infant so as to respond appropriately to the stage of development and its attendant tasks.

The fact that the treatment setting does not blend with the pathology of the patient emphasizes his separateness and the boundaries of the self. This aspect of work with the patient with a primitive and pathological organization of the self and the object world can be difficult to maintain in the face of projective identification, a defense common in these patients.

Klein, Heimann, Isaacs, and Riviere (1952) describe "projective identification" as a mechanism in which parts of the self are projected into the object. They comment that "in psychotic disorders this identification of an object with the hated parts of the self contributes to the intensity of the hatred directed against other people" (p. 301).

Bion (1959) notes what happens to the analyst when he is on the receiving end of the projective identification of the patient. There is a particular countertransference experience characteristic of this situation. "The analyst feels he is being manipulated so as to be playing a part, no matter how difficult to recognize, in somebody else's phantasy. . . ." There is usually a temporary loss of insight on the part of the analyst as he experiences strong feelings that seem justified by the objective situation. And "there is a sense of being a particular kind of person in a particular emotional situation." One feels that one has actually become the kind of person he is identified with. Bion comments that the "ability to shake oneself out of the numbing feeling of reality that is a concomitant of this state is a prime requisite of the analyst . . ." (p. 149).

Bion later (1963) uses the term *containing* for this process. Langs (1976) speaks of the unconscious needs of the therapist to be a pathological container in some instances. Reciprocally, some therapists need to projectively identify their own sickness onto the patient and make the patient the pathological container for that sickness (p. 205). This of course is the acting out of the countertransference in its original meaning as a manifestation of the therapist's own psychopathology. Langs (1975a) refers to the situation in which the therapist participates in a pathogenic interaction as a "therapeutic misalliance."

One woman who used this mechanism as a defense against the emergence of the hating and hated and feared maternal introject, managed to embroil several individuals of her interpersonal network, including her therapist, in a hostile, interlocking system. When this situation was interpreted and the analytic setting restored, she was able to comment of herself, "I had to get the anger out of me. I wrote the letter. Then I wanted to get it out further and send it, but I was afraid it would come back to me." The interpretation was made that she had to put the anger outside herself because it tied her to the rageful and feared mother. This repetitive form of acting out constituted her main defense against the negative transference involving the bad object of symbiosis.

Giovacchini (1972a) observes that this immersion of the therapist in the content of the patient's early developmental phase is disturbing and forces him to gain insight and share it with the patient: "he has to emerge from the patient's frame of reference and, once again, return to an analytic, observational context" (p. 126). Giovacchini comments that although it might be better if the therapist did not have such countertransference reactions, they occur fairly frequently when treating patients with characterological psychopathology. If one is able to maintain one's own observing ego and analytic attitude in the face of these countertransference reactions, they become a source of valuable information about the patient's psychic structure. Even if the therapist does become the "container" and participates in the "therapeutic misalliance," it is possible to recover and to make use of the event for further analytic work. The momentary lapse will reveal the therapist's lack of perfection and omnipotence. How the patient reacts to this offers further material for exploration.

In the case of projective identification, the definition of the setting is manifest in the therapist's refusal to participate in the situation. Maintenance of the analytic attitude also defines the boundary between the psyche of the patient and that of the therapist.

The therapeutic situation is explicitly defined in the following interchange with a young woman who had just recently begun treatment.

> I've been avoiding stuff. . . . (Perhaps that lets you feel some sense of control of the process.) But I don't let you do anything. (Perhaps if I don't fight you for control, you will come to feel safe enough to give it up.)

And in the situation with the patient with anorexia nervosa, issues of identity and boundaries and autonomy are spelled out, and the alliance is explicitly defined in a way that carries no threat of either loss of autonomy or abandonment.

> I could starve to death and no one would notice. (It's one way to find out if they care.) Yes, it is. (That puts you in a difficult bind—either it feels as though people are neglectful and don't care or as though they are being intrusive.) It's not so much the intruding I resent. It's more the actual control, the presumption that what they say—when I get irritated and panicky if someone says I should eat. I don't like that. They should leave me alone and let me go the course I've set for myself. (That interferes with your autonomy.) Yes. Even if

I can say no, just the fact that they think it. (When I said I
wanted you to see Dr. L. to make sure you don't get sick, did
that feel like I was interfering with your autonomy?) No. I felt
guilty because I know you're right. You have the right to say
that because you're looking after my psyche. If I had a more
sure sense of myself I wouldn't have to put on a label, a quantity, to everything. This identity thing is definitely true. If I
can put good or bad labels on myself, it gives me the sense of
who I am if I don't have the gut feeling.

And later in the session:

(It sounds like you fear that your wish for passivity will get the
better of you.) I have to struggle against it, to have to do things
I don't want to do. I guess that's not really cracking up. (I
hear a protest: "I don't want to. Don't make me.") I'm afraid
I would be sucked into a vortex of helplessness. Tell me I
won't. (I don't think you will so long as we keep plugging
away.) That makes me feel better. (You're not alone in your
struggle. You do have a partner.) But no one else is. If anyone
else is my partner, they go away. (Like I did last week?) But
you'll be back. I know you're there.

In this session I emphasized the issue of the alliance and by so
doing, also defined the situation as one in which she will not be abandoned. But I had to be careful to say that although I will "hold"
you, I will do so in a way that will not overpower you. The use of
"we" defines this aspect of the situation. At this point I gratified the
need for a powerful object with a statement of reassurance. I found
that neutrality was sometimes experienced by her as an abandonment, which she could not work with therapeutically at this time.
When I gratify the need here, I provide the holding environment she
needs at this stage of vulnerability. Greenson (1970) writes:

The most brilliant interpretations of unconscious meaning are
valueless, even harmful, if the patient feels he is losing contact
with his inner self and outer reality and desperately needs

emotional and visual contact with me as a concrete, real, and predictable person. . . I must become the bearer of reality, the emissary between reality and fantasy, for the patient.. . . I have to supply for my borderline patient what my neurotic patient does for himself.

AD HOC DECISIONS IN
THE TREATMENT OF CHARACTER DISORDERS

Giovacchini (1972b) remarks that with some patients one can adopt a wait-and-see attitude (p. 240), whereas with others one cannot. He notes that the two types of patients cannot be distinguished on the basis of the severity of their psychopathology.

There can be no hard and fast rules with respect to the interpersonal ambience in working with borderline patients. The degree of emotional presence or of activity on the part of the therapist must be determined in each situation on the basis of their impact upon the individual. This may involve some degree of trial and error at the beginning of treatment, with very close attention to whether one's approach is experienced as a danger to the self or as facilitating its emergence and growth. The use of the couch comes under the same considerations.

Both Miss R. and Miss C. characterized their real core self as unformed and barely accessible. Both had highly developed false-self identities consolidated around the use of the intellect. And both were emotionally detached.

Miss R. welcomed the detachment and was grateful for my respect for her defense. It was never interpreted as a resistance, but its import as protective of the boundaries of the self was duly noted. She later viewed my willingness to stay back and bide my time as an important factor in her improvement.

Miss C. found the detachment and lack of affective contact dystonic and distressing. Yet she was also highly sensitive to impingement, which she found difficult to ward off without being detached. Although I still maintained an analytic attitude, I realized that my manner with her was causing her an intolerable degree of anxiety and allowed myself a greater degree of emotional presence, which she seemed to need to ameliorate the severe separation anxiety. At one point she complained about the lack of structure and almost begged that I provide some.

> I have no control of making myself be what I want. Coming here—it's random, free from a way of making it come together. (Does the lack of structure here cause you even more distress?) It makes me anxious. It makes the day before and after hang over my head. I'm forced to sit here to think and talk. I don't have an easy handle. (Do you need more help from me?) I would like tasks—homework—that give me control. I would feel as if I had more control.

At this point I realized I had the task of responding in a way that would (1) facilitate the emergence of the real self and integration, (2) not exacerbate the problem of feeling out of control, a problem she was "curing" by not eating, and (3) not have the impact of an impingement so that she would have to use even more detachment to ward me off, which would then exacerbate the separation anxiety. At such points in treatment when I am faced with a decision of what to do, I find that I can define my task by clarifying for myself what the structural issues are and what the immediate goal relevant to structuralization should be. Once having defined the task in this situation, I "invented" an intervention that I believed would have the desired effect without untoward, negative therapeutic reactions. It was certainly not an analytic technique, but I do not believe that it was "antianalytic" inasmuch as it did not interfere with the goals of treatment. I suggested that she make a list of statements about herself that she felt to be true so that she could begin to organize for herself all the different aspects of herself. She could then talk about them if she wished in any way that she felt would be useful. She responded, "I think I will do that." She did, in fact, although she chose not to discuss the content of her list.

My way of being, which had been so useful in the situation with Miss R., had been making Miss C. worse. Perhaps the difference lay in the degree of adaptiveness of the defense of detachment.

Miss R.'s detachment was adaptive insofar as it promoted structuralization of the boundaries of the self. Because of a sufficient degree of cohesion, although there were deficits of integration, the detachment could be tolerated. For Miss C. the detachment that protected the boundaries of her self also brought a severe separation-anxiety reaction. This in turn led to renewed reliance upon the grandiose self and the need to reject food, a symptom that was life threatening. The paradoxical reaction to her defense of detachment complicated the course of treatment. The issue continues to confront me with the need to be emotionally present to an adequate degree to mitigate the experience of object loss but not to the degree that my behavior is experienced as an impingement to be warded off. This is the kind of paradoxical bind that leads to a negative therapeutic reaction. In this kind of situation, interpretation of the bind and its impact on the interaction is indicated.

Greenson (1978) points out the difference between "unanalytic" procedures and "anti-analytic" procedures. An antianalytic procedure is one that blocks or lessens the patient's capacity for insight and understanding. "Any measure which diminishes the ego's function or capacity for observing, thinking, remembering, and judging would fall into this category." Under these conditions the patient may develop "more doubts about his ego functions and his capacity to empathize, all of which would have impaired his capacity for sound ego functioning and retarded his analysis" (p. 366).

With some patients such as Miss C., "unanalytic" intervention may be necessary, but always with due consideration for the nature of the character pathology and the treatment goal. These interventions need not be "anti-analytic." This kind of situation calls for a sound structural, developmental diagnosis, an attitude of guardianship toward the survival of the self, and some degree of moment-to-moment creativity on the part of the therapist. Giovacchini (1972b) notes that some patients do not want any intrusion whereas others require the analyst's interventions as a unifying experience (p. 242).

The organizing presence of the therapist can be exercised with the use of the patient's name. I view the first name as an important organizer inasmuch as it is heard from the first day of life onward in connection with self and object interaction. I use the first name at times, quite deliberately, in the service of facilitating attachment and organization. For instance, the use of the name as part of a response to an affect-laden communication from a detached patient facilitates the integration of the self-representation with respect to both affect and object relatedness. Miss R. reacted to my using her name in the following way.

> Tonight you called my name. You never did that before. It seemed to be a further affirming of self. To some extent it gives me some reality here I wasn't conscious of; it makes me a person here—not just a disembodied voice describing pictures. For some reason it is disturbing. I don't want to be a person here. I don't want human interaction. It's scary to me. It also put into my head the notion that you would think of me as Evelyn. I have a feeling that I'm a good patient, a classic case, a feeling that you must think about that. Your calling me by name reminded me that you might think about me.

I had, in fact, used her name on other occasions. Her awareness of it at this stage in treatment becomes possible with the progress in differentiation, with the letting down of the wall of detachment and denial of my existence—in short, with the firming up of differentiated self- and object-representations.

In the material from this session we got a sense of two effects of the use of her name. It was organizing of the self, and it made her aware that I was aware of her. The first felt good. Of the second she was afraid but ambivalent. I had used her name in the previous session when she was in a state of great distress, to which I had responded using her name as a way to say "I am here with you" as well as to make use of its organizing, and therefore anxiety-reducing potential. The use of the sound "hmm" comes under similar considerations.

RESISTANCE AS AN ALLY
IN THE SERVICE OF STRUCTURALIZATION

Giovacchini (1972b) reminds us that the concept of resistance "as something to be overcome creates an atmosphere, a moral tone, that is antithetical to the analysis of many patients. . . . Analysis of resistance . . . is not the same as overcoming resistance" (p. 291). The analysis of resistance must not become an exhortative struggle to make the patient give up something in the interest of analysis.

Doroff, in unpublished notes, writes:

In a case recently presented to me for supervision, the patient was described as coming into the session with an organized and detailed written agenda relating to issues he wished to discuss. The therapist felt disturbed by this behavior and labeled the patient's actions as "resistance." Efforts were made to separate the patient from his written agenda with the expectation that if this could be done, something "real" in the session might take place. The result was that a tenuous patient-therapist relationship became increasingly strained.

If we assume that the patient's behavior reflected his efforts to organize his experience in the face of ego defects that did not permit him to do so in a more mature manner, then to comply with the therapist's demands would mean the risk of fragmentation. Thus the patient was confronted with the dilemma in which he could either give up his therapist or risk psychological disorganization.

I suggested to the therapist that the patient was not being resistive so much as he was struggling to organize his experiences in the face of an ego that was unable to do so in a less rigid manner. I further suggested that an abrupt reversal of strategy was called for and indicated that the main thrust should be to provide as much as possible, a matrix within which the patient could experience the therapist as supporting his efforts to organize his experience. I suggested that not only should the therapist permit the patient to use them, but should participate with him, at least to the extent of listening carefully and occasionally making "mothering sounds" so as to let the patient know she was there. This would be to help the patient experience a therapist-mother who helps him to further develop his ego functions.

Defense against the development of transference can be viewed as a serious resistance from the point of view that working within the transference is the most important focus of our interventions. When there is a danger of a psychotic transference, it may be deliberately avoided in planning therapeutic strategies, limiting the treatment to more circumscribed areas of concern. Resistance to developing a transference is also seen with the borderline patient. There are some patients for whom the transference interpretation will constitute an impingement, an insistence on the part of the therapist that the patient acknowledge his existence when the patient prefers, for important defensive reasons, not to acknowledge it. Yes, this is resistance. But as a defense is it at the moment protecting the survival of the self? And if it is, should we interfere with this defense at this point of treatment? The work with Miss R. is a good example of going along with the defense and working outside relatedness issues. She commented in her one hundred and thirty-sixth session—now experiencing the solidity of a cohesive and integrated self.

What I don't understand is that you haven't existed very long, and all I've read about transference. Now it seems that it was very important that there was none—whether because I refused to allow it, or the essence of my problem precluded considering you as a person. I want an intellectual answer for that more than I need an answer emotionally. I'm curious about how transference is important.

I explained that there had indeed been transference, at the start of our work, when she expressed the feeling that I had put up a certain picture just to draw a reaction from her, that she had experienced me as the intruding and impinging mother. I explained that the transference was manifest negatively, in its absence, by what its absence protected her from.

With the structuralization that took place in this context, she is now able to let herself experience me as a person and to deal with transference issues at this more evolved level. With the achievement of cohesion and integration, rapprochement issues emerge. A dream suggested that she feared my anger at her wish to cut down from three times a week to twice. She acknowledged that she had a "lingering fear" relative to that issue. Will this mother abandon her with emotional withdrawal as punishment for asserting her separateness and growing autonomy?

Relationship issues will come to the fore as she knows she does not want to remain in emotional isolation and is concerned if she will be able to "coexist" in a relationship. The therapy situation, though not "needed" as acutely as before, should enable her to resolve these remaining concerns.

The therapeutic alliance is directly related to the attachment to the therapist. Even when the patient is detached, as in the situation with Miss R., the obvious presence of the alliances is an indication, in my opinion, that there is also an attachment, albeit denied. Easy rupture of the therapeutic alliance mitigates against the establishment of the attachment through which the therapist, like the primary mothering person, becomes the mediator of organization and the eventual source of those internalizations and identifications that promote autonomy. A rupture of the therapeutic alliance, once there has been an attachment, will evoke the experience of object loss and its attendant anxieties and defenses.

Like Dickes (1975) I prefer to distinguish the therapeutic alliance from the working alliance. Dickes says that "the term 'therapeutic alliance' should be reserved for the full-scale therapeutic rapport which includes all elements favorable to the progress of therapy" (p. 6). Thus it encompasses the working alliance. The working alliance depends upon the mobilization and preservation of the observing ego. "It centers on the patient's ability to work in the analytic situation" (Greenson 1967, p. 192).

The working alliance comes to the fore in the analytic situation in the same way as the patient's reasonable ego, the observing, analyzing ego is separated from his experiencing ego.[p. 193]

There are many instances in the treatment of the character disorder that we may have a therapeutic alliance based simply on the gratification inherent in the one-to-one situation, without the development of a working alliance. Frustration ruptures the therapeutic alliance, and there seems to be no way to mobilize the working alliance. We may find this situation with the narcissistic individual who uses the therapeutic relationship as part of the acting out of the masochistic triangle. There are some "patients" who also seek treatment for the gratification inherent in it and who are not motivated for change. Unless the working alliance can be mobilized, there is no treatment.

COUNTERTRANSFERENCE ISSUES

The therapist who works with patients with severe characterological psychopathology is required to bring to the task an attitude of what Winnicott (1951) calls "primary maternal pre-occupation" (p. 300). This attitude is necessary for the provision of the therapeutic matrix within which deficits in structure may be repaired. The therapist must also have a thorough cognitive understanding of the nature of the patient's psychopathology and its relevance to the treatment goals. From the personal side, he or she will need a clear sense of the boundaries of the self and a well-secured self-esteem that does not depend upon the patient to nurture it with his love, his gratitude, or his improvement. Not that these qualities are not needed in the treatment of all patients; in working with the more primitive patient, all these qualities will be sorely taxed.

Kohut (1971) writes of the "specifically frightening implication of feeling drawn into an anonymous existence in the narcissistic web of another person's psychological organization" (p. 276). Giovacchini (1972a) describes the situation in which the patient projects onto the therapist his own amorphous self-image, creating an "existential crisis" in the therapist (p. 121).

These are not countertransferences that are idiosyncratic to the therapist, but rather those that are typically generated by the particular character structure of the patient. Identified as such, they provide valuable information for the therapist, helping him to anticipate and guard against acting out himself, and also to inform him of the meaning of the patient's behavior.

I view the countertransference problems of working with patients with character disorders as running parallel to, or as analogous to, the characterological vulnerabilities of the patient. Inasmuch as we have all traversed the same developmental route—some more successfully than others—the same issues of self will pertain to us all. Negative countertransference reactions may run the gamut from an existential annihilation of the self to feelings of intrusion or impingement, or narcissistic wounding with the confrontation of one's realistic limitations. We may have to contend with the mobilization of our own unassimilated introjects when the bad mother is projected upon us by the patient. This may make us susceptible to becoming the "container" for the patient's projective identifications, or we may have to fight against these projections so that we lose the analytic attitude, which calls for interpretation and not a reaction.

We must be able to tolerate the abandonment by the detached patient without losing our own sense of presence in the situation. We have to be able to tolerate the idealizing transference and our discomfort with the mantle of omnipotence. Our own reality testing is our ally under these circumstances.

Although these may not be present-day issues in the character of the therapist, or although they may be issues that have been analyzed and worked through, every one of them can come into play in the course of our professional work.

To the extent that we can maintain an analytic attitude in the face of these reactions and not react overtly, we also maintain the therapeutic matrix. When we do react, when we become caught up in the patient's acting out, we then contribute to the blurring of the boundaries of the self of the patient, we reinforce his splitting, and we realize his worst fears about the interpersonal environment. His projections become reality, and the working of integration is defeated. A continuing self-analysis or, when indicated, consultation with a colleague may be useful when it becomes apparent that the situation has taken such a turn.

THE THERAPEUTIC MATRIX AND
THE BIRTH OF THE SELF

Toward the end of the second year of Miss R.'s therapy, structuralization was proceeding rapidly, particularly with respect to the cohesion and integration of the self-representation. In response to material reported, I explained briefly the toddler's experience of omnipotence associated with the maturation of the autonomous functions and the analogous omnipotence of the "obnoxious thirteen-year-old" who believes he or she has invented both sex and ideas. My goal was to demystify the magical feelings that Miss R. associated with experiences arising from the operation of her autonomous cognitive functions, particularly her visual imagery. The integration of these experiences, presently part of the schizoid, core self (which was not related to reality and which was grandiose in quality) into the real, differentiated and object-related self, would be a critical organizational shift.

When you were talking just now about omnipotence—those ideas were there. One thing that disturbs me about the visual images is the same—it's something that just happens—it's my brain, its makeup. It seems to be a good thing. For this process, it's been what I ascribe benefit to. It's the same problem as the obnoxious thirteen-year-old. (Did my using that word upset you?) [*Laughs.*] No. It rang true. I feel I'm stuck at being an obnoxious thirteen-year-old. (Do you think holding on to it could be protective—that it could have survival value for you, Evelyn?)

Once again I make a point of using her name so as to enhance the integration of the autonomous thought processes with external reality in the context of an empathic and safe object relationship. I again emphasize that I am on the side of the survival of the self. She goes on:

When you were just talking, I became aware of having a vagina. It seems that what you were saying had something to do with a sense of wholeness, of a fundamental identity. I think that's a very unusual feeling for me. . . . My initial bias was that things aren't as related to sex as everyone thinks. On the other hand, I can't deny that I have that sensation. When I had that dream about my father in the bathroom I was shocked that I should have such a dream. It was so explicit. It seemed to be very major—a breakthrough. (You begin to feel your sexuality as integrated into your self.) When it wasn't integrated, it had no existence.

The dream to which she referred could also have had an oedipal interpretation. I elected to stay with the theme of integration and wholeness. Oedipal issues were to rise again in her dreams before too long, and with the firming up of structure, we would be able to shift to feelings and wishes vis-à-vis her father. The next day she reported:

I had a happy feeling yesterday that I had the dream and what you pointed out. It gave me a very contented feeling. It's hard to explain why I felt so good about it. I'm happy and grateful.

In this session—the one hundred and twenty-ninth—she talks about her growing awareness of me as a person separate from her. That is, with the integration of the self and the firming up of her ego boundaries, the object is also differentiated and takes on its own structure. Her continued elation at the experience of realness and wholeness is expressed the following day.

At this point I'm more conscious of you as a person. I don't want that, but I suspect it's a necessary next step. I want to say no, that's enough. . . . I was thinking that I was born this April 13. The last two days I have felt more mellow here. I hear a difference in my voice. It sounds more self-assured. I've been thinking about my dreams and what we said Tuesday about them. The greatest enterprise seemed to be to think about thinking. To understand the thought processes was an endeavor that was pleasing and worthwhile. I like thinking about how excited I was about my own thoughts, a fascination and real affection for my mind. . . . I'm conscious of being very close to tears. I don't understand that. (When you talk about your thinking, you are also talking about your real, core self. Perhaps the tears may have something to do with the feelings you have about the "birth" of your self.)

The therapist who views his or her role as the mediator of organization within the therapeutic matrix will sometimes have the opportunity of sharing with the patient the joy of the emergence of the self out of the darkness of existential despair.

Chapter 14

ANXIETY
AND THE INTEGRITY
OF THE SELF

In healthy development, the individual gradually becomes able to manage anxiety with a stable repertoire of defenses that are readily available to the ego in the face of psychic danger. "Signal anxiety" (Freud 1926) refers to this reliable defensive capacity, in which anxiety acts as a signal to the ego to activate these (usually unconscious) defenses.

This capacity must be viewed developmentally in order to understand the implications, theoretical and clinical, of the failure to develop signal anxiety.

In delineating the kinds of anxiety characteristic of the stages of attachment and the separation–individuation process, Schecter (1980) pinpoints missing someone who is loved as the key to understanding anxiety. For the infant love "means the security of empathic responsiveness to his needs by the mothering one" (p. 546). Both the mothering one and the analyst are characterized as providing the steady holding environment that enhances the integration of the self.

Whereas Schecter emphasizes the importance of the relationship per se, I shall consider the relationship in terms of its developmental

*Adapted from an article that appeared in *Journal of the American Academy of Psychoanalysis*, Vol. 8, No. 4, 565–573 (1980) © 1980 John Wiley & Sons, Inc.

0090-3604/80/0008-0565$01.00

function, that is, the promotion of structuralization, and to recon-
ceptualize the key to understanding anxiety as any danger to the
integration of the self.

Schecter alludes to this view when he differentiates traumatic
anxiety from signal anxiety: with traumatic anxiety, "the ego is
overwhelmed or disorganized . . ." (p. 539). Later he notes that
"resistance often functions in the service of maintaining a sense of
self-constancy and continuity, warding off a sense of discontinuity in
one's identity" (p. 551).

Following this line of thinking, I shall approach the issue of
anxiety from a structural point of view, by considering the developmental roots of anxiety from the perspective of the implications for
adult character structure and for the psychoanalytic treatment of
character disorder. From my own theoretical viewpoint, I shall explore
the structuring of affect (as well as the structuring of drive and
thought) within a cohesive, reality-related, object-related self.

I find it useful to consider anxiety from the broad general perspective as a concomitant of any threat to the integrity of the self. The
specifics of this threat will depend on the character structure of the
individual. For the more primitive character whose self structure is
deficient in its cohesion and differentiation, the threat may be to the
structure itself. This threat may be disorganization or what Kohut
(1977) refers to as the dissolution of the self. For a more evolved
character in whom ego and superego structuralization has taken
place, the threat may be to the sense of consonance and internal
harmony of the structure—the structural and dynamic underpinning
of neurotic conflict. Basch (1976) comments: "Emotions are sub-
jectively experienced states and always related to a concept of self vis-
à-vis some particular situation" (p. 768).

Perhaps the most important distinction that needs to be made here
is that between the traumatic state and signal anxiety. Krystal (1978)
describes psychic trauma as the outcome of being confronted with
overwhelming affect. In this situation the "affective responses produce
an unbearable psychic state which threatens to disorganize, perhaps
even destroy all psychic functions" (p. 82). That is, the ego is
overwhelmed. In the case of signal anxiety, there is a sense that
something bad is *about* to happen, and if adequate defenses can be

mobilized, the something bad can be averted. When the defense fails, anxiety can escalate to panic and become a traumatic state.

Let us consider the developmental implications of repeated traumatic states in the first year or so of life. Khan (1963) attributes what he calls cumulative trauma to the mother's failure to function adequately as a protective shield for her child. This may be due to an absence of empathy or to illness and pain in the child that she is powerless to alleviate. Whatever the reason, the child is subjected to repeated traumatic states that interrupt and interfere with the budding organization of the ego and the synthesizing of a cohesive self-representation. Krystal notes that in adult life the fear of affect may represent a dread of returning to the infantile type of trauma. This is not only a dread of returning to the traumatic state but also an *expectation* that it will occur (p. 98). Winnicott (1974) views the fear of breakdown in a similar way: "The ego organizes defenses against breakdown of the ego organization and it is the ego organization that is threatened" (p. 103).

The defenses erected against the traumatic state in early life lead to pathology of structure even as they protect it. This is unlike the defenses put into operation by an already structured and differentiated ego, as in the case of signal anxiety. The primitive defense against the traumatic state in infancy is not derived from the object relationship. In fact, it may be manifest in a schizoid development that emotionally excludes the object. As Tolpin remarks (1971), "the infantile psyche begins early to resort to pathogenic mechanisms . . . that are expedient substitutes for maternal buffering . . ." (p. 336).

Anxiety as a signal is derived from the gradual internalization of the comforting functions of the primary mothering person. This comes about when the good-enough mother characteristically intervenes so that the experience of distress or unpleasure is consistently followed by the experience of being comforted *before* a traumatic state can develop. In this manner, affect becomes structured within the emerging self–object–representation and does not remain unstructured or lead to disorganization. Tolpin describes the role of the transitional object (Winnicott 1951) in the developmental shift from dependence on the mothering person for the alleviation of distress to the achievement of signal anxiety. The child "usually creates this object," that is, the transitional object, "when he has emerged enough from the symbiotic state to begin to perceive his mother as the chief instrument of his sense of well being and relief from distress" (p. 321). He has endowed, for instance, a blanket with her functions. Tolpin observes that "although the infant begins to perceive the mother as a not-me . . . by the time the transitional object is formed, her soothing functions are perceived as part of the self . . ." (p. 326). Experiences with the object of the stage of symbiosis are self experiences as well, and they are retained as part of the self-representation even as differentiation from the object proceeds.

The blanket, or teddy bear, is decathected little by little as its soothing functions are further internalized. With fixation at the transitional object level of dealing with anxiety, the individual still needs something from the outside. This dependency may be on food, which functions as the transitional object, or on an idealized other. The degree to which children are able to soothe themselves with a blanket or to which they cling·anxiously with little comfort will affect the outcome of the internalization process. The quality of the comforting interaction with the mother will help determine the quality of the interaction with the transitional object. Tolpin notes that the "demanding and possessive behavior of the child during the separation-individuation phase is thus seen as the expression of the phase-appropriate psychic organization that treats the mother's activities and functions as the child's own until they can be acquired from her to form the emerging self" (p. 341). At this time the mother is narcissistically viewed as an extension of the self. The mother's capacity to tolerate this phase with equanimity and empathy will enable the child to move beyond it.

Part of the process of assimilating maternal comforting functions into the self is achieving a sense of mastery. When the mother responds to her child's cry, the child can connect its own activity with relief from distress. But when the mother does not respond, the child must passively endure. Because this situation can lead to the traumatic state, passivity, which is enforced at this stage of development, comes to be associated with anxiety and panic. I have observed that several patients who do not have that sense of mastery and potential effectiveness with activity and who do passively endure with anxiety report severe anxiety upon awakening in the morning as long as they remain in bed. They feel better as soon as they get up and begin to get themselves organized for the day.

The process beginning with distress and followed by maternal comforting lays the groundwork for the gradual internalization of comforting functions, for the achievement of ego defenses against anxiety (which functions as a signal), and for the development of basic trust. It is also critical for an image of a self that has the capacity for active mastery. Tolpin notes that with the emergence of the transitional object, children now actively do for themselves what previously had to be done for them. The very issue of taking active charge of the comforting situation, I believe, relates to the sense of mastery that comes with being able to have a positive effect on the mother. Children who know they have a negative effect on their mothers may become frightened of their power to destroy.

The development of signal anxiety is a concomitant of the achievement of object constancy. The end of the separation–individuation process is marked by the further assimilation of maternal (or parental) functions into the self even as the object is separated out as fully differentiated from the self. This involves the assimilation of both nurturant and executive modalities (Giovacchini 1979) and the imperatives that leads to the structuring of the superego. Schecter (1979) speaks of the formation of the superego as "the organization of experience in the imperative mode" (p. 362).

With the structuring of the superego, a new danger to the self emerges. Indeed, for each of the stages in object relations development, there is a specific danger to the integrity of the self. Freud (1926) describes a sequence of danger situations that can be conceptualized from the perspective of the structure and integrity of the self.

The first danger situation is overwhelming excitation. This we can relate to the infantile traumatic state that overwhelms the budding ego. Next is the loss of the object. The undifferentiated object of symbiosis and of the earlier substages of the separation-individuation process is essentially a prosthesis that holds together the budding organization of the self. Object loss at this stage threatens the cohesion of the self. Schecter (1980) writes of the infant's fear of the strange. I see this as related to the developmental and structural immaturity of the child for whom the external structure, including the interpersonal environment, still functions as an organizer. When there are internal structural defects, this dependence on external structure may become manifest in what is referred to as culture shock. The autistic child's pathological need for sameness is probably in this same category.

Next, Freud points to the danger of losing the object's love, which threatens emotional abandonment at a time when the object is still needed to alleviate distress and to prevent the emergence of the traumatic state.

Castration anxiety of the oedipal period endangers the integrity of the bodily self and the body ego. Finally, the danger of losing the superego's love risks losing the internal harmony within the self structure—a loss of integrity that does not threaten dissolution of the self, but a loss of integrity nonetheless.

Departing from Freud's formulation and thinking in terms of present-day object relations theory, we can also list other kinds of dangers to the integrity of the self. For example, the anxiety of humiliation manifests a threat to the grandiose self structure, which itself may serve as an important defense against the dissolution of the self that goes with object loss. We see this with the borderline patient. The splitting of self and object representations creates an intolerable intrapsychic disharmony which is alleviated by projective identification. Externalization and acting out promote the illusion of intrapsychic unity and harmony. The anxiety of shame comes with the awareness of the discrepancy between the ego ideal and the immediate experience of the self.

Defenses can be viewed in general as those available behaviors that will restore the sense of integrity of the self, be it schizoid withdrawal, whuch shuts out the object and its distressing and traumatizing impact, or repression, which prevents awareness of intrapsychic conflict among structured aspects of the self.

This structural view of the self and anxiety has implications for treatment. As I wrote in an earlier chapter, the consistent and predictable presence of the primary mothering person throughout the early months of life serves to tie together the infant's experiences in a particular way. It is through her that the body, impulse, feeling, action, and eventually thought become organized as parts of the self and integrated, both with one another and with external reality, of which she is a representative. The mothering person is a bridge between the child's inner world of experience and the outer world of reality. She not only mediates this process of organization and reality-relatedness, but her image also is part of what is organized and is the basis for the development of object relatedness. When early development within the maternal matrix goes well, the outcome is a cohesive, reality-related, object-related self.

Within this context, early primitive distress does not result in traumatic states that overwhelm the budding ego organization but are gradually transformed into signal anxiety. With this structuralization, anxiety is no longer associated with a threat to the very structure of the self. It will instead be associated with a threat to the sense of harmony and consonance within the structure, and the ego will have developed a repertoire of defenses against it.

What the therapist does, or should do, in any given treatment situation must bear directly on the developmental, structural diagnosis. This diagnosis will take into consideration the qualities of cohesion and integration and reality relatedness and object relatedness. When a failure or deficit in the organization of the self is found, we can view the major function of the analyst as analogous to that of the primary mothering person or persons of infancy—that is, as the mediator of organization within the therapeutic matrix.

This therapeutic matrix sets the stage for repairing the deficits in the character structure. It facilitates organization and integration of the various aspects of the self, some of which may have been cut off, denied, or repressed and which may have a disorganizing impact when experienced. With such disorganization we shall observe not anxiety, which can be interpreted, but panic, the traumatic state that accompanies the dissolution of the self.

To the extent that we are able to alleviate the traumatic state readily and effectively within the context of continuing structuralization, the experience of anxiety as a signal will gradually come to replace the experience of panic. The therapeutic matrix facilitates the attachment process which eventually provides the basis for the internalization of maternal–therapist functions.

I believe that the single most critical and powerful message that we can communicate to the borderline patient—or indeed to any patient with a character disorder—is our concern for and dedication to the survival of the self. The therapeutic alliance depends ultimately on this fundamental trust. As we monitor the patient's level of anxiety, we can also assess our relative success or failure in this regard.

If our goal is to further ego development and the structuralization of the self, then the way in which we manage the patient's anxiety level will be a central concern. Do we, like the unempathic mother, allow it to escalate into a traumatic, ego-overwhelming state, or do we begin pairing distress with our alleviation of distress, a process that we hope will eventually become internalized? Alleviation of distress refers to whatever technique is indicated. It may be an empathic statement or an interpretation that promotes structuralization. Clearly, we must have an accurate picture of the patient's character structure and the deficits in self structure so that we can distinguish a tolerable anxiety from a traumatizing one.

It is my guess that many so-called negative therapeutic reactions are reactions to something the therapist does or says that threatens the integrity of the patient's self, that traumatizes the patient. Thus the term negative therapeutic reaction is a misnomer. Panic reactions may be flight from treatment or acting out. If we do make such an error, it should be verbalized to the patient in such a way that we restore the patient's sense of safety and thereby also the therapeutic alliance. Properly managed, such errors and their sequellae can be constructive. The empathic recognition of the traumatic experience will alleviate the traumatic state, and subsequent interpretation of the event will promote structuralization. This is not to say that we should deliberately induce trauma. Basic trust is always at stake in this situation, and cumulative trauma in the treatment situation will eventually necessitate flight from it.

Chapter 15

REFUSAL TO IDENTIFY: DEVELOPMENTAL IMPASSE

Identification is the process required for the completion of the separation-individuation process and the resolution of the Oedipus complex. Freud (1923) writes that with the dissolution of the Oedipus complex there is a father identification as well as a mother identification. The father identification preserves the object relation to the mother that belongs to the positive complex (in males), and at the same time, it replaces the object relation to the father that belongs to the inverted complex. "The same will be true, *mutatis mutandis*, of the mother–identification" (p. 34).

Freud sees the broad general outcome of this phase as forming a precipitate in the ego which consists of these two identifications in some way united with each other. This modification of the ego then *"confronts the other contents of the ego as an ego-ideal or superego"* (p. 34).

The end of the separation-individuation process (Mahler, Pine, and Bergman 1975) is marked by a fully established sense of a separate identity and object constancy. These are the outcome of a series of indentificatory internalizations, particularly maternal functions and modalities (Tolpin 1971, Giovacchini 1979). What once came from the object now resides within the self.

From an object-relational viewpoint, failures of identification result in an ego insufficiency that constitutes the port of entry to regressive preoedipal symptomatology under the impact of oedipal anxieties.

This insufficiency—the incomplete securing of object constancy and emotional autonomy—is the basis for an ongoing dependency on the object and for the lack of intrapsychic autonomy that generates fears of abandonment, separation-anxiety, and depression.

In the clinical setting, we see a steadfast "refusal" to identify that interferes with the completion of the separation-individuation process and the resolution of the Oedipus complex. The purpose of this refusal is to protect gender identity and the ego ideal.

We need to clarify the term *identification* and to distinguish the primary identifications of early object relations development from later identifications. We also must differentiate identification as a process changing the structure of the ego from that which defends the ego against object loss or other dangers. The internalizations that allow one to *give up* the object—as with the completion of the separation-individuation process and the resolution of the Oedipus complex—are not the same as the identifications that *defend against* the anxiety and depression of loss. One woman, after the death of her mother when she was a young adolescent, essentially became her mother, a defense that propelled her into an incestuous relationship with her father. Identification with the aggressor defends against the anxieties inherent in the role of passive victim. One patient, attempting to resurrect his relationship with his beloved grandfather, developed Parkinson-like tremors. These identifications, like any other ego defense, need to be analyzed.

Defensive identification does not lead to a structural change in self-representation, but developmental identifications do. In his discussion of the relationship between identification and individuation, Schecter (1968) defines the process of identification as "the means by which part of the psychic structure of one person tends to become like that of another to whom he is emotionally related in a significant way" (p. 50).

Schecter also distinguishes the conscious wish to become like another person (as happens in the formation of one's ideals) from the actual tendency to become like another, that is, from the basic developmental processes leading to structural likeness. He also differentiates both of these from "pseudo-identification which involves an attempt to reconstruct an internalized object with which the self may then fuse. The severely disturbed, often psychotic patient attempts to cling to the internal object, to fuse with it, to 'become' it, or to destroy it" (p. 74).

Schecter concludes that identification grows out of primarily active and relatively conflict-free individuating processes and that it contributes to the ego structure or strength necessary for the gradual relinquishing of the more primitive object ties. "Identification and the partial loosening of primitive object attachments may be simultaneous and part and parcel of the same individuation process . . ." (p. 64). Freud (1923) writes that the ego is a precipitate of abandoned object cathexes and notes that it may be that "identification is the sole condition under which the id can give up its object" (p. 29). When this process of identification loses its conflict-free status— when identification stands in conflict with gender identity and/or the ego ideal—there is a developmental impasse.

Schafer (1968) defines internalization as referring to *"all those processes by which the subject transforms real or imagined regulatory interactions with his environment, and real or imagined characteristics of his environment, into inner regulations and characteristics"* (p. 9). Meissner (1981) sees internalization as the manner in which "characteristics of external objects are taken in and become part of the inner psychic organization" (p. 15).

According to Meissner (1981), the three kinds of internalization are incorporation, introjection, and identification. Incorporation is a relatively primitive process. With this form of internalization, the quality of the object is merged into the organization of the self, while the object, quaobject, is obliterated. "Through incorporation, the object representation becomes wholly and indistinguishably merged into a subject's self-representation" (p. 51). In normal infant development, this is characteristic of the undifferentiated self-object representation of symbiosis. In the development of the pathological grandiose self, this condensation also occurs and is accompanied by the emotional and cognitive exclusion of the object.

Meissner finds (1981) introjection deriving from a less primitive relationship to the object. "Elements or aspects from the object are taken in in such a way as to preserve the relationship between the derivative aspects of the internalized object and the external object"

(p. 52). In effect, the introject, which is the product of introjection, is part of the ego but is not assimilated into the self-representation. Meissner notes its resemblance to the transitional object, except that in this instance the transitional object is internal. The introject may be projected and constitute the basis for transference reactions, the dynamic of projective identification.

As always, we must keep clear the distinction between normal developmental processes and the products from those that occur with regression or defense. The unassimilated introject (Giovacchini 1979) is the product of a stage in the separation-individuation process, somewhere between the undifferentiated self-object of symbiosis and the fully differentiated object that comes with the achievement of object constancy and identity. The original product of incorporation is *transformed* into an introject through the hatching process (Mahler 1968).

Meissner states (1981) that with identification nothing is "taken in." Rather, internal differentiation and organization are enhanced. "Thus, while incorporation and introjection can be understood as defensive measures and ways of dealing with the intolerable threat of separation from or loss of the object, in identification the object is left totally intact and distinct and its inherent separateness is not only tolerated but preserved" (p. 53). Meissner views identification as essentially a modeling and self-organizing process.

I wish that Meissner had more clearly distinguished between identifications with the primary attachment object of symbiosis that *remain* as part of the self after differentiation of self from object, and the later identifications made by a now differentiated self. To me, when he speaks of a modeling process that preserves the separateness of the other, he seems to be referring to the second of these.

The self and object representations of the first three or so years of life develop hand in hand out of the undifferentiated image of the symbiotic stage. Primary identifications are those resulting from the separation-individuation process in which identifications with the primary attachment object lead to the intrapsychic autonomy of a fully differentiated self. Through this process and through transmuting internalizations (Kohut 1971), part of the earlier undifferentiated object representation becomes part of the self-representation, even as the self is being differentiated from the object. We see this shift in a toddler's relationship with a transitional object, a blanket or teddy bear. Unlike the incorporation or condensation of object attributes into the self, as with the pathological grandiose self in which the object is excluded emotionally and cognitively, the identificatory processes, which mark the end of the separation-individuation process in which object attributes become part of the self-representation, the object is both differentiated from the self and preserved emotionally and cognitively. Both of these differ from the unassimilated introject which is neither part of the self nor completely separate from it.

The issue of identifying with the primary attachment object is especially relevant to the issue of gender identity for the male and, as I shall discuss later, becomes the source of conflict that leads to the defensive refusal to identify.

With the achievement of identity and object constancy after separation and individuation, later identifications continue to modify the self-representation throughout life. Identification with the later mother of reality, with the father (including that identification accompanying the resolution of the Oedipus complex), with a loved grandparent, with heroes and heroines, or with other important models continues throughout the life cycle. Identification is important to analytic treatment, in which the analytic attitude and functions of the analyst are absorbed into the self and eventually enable the individual to become his or her own therapist, as it were.

Kohut (1977) notes that we should focus on repairing secondary structures when the pathology of primary structures is too severe to allow repair. Here we must draw on later identifications that both defend against the emergence of a pathological self and object representation situation and compensate for it, allowing for a healthier functioning that overlays the repressed pathology. We have to decide early in treatment whether to repair the primary or the secondary pathology. This will often depend on the degree of cohesion of the self-representation and on the presence of a significant positive object representation. In my experience, those patients whose primary pathology I elected not to treat had a paranoid core in which organization around an undifferentiated bad self and object were suffused with anxiety and rage. Early positive images, if there were any, had become condensed (Meissner would say "incorporated") into an idealized, schizoid, grandiose self, and herein lies the danger of a psychotic transference. Emotional object relatedness leads directly to the paranoid core. Schizoid defenses ward off the dangers of psychosis, and later identifications enable a higher level of functioning than might be anticipated.

Developmental identifications are important, first, in achieving identity and object constancy upon completing the separation-individuation process and in leading to the emergence of intrapsychic autonomy and, second, in resolving the Oedipus complex so as to allow the individual to give up the parent as the object of libidinal strivings and yet retain the relationship intrapsychically in the form of the mature superego. Thus identification is a process that leads to the structuralization of both the ego and the superego.

IDENTIFICATION AND OBJECT CONSTANCY

The overall process of object relations development (along with the general ego development to which it is central) ideally culminates in libidinal object constancy (Hartmann 1952) and a consolidation of individuality (Mahler, Pine, and Bergman 1975). Burgner and Edgcumbe (1972) understand the concept of object constancy as "the individual's capacity to differentiate between objects and to maintain a relationship to one specific object regardless of whether needs are being satisfied or not . . ." (p. 315). It is the "capacity to recognize and tolerate loving and hostile feeling toward the same object; the capacity to keep feelings centered on a specific object; and the capacity to value an object for attributes other than its functions of satisfying needs" (p. 328).

Eventually this must entail the ability to see parents as they really are without a dependent idealization or a defensive disparagement. This also is one of the steps in resolving the Oedipus complex.

Mahler describes object constancy in terms of the internal good object, the maternal image that is psychically available to the child, just as the actual mother was previously available for sustenance, comfort, and love. Mahler, Pine, and Bergman comment that object constancy seems to come about during the third year and that with this achievement the mother can be partly replaced by the now reliable internal image. The security that comes with this step toward intrapsychic autonomy enables the child to sustain the anxieties of the oedipal conflict and thus to maintain forward development. Fear of abandonment or loss of the object's love heightens the anxieties of the competitive situation.

The further delineation and enrichment of the self also takes place at this time, and the establishment of individuality is the developmental task that is paired with the achievement of object constancy. The self-representation is enriched by the assimilation of maternal functions into the self. Giovacchini (1979) focuses on the connection between the self-representation and the nurturing modality of the maternal introject: "The evaluation of the ego's functional capacity becomes incorporated into the identity system and contributes to the self's feelings of confidence, security, and esteem" (p. 276). This assimilation of caretaking activities into self-representation is important to the structuring and equilibrium of self-representation.

The end of the separation-individuation process is marked by this assimilation of maternal functions into the self, even as the object is separated out as fully differentiated from the self. This assimilation includes both nurturant and executive modalities and maternal anxiety-reducing interactions and leads to the development of signal anxiety (Horner 1980). The assimilation of the "imperatives" that leads to the structuring of the superego (Schecter 1979) also leads to the resolution of the Oedipus complex.

The assimilation of the functions and qualities of the object into the self-representation—the process of identification—is thus essential to achieving intrapsychic autonomy and increasing autonomy from the object relationships of the oedipal period. With the differentiation that accompanies identification, the object loses its introject status. What remains are the identifications that are part of the self and valued object relationships based on reality. That is, the incorporated object of symbiosis that was then transformed through increasing differentiation into an introject is now replaced by an identification.

Of the stages of the separation-individuation process, the end point, the achievement of object constancy and an autonomous identity, has perhaps been given the least attention in the literature. It has come to my attention that some patients fall just short of completing this developmental task, which prevents their achieving dependable intrapsychic autonomy. I shall refer to this group as "preneurotic." They are not borderline or narcissistic personalities; yet they have not yet achieved the degree of intrapsychic structuralization and individuation that is assumed in the neurotic character structure, as opposed to the character disorder.

I now believe that the "pure" neurotic character is a developmental ideal that is rarely seen. The persistence of the Oedipus complex indicates an incomplete development with respect to the identifications necessary for the full structuralization of ego and superego. Thus we must deal not only with intrapsychic conflict but with structural deficit as well. From this point of view, all psychological disorders are at least in part characterological—characterized by both structural deficit and intrapsychic conflict.

When an individual fails to make the identifications that mark the close of the separation-individuation process, we can assume that he or she will also display prominent oedipal problems, as the exaggerated dependency strivings will conflict with the competitive strivings and as the same identificatory process is essential to its resolution. Anything that interferes with this process will prevent the resolution of both separation and individuation and the Oedipus complex.

As long as significant attributes of the object belong to the object rather than to the self, the self will remain dependent on the external object relationship for these attributes and their contributions to the individual's security and self-esteem. Clinically these patients present a picture of exaggerated dependency and depression in the context of a relatively well differentiated and structured ego. These dependencies are often played out in current adult relationships, and there is often a clear oedipal cast to them as well. In addition, they will be manifest in the transference, often constituting the major—and sometimes quite subtle—source of transference resistance.

IDENTIFICATION AND THE STRUCTURING
OF THE SUPEREGO

Loewald (1979) does not believe that there ever is a final resolution of the Oedipus complex but observes that there is a "waning" that can be expected both developmentally and as the outcome of treatment. With respect to the outcome of analysis and the establishment of a relationship of equality with one's parents, he writes: "It is not established once and for all, but requires continued internal activity; and it is not necessarily obvious at the point of actual termination" (p. 764).

According to Freud (1923), as the object cathexes of parental objects are relinquished, they are replaced by identifications that form the nucleus of the superego. The superego takes over the father's severity and his prohibitions against incest, securing the ego from the return of the libidinal object cathexis. "The libidinal trends belonging to the Oedipus complex are in part desexualized and sublimated . . . and in part inhibited in their aim and changed into impulses of affection" (p. 176).

Here we see how identification in resolving the Oedipus complex leads to the structuralization of the superego and a more realistic and appropriate relationship with the parents. At the same time those identifications originating out of the primary object attachment lead to a further structuralization of the self-representation and to the capacity for mature relationships. They are parallel processes that mutually facilitate one another. On the less favorable side, an impediment in one may become an impediment in the other.

INTERACTION OF PREOEDIPAL
AND OEDIPAL DEVELOPMENT

The Oedipus complex is triadic, and preoedipal issues are dyadic. Competition for the exclusive possession of the preoedipal mother is the same for boys and girls and is based on the narcissistic need for the object, for the maintenance of the self and positive self-feeling.

The competitive aspect of the oedipal situation is different insofar as the mother and father are differentiated from each other and each has his or her own significant relational meaning for the child as real people and not simply as extensions of the self. In the preoedipal need to possess the object, the competitor has minimal or no intrinsic importance as yet.

If we think in terms of a sexualization of the preexisting object-relational situation, we can see how these two lines of development become intertwined. The following material is from a session with an unmarried thirty-year-old woman:

> I hated it when my parents sent me to camp, and then they went out west. I thought my father was mean to do it, but I felt it was my mother's fault, that she made him go. I thought he'd rather be with me. When I was ten I left camp and went traveling with them. It was like a sexual relationship with my father in the car. I scratched his head and rubbed his shoulders the whole time. I was always hungry and wanted to stop and eat, like I wanted sex with him. I wanted to be with him alone. I imagined my mother hated me. When she did nice things for me, I was paranoid about it. Why was she so nice to me? I thought my father liked me as much as I liked him. When we stopped over, I was by myself and they were together. [Therapist: At some level you recognized that she was special to him, and you hated her for that. She was the one who got to sleep with him. The hate you had for her you projected onto her when you felt you were the special one.] I did! I hated her! I feel I have to get even with my mother because she had my father. I'm thinking of something I can't put together. It was a feeling from my mother. I wanted to be special to her, too. I wanted to believe something about me when I was younger, that I was sexually appealing to her, too. I was afraid my mother was going to do something to me. I wanted to feel that she was attracted to me in a sexual way, too. It spread over from my father to my mother. It sounds nuts! I was afraid she'd get into my personal business. I tried not to get dressed in front of her. I felt I had to because she wanted me to. I thought I had to leave the door open because she was supposed to see everything I did. It was like punishment for my feelings for my father. I had

to suffer that. I remember I'd be touching myself and be afraid of my mother coming. I remember in the bathroom when I'd wipe myself; I knew it felt really great. I know I couldn't tell her I had this feeling. I didn't want to think that she had that feeling, that my father touched her. No one else had that feeling, and she'd better not find out because she'd know I had the idea to have that feeling with my father.

The patient's wish to be special with her mother had a preoedipal, narcissistic quality. She envied her mother not only for having her father but also for her every capability and strength. Her feelings toward her mother became sexualized when the feelings "spread over" from those for her father. Her fear of her mother's envy led to a defensive characterological regressive stance in all of her relationships and constituted a major transference resistance in her treatment. Although this dependent idealizing and its secret but acknowledged counterpart—an attitude of superiority—seemed very much like the transferences of the narcissistic personality disorder as described by Kohut (1971), this patient nonetheless showed far greater differentiation and integration of internal representations, as manifest in her interpersonal relationships. The availability of the observing ego and the working alliance in regard to these issues added a picture of regression rather than a developmental arrest, a diagnostic distinction that we must be very careful to keep in mind. The hatred that this woman felt toward her mother prevented the very identifications that would have enabled her to move out of dependency. Her secret need to disparage her mother (and her therapist) in order to mitigate the hatred of envy made those identifications undesirable.

THE REFUSAL TO IDENTIFY: GUARDIAN OF THE EGO IDEAL AND GENDER IDENTITY

I have observed that the male's need to protect his sense of masculinity is a deterrent to the identifications with his mother, the primary attachment object, that are essential to intrapsychic autonomy. Greenson (1968) writes about the importance to the little boy of "disidentifying" from his mother in order to secure his male gender identity. Greenson uses the term *disidentify* in his discussion of the little boy's struggle to free himself from his early symbiotic fusion with his mother: "The male child's ability to disidentify will determine the success or failure of his later identification with father. These two phenomena, disidentifying with mother and counteridentifying with father, are interdependent and form a complementary series" (p. 306). The outcome of this process is determined by the mother's willingness to let the boy identify with the father figure and by the motives that the father offers to the child for identifying with him. Part of the motivation to identify with the father also arises out of the mother's love and respect for the father. This process is often made nearly impossible when the real qualities of the father—for example, if he is an alcoholic failure—make him unacceptable as a model for the boy. In instances of loss of the father through death or separation before the Oedipus complex is resolved, the question of maleness is bound to be an issue when there are no other available male figures to take his place.

Greenson asks what happens to the original identification with the mother and wonders whether it disappears or becomes latent: "How much of the boy's identification with father is a counteridentification, actually a 'contra'-identification, a means of counteracting the earlier identification?" (p. 312). Greenson postulates that it is in this area that we may find an answer to why so many men are uncertain about their maleness. I pose an additional question: What is the relationship between the inability of many men to experience and express tender emotions and an early splitting off and repression of identifications with the nurturant mother in order to protect their sense of maleness? The consequences of this for the adult relationship in which the oedipally fixated woman brings her need for maternal nurturance to the male figure are all too common in the marital situation.

I believe that this very need to disidentify with the mother to protect the sense of maleness precludes the male's achievement of object constancy and intrapsychic autonomy. He is then thrust into an emotionally dependent stance in his adult object relationship, although this dependency is likely to remain repressed or denied.

A thirty-five-year-old unmarried man complained of not being able to establish a lasting relationship with a woman. On the basis of his positive identifications with his loved and admired father, he was able to achieve a high level of business success. But he still maintained a posture of inadequacy with respect to certain executive functions and strengths attributed to the mother, a posture he played out in his relationships with women, thus inviting their domination and contempt. His fear of identifying with his mother and the dangers associated with his oedipal fantasies had been explored before the session from which the following exerpt is taken. Grandiosity as an ego defense, which was prominent in his dynamics, must be distinguished from the existence of a pathological grandiose self, which is a distortion of the ego. Grandiosity is a trait of an integrated and differentiated self-representation, and a pathological grandiose self is a self-representation not integrated with other self-representations and deriving its power from the incorporated omnipotent object of symbiosis.

It's the issue of being inferior or superior. I discussed it in my relationship to you. I never felt superior: at times inferior and at times a peer, but never superior. Being superior gives me an overblown sense of myself and of controlling others by being patronizing or protective. Or there's a sense of inadequacy when I feel less, when I feel incompetent, unable to do something. When I feel inadequate and less than myself, I acquire characteristics of the other, and there's a role confusion. It's hard to separate myself from you.

Here the patient is describing not the defensive merger of the borderline patient but a defensive pseudoidentification that protects him from humiliation and the anxiety of felt dependency. He continues:

I become that person and not a separate entity. I need to identify the elements of my dependency and work on them. In enough of my relationship with you I feel inadequate. I wish your strength to be mine; I rely on your judgment. [Therapist: The trick will be to learn from my strength and make it part of you and still be able to maintain your sense of separateness from me.] I still need to identify what you got that I ain't got, and why I feel I don't have it. If I can come to terms with it I will have the ability to relinquish my need to acquire your strength, yielding the separateness. [Therapist: Because you had to hold on to your sense of maleness as a boy, you couldn't let yourself acquire your mother's strength.] The achievement of maleness is also the problem of losing the strength she represents to me in terms of emotional self-sufficiency. Like my apartment—if I wasn't fearful of identifying with her I would have been able to acquire her strength in this area. I saw *not* taking care of my apartment as a rebellion and as positive. I was determined to be male and to be independent.

Oedipal issues were predominant for this man. Fantasies of intercourse with his mother led to fantasies not only of castration—by his mother—but also of annihilation of a separate self. Fantasies of killing his father so that he could have his mother evoked anxiety because he perceived his father and his identification with him as rescuing him from his engulfing preoedipal mother. He remained dependent because he could not allow the identifications with his mother that would lead to intrapsychic autonomy. With the dependency, he perceived her (women) as strong, and he wanted her (their) strength. He could imagine gaining it only by means of an identificatory merger (pseudoidentification) with the annihilation of the self as a result, which led to anxiety, or by destroying the woman and stealing her power from her, which led to feelings of guilt.

Loewald (1979) concentrates on the interaction of oedipal and preoedipal issues and observes that the incest barrier promotes the shift from identification to object cathexis, particularly in the boy: "The preoedipal stage of primary lack of subject/object differentiation is evolving into the object stage. . . . The incestuous object, thus, is an intermediate, ambiguous entity, neither a full-fledged libidinal *objectum* nor an unequivocal identificatum" (pp. 766–767).

The patient just described had fears of annihilation beyond castration that accompanied his fantasies of intercourse with his mother and illustrates the more terrifying oedipal dangers for the boy.

Again we need to distinguish between the primary identifications that originate in the symbiotic bond in early object relations development and the later identifications that come with the resolution of the Oedipus complex. Loewald (1979) states: "If . . . parents foster the predominance of incestuous trends, that development is interfered with. The older, primary identifications inherent in the incestuous trends, are then not allowed to become partially transformed into superego identifications, as the oedipal relationship is not relinquished but perpetuated" (p. 767). That is, when the oedipal-incestuous ties are relinquished and the restitutive identifications with aspects of the oedipal objects leads to superego formation, "it is implied that to a significant degree primary identifications give way to secondary or superego identifications" (p. 768). Loewald comments that in the classical neuroses, what he calls the "psychotic core," or the residuals of the primary identifications in the unconscious, may not need specific analytic work.

I do not agree that the primary identifications give way to secondary identifications, at least not those identifications essential to completing the separation-individuation process. These two kinds of identification may complement each other, or they may conflict with each other. I think Loewald is referring here to the earlier unassimilated introject or to the even earlier incorporation of the object as an identification.

But with the girl, oedipal strivings pull her away from the mother of primary identification and, if anything, emphasize the separation and support individuation. In this instance, both rejection of the mother as a desirable model in the service of individuation and the need to disparage her as a rival for the father are the basis for refusing to identify, resulting in the failure to achieve object constancy and intrapsychic autonomy.

On the other hand, the oedipal wishes of the boy pull him back to the preoedipal mother and hinder his drive toward individuation. Such wishes tend to have a regressive impact. I hypothesize that the little boy who turns to his father as oedipal object-choice (the so-called inverted complex) must do so, in some cases, to counter the threat to differentiation from the primary attachment object, his mother. It is a flight from engulfment and annihilation of the separate self. At the same time, a secondary identification with the mother compensates for losing her. The inverted complex in the male child may also come about in the combination of an emotionally unavailable mother and a more available father.

In effect, for both boys and girls, the father as an oedipal object-choice assists individuation and/or substitutes for the inadequate mother. The specific balance of maternal and paternal emotional availability and their support of individuation will be different in each situation, and the outcome of any development can be understood in these terms.

The little girl's refusal to identify with the disparaged mother may also help protect her ego ideal. As well, it may guard against potential oedipal punishment, inasmuch as the daughter perceives certain qualities or abilities as belonging to her mother and forbidden to her, being as taboo as are her wishes for her father. Her mother is the only one allowed to be sexual and the only one allowed to be talented, strong, or whatever else has been designated as the mother's domain. Identification itself becomes competitive, and competitive strivings of any sort are guilt ridden and repressed because of their close association with oedipal strivings and the fear of the mother's envy and retaliation. The predominant defense mechanism in refusing to identify is reaction formation. Not only am I not like my mother; I am just the opposite.

It became clear in the course of psychoanalytic psychotherapy with a middle-aged homosexual woman that her relationships with women were based on a felt dependency and fear of women and on her attempts to placate them. Her associations, memories, and dreams strongly suggested a heterosexual character.

The departure of her father from the home when she was five years old threw her back on her dependent tie with a narcissistic and exploitative mother. Her relationships with women were predominantly masochistic, with the hope that by pleasing and placating she would be loved and not abandoned. As Freud notes (1931), when the father is disappointing, the little girl will return to her attachment to her mother and to the sexuality of the "negative Oedipus complex." I view this as the sexualization of a preoedipal dyadic situation, a "contamination" of an earlier developmental stage by feelings or impulses belonging to a later one. Nevertheless, despite this theoretical divergence, I agree with Freud in respect to structural and developmental implications.

In treatment this patient experienced severe anxiety whenever she reported a pleasant or gratifying experience. She considered, transferentially, the therapist as the envious mother who would not tolerate her having anything good. She tended to offer gifts in a seductive manner when her own anger threatened to emerge from repression. Inevitably she blamed the maternal figure for the deprivations that resulted from her own placating renunciations.

As we began to discuss termination, she reported two dreams:

One dream was violent. Someone had been killed, and I needed a note to say that I wasn't present. In the second dream, I was in a therapy session. The therapist didn't look like you, but it was you. There were a lot of people around. I got angry. I said I wouldn't pay when I had to share and be interrupted.

Her anger at her mother who failed to meet her needs, who went out with boyfriends, and who left her to look after her younger siblings is evident in these dreams. The patient saw the idea of termination as an abandonment, even though she had initiated the topic. The patients who would be staying in treatment with the therapist were the envied siblings. Her guilt and her need to deny her anger were expressed in the first dream.

Toward the end of her treatment the patient became romantically involved with a man. He responded to her in a manner that allowed her to reexperience the lost bond of tender affection and sexuality she once had had with her father. At this time she began to view the coming termination as a punishment for her relationship with a man. She reported being strongly drawn to a woman and offered dreams that said, in effect, "I still want only women; that is, I still want only you, Mother." Interpretation mitigated the anxiety and the flight from her emerging heterosexual interests.

It also became clear that the patient's renunciation of strength with all its feared ramifications left her dependent on a powerful maternal figure. The renunciation was partly due to her fear of her own aggression and her view of her mother's aggression as bad. In all events, she would be "nicer" than her mother was. Her need to cling to an image of herself that she came to characterize as a "goody two-shoes" prevented her from internalizing her mother's positive and effective strength. Her need to protect this image of an unrealistic, "sanctified" self was addressed throughout her treatment.

That the inhibition of aggression was also tied to oedipal issues is clear from the following dream:

There was a woman, my mother. She was pregnant and married to her second husband. In the scene I seduced him. I kissed him and held his body close to mine. I enjoyed it. I didn't care that my mother was there.

After relating the dream she asserted rather fiercely that she had no intentions of letting her mother keep her any longer from what she wanted in life. It should be noted that her mother was no longer living at this time. Her aggression had been tied not only to her anger at the maternal failures but also to carrying out the forbidden oedipal wishes. After accepting her real mother and a more realistic view of her nature, the patient was able to accept the identifications with mother's strengths, strengths that had been attributed solely to her mother and that had been viewed as bad. With this shift the patient began to think of ending treatment with far less ambivalence and with a sense of accomplishment.

I have found in many instances that a woman's continued stance of dependency is a direct consequence of her rejection of maternal power, which is viewed as bad as it has been experienced as opposing the wishes of the self. The good, nonpowerful self, in addition, will be preferred by her father and is more consistent with the child's developing ego ideal. At the same time, by rejecting the identifications with the now disparaged mother, the little girl may identify with a now idealized father. She strives not only to be specially loved by him but also to be like him. The identifications with the mother and father are now experienced intrapsychically as conflicting in a manner that reflects the problems in the original interpersonal situation. To be intellectual and professionally successful or to stay home and be a mother are current psychosocial issues, and role conflicts may be further derivatives of the internalized oedipal conflict.

THE SUPEREGO AND THE EGO IDEAL

Freud's concept of the ego ideal changed over time. In his *Introductory Lectures* of 1917, he writes that the ego ideal is created "for the purpose of recovering thereby the self-satisfaction bound up with the primary infantile narcissism, which since those days has suffered so many shocks and mortification" (p. 429). In object relations terms, this view of the ego ideal is related to the grandiose self, the defensive and compensatory structure that may be activated by those very "shocks and mortification." A defensive and compensatory ego ideal must be distinguished from that of the mature superego which is the outcome of the transmuting internalizations of parental imperatives (Schecter 1979) at the end of the separation-individuation process and the parental identifications that are part of resolving the Oedipus complex.

Freud made that shift in 1933 in his *New Introductory Lectures* in referring to the superego as the "vehicle of the ego ideal, by which the ego measures itself, towards which it strives and whose demands for ever-increasing affection it is always striving to fulfill" (p. 65). Freud views this ego ideal as a "precipitation of the old idea of the parents, an expression of the admiration which the child felt for the perfection which it at that time ascribed to them" (p. 65).

Sandler, Holder, and Meers (1963) relate the ego ideal to the ideal self, which they view, in object relations terms, as one of the shapes that the self-representation can assume. They trace the development of a mature, reality-oriented ideal self as it takes place in the healthy individual. The ideal self contains a solid core of identifications with the admired parents of the earliest years. However, "in the well-adapted individual the content of the ideal self will undergo continuous modification in the light of the person's experiences in reality" (p. 154). Parental ideals are modified and displaced over time and integrated with ideals taken over from other figures throughout life. The authors note that in states of regression the ideal self will more closely adhere to aspects of the idealized pregenital objects.

Loewald observes that the essence of the superego as an internal agency requires recognizing one's needs and impulses as one's own. This means "granting them actively that existence which they have in any event with or without our permission" (p. 761). Loewald adds that this involves facing and bearing guilt for acts considered criminal, even if these acts exist only in fantasy. The criminal acts he refers to are the incestuous fantasies of the Oedipus complex and what he views as a form of parricide: the murder of parental authority and the assumption of responsibility for one's own life that takes place with the severing of emotional ties with one's parents. Incest is the "crime" associated with oedipal wishes, and parricide is the "crime" associated with the resolution of the Oedipus complex. "Not only parental authority is destroyed by wresting authority from the parents and taking it over, but the parents, if the process were thoroughly carried out, are being destroyed as libidinal objects as well . . ." (p. 757). Loewald does state that if things go well, tenderness, mutual trust, and respect—the signs of equality—will remain. Freud, too, notes (1924) that the libidinal trends of the Oedipus complex are desexualized, aim inhibited, and changed into impulses of affection (p. 173).

Loewald sees the repression of the Oedipus complex as avoiding the emancipatory "murder" of the parents and as a way to preserve infantile, libidinal-dependent ties with them. When the intrapsychic autonomy of a fully differentiated self is not achieved, this "murder" can have terrifying consequences. Loewald finds that when this parricide is carried out, "aspects of oedipal relations are transformed into superego relations (internalizations), and other aspects are, qua relations with external objects, restructured in such a way that the incestuous character of object relations gives way to novel forms of object choice" (p. 758). Even so, he tells us, these novel choices will still be under the influence of those internalizations.

Loewald concludes that oedipal issues are new versions of the basic union-individuations drama. But I do not think that they can be so neatly equated. Their complex interrelationships must be understood. The failure to achieve object constancy and emotional autonomy will interfere with the resolution of the Oedipus complex, and wishes and anxieties relevant to oedipal strivings will hinder the achievement of object constancy and emotional autonomy. And the converse also obtains: achievement of either developmental goal, in whole or in part, facilitates the achievement of the other. They go hand in hand and affect each other reciprocally. The accuracy of our interpretations, and thus their effectiveness, depends on the precision of our understanding.

DEVELOPMENTAL DEFICIT OR DEFENSIVE REGRESSION?

Earlier in this chapter I stated that the failure of identification will result in an ego insufficiency that constitutes the port of entry to regressive preoedipal symptomatology under the impact of oedipal anxieties. The insufficiency—the incomplete securing of object constancy and emotional autonomy—is the basis for an ongoing dependency on the object and for the lack of intrapsychic autonomy that generates fears of abandonment, separation-anxiety, and depression. Because of this susceptibility to regression, well-differentiated patients are treated clinically as though they suffered from serious structural deficit.

I have observed an increasing, inappropriate use of the borderline diagnosis, particularly with patients who use regressive defenses, such as splitting as a defense against the pain of an ambivalence of which they are structurally capable, and who retreat from the competitive, triadic, oedipal situation to a dyadic, preoedipal stance. Similarly, therapeutic principles appropriate to the treatment of the more primitive character structure, such as the holding environment and the function of the therapist as self-object, are being misapplied in a manner that reinforces regression.

Zetzel's (1971) distinction between the borderline personality and borderline states addresses similar issues. She proposes differentiating among problems derived from unresolved intrapsychic conflict, regression in response to serious developmental or situational stress, and, finally, a serious failure to establish certain basic ego functions (p. 869).

The difference is readily apparent clinically. If the therapist responds to the more structurally primitive patient with an interpretation, the effect will tend to be disorganizing and boundary blurring. The patient will experience this as an intrusion, an impingement that overwhelms the structurally vulnerable self, perhaps evoking a paranoid reaction, unless the interpretation empathically mirrors the patient's problematic experience of the self.

Quite the contrary is true with the patient who uses regression defensively, who views a correct psychodynamic interpretation as offering a higher level of functioning by alleviating distress and increasing insight.

In his paper "Thoughts on Narcissism and Narcissistic Rage," Kohut (1972) distinguishes between "pseudohysteria" and "pseudonarcissistic disorder." The pseudohysteric, who initially gives the impression of a classical neurosis, reacts to interpretation in a near-catastrophic manner, with wild acting out, oedipal love demands directed toward the analyst, and threats of suicide. Kohut writes that "although the content . . . is all triangular oedipal, the very openness of their infantile wishes, the lack of resistances to their being uncovered, is not in tune with the initial impression" (p. 370).

Kohut describes the pseudonarcissistic disorders as trying to come to terms with both the object-instinctual conflicts of the oedipal period and the narcissistic injuries to which a securely established self is exposed within the context of the oedipal experience. He tells us that the presence, and even the initial predominance, of the narcissistic features "does not alter the fact that the essential psychopathology is a classical psychoneurosis" (pp. 371–372).

We also must distinguish between the benign regression that enables repair through interpretation, an empathic response, or construction and a malignant regression with a downward spiral of ego competency. Our intervention must be appropriate to the immediate availability of the patient's reality ego. Even when regression is defensive, a holding response may be indicated. With the malignant regression, the therapist may have to function as an auxiliary reality ego in order to restore that of the patient, at which time an interpretation can be made.

There are certain developmental issues to be considered in regard to the patient who uses regression as a defense. Why this particular mechanism? Generally there will be significant rapprochement issues involved. The assumption that all cases that entail rapprochement issues are borderline makes it a wastebasket diagnosis. Rapprochement issues will be evident in everyone, no matter how well differentiated and integrated. The polarity of self versus other is present from the first day of life, with its alternating inwardly and outwardly directed attention. Unless the importance of the other is defensively denied, this polarity will continue throughout life, often creating conflict. It is a major developmental conflict of adolescence. Narcissistic issues also will be evident in everyone. To fall short of a well-developed ego ideal is to experience shame. Resolution of the Oedipus complex entails the narcissistic wound caused by the realization that, as the child, one is the loser in the father-mother-child triangle, especially when there is a powerfully cathected illusion that one is the winner.

When the mother of the rapprochement period fails to reinforce the child's steps toward individuation—and this includes moving toward father as a desired object—those steps will become fraught with anxiety, with a consequent paralysis of will and intentionality. No matter how cohesive, differentiated, and relatively integrated a child of three or four or five (or even fifteen) may be, the threat of maternal rage or abandonment will evoke both anxiety and depression. The depression comes with losing the love of the object and, thus, the loss of self-love that is still dependent on external reinforcement. With the borderline personality disorder, this same loss evokes dissolution anxiety with attempts at restitutive merger. With the narcissistic personality disorder, the defensive pathological grandiose self is mobilized (Kohut 1971).

When a patient uses regression defensively, he or she may return to the preoedipal object-relations situation in which issues become dyadic rather than triangular and in which the object is related to in a less differentiated manner, even though structurally the self is cohesive and well differentiated from the object.

In his discussion of the differences between the pathology of relations with a differentiated other and the pathology of relations with an undifferentiated other, Pine (1979) reminds us that we should not underestimate the importance of the major cognitive achievement of awareness of separateness which is anchored in perceptual reality. He notes that this awareness is not easily lost but is an achievement that is consistently present throughout a full analysis that includes important regressive features in the transference (p. 240).

When both defensive and malignant regressions are operating, the therapist must be prepared to shift his or her level of working, from an interpretive stance when the patient is at the oedipal level, to an empathic stance when the patient is more regressed and unable to tolerate the anxiety (Bromberg 1980), to the role of auxiliary reality ego when traumatic events further undermine the regressed ego. Nevertheless, consistent interpretation of the defensive function of the regression is critical, and reinforcement of the regression is to be assiduously avoided.

Balint (1968) states that at the oedipal level, adult language is an adequate and reliable means of communication but that adult language is often useless or misleading in describing events at the level of what he calls the basic fault, because here words do not always have an agreed-upon meaning. In a session with one patient, a twenty-eight-year-old professional woman, I was communicating at the higher level and was unaware of the extent of the regression into which she had moved. In the next session she reported a dream in which I was speaking French to her and a baby. There was no dissolution of the self or loss of the positive alliance with my empathic failure, as she was able to symbolize it under the aegis of the ego.

It is the basic cohesion and differentiation that reveals that the problem is not the deficient structure of the self-representation, even though libidinal object constancy has not been well secured and even though there may be conflicting identifications within the self-representation. Conflicting identifications are not the same as a developmental split. They are experienced as part of the self rather than as unassimilated introjects to be externalized through projective identification. The conflicting identifications often reflect the libidinal conflict within the oedipal triangle. The difference is apparent in the therapeutic relationship, the quality of affect, and the nature of certain cognitive assumptions. Treatment may be no less difficult, but it requires different interventions.

References

Abelin, E. L. (1971). The role of the father in the separation-individuation process. In *Separation-Individuation*, ed. J. McDevitt and C. Settlage, pp. 229–252. New York: International Universities Press.

Ainsworth, M. (1963). The development of infant-mother interaction among the Ganda. In *Determinants of Infant Behavior*, Vol. 2, ed. B. M. Foss. New York: Wiley.

Ainsworth, M., and Bell, S. (1969). Some contemporary patterns of mother-infant interaction in the feeding situation. In *Stimulation in Early Infancy*, ed. A. Ambrose, pp. 133–170. London: Academic Press.

Atkin, S. (1974). A borderline case: ego synthesis and cognition. *International Journal of Psycho-Analysis* 55:13–19.

Balint, M. (1968). *The Basic Fault*. London: Tavistock.

Basch, M. (1976). The concept of affect: a re-examination. *Journal of the American Psychoanalytic Association* 24:759–778.

Beres, D. (1956). Ego deviation and the concept of schizophrenia. *The Psychoanalytic Study of the Child* 11:164–235.

Bion, W. R. (1959). *Experience in Groups and Other Papers*. New York: Basic Books.

——— (1963). *Elements of Psycho-Analysis*. New York: Basic Books.

Blanck, G., and Blanck, R. (1974). *Ego Psychology: Theory and Practice*. New York: Columbia University Press.

Bowlby, J. (1946). Forty-four juvenile thieves: their character and home-life. London: Baillère, Tindall and Cox.

—— (1960). Grief and mourning in infancy and early childhood. *Psychoanalytic Study of the Child* 15:9–52.

—— (1969). *Attachment and Loss, Vol. I: Attachment*. New York: Basic Books.

—— (1973). *Attachment and Loss, Vol. II: Separation: Anxiety and Anger*. New York: Basic Books.

—— (1975). Attachment theory: separation anxiety and mourning. *American Handbook of Psychiatry*, Vol. 6, Chap. 14, pp. 292–309.

Bradshaw, S. (1982). Review of *Object Relations and the Developing Ego in Therapy*, by A. J. Horner (1979). *Bulletin of the Menninger Clinic* 46(3)295–296.

Bromberg, P. (1980). Empathy, anxiety, and reality. *Contemporary Psychoanalysis* 16:223–236.

Bruch, H. (1973). *Eating Disorders*. New York: Basic Books.

Buhler, K. (1927). *Die Krise der Psychologie*. Jena: Fischer.

Burgner, M., and Edgcumbe, R. (1972). Some problems in the conceptualization of early object relationships. Part II: the concept of object constancy. *Psychoanalytic Study of the Child* 27:315–333.

Burnham, D. (1969a). Child-parent relationships which impede differentiation and integration. In *Schizophrenia and the Need-Fear Dilemma*, eds. D. Burnham, A. Gladstone, and R. Gibson, pp. 42–66. New York: International Universities Press.

—— (1969b). Schizophrenia and object relations. In *Schizophrenia and the Need-Fear Dilemma*, eds. D. Burnham, A. Gladstone, and R. Gibson, pp. 15–41. New York: International Universities Press.

Burnham, D., Gladstone, A., and Gibson, R. (1969). *Schizophrenia and the Need-Fear Dilemma*. New York: International Universities Press.

Campbell, S. (1977). *Piaget Sampler*. New York: Jason Aronson.

Chrzanowski, G. (1978). From ego psychology to a psychology of the self. In *Interpersonal Psychologies: New Directions*, ed. E. Witenberg, pp. 33–46. New York: Gardner.

Corwin, H. (1972). The scope of therapeutic confrontation. *International Journal of Psychoanalytic Psychotherapy* 1:68–89.

—— (1974). The narcissistic alliance and progressive transference neurosis in serious regressive states. *International Journal of Psychoanalytic Psychotherapy* 3:299–315.

Crewdson, F. (1978). Presentation at twenty-second annual meeting of the American Academy of Psychoanalysis, May 6, Atlanta, Ga.

Dickes, R. (1975). Technical considerations of the therapeutic and working alliance. *International Journal of Psychoanalytic Psychotherapy* 4:1–24.

Doroff, D. (1975). Behavior as a dream: a therapeutic paraphrase. *Journal of Contemporary Psychotherapy* 7:117–119.

—— (1976). Developing and maintaining the therapeutic alliance with the narcissistic personality. *Journal of American Academy of Psychoanalysis* 4.

Erikson, E. (1950). *Childhood and Society*. New York: Norton.

Escalona, S. (1968). *The Roots of Individuality*. Chicago: Aldine.

Fantz, R. L. (1966). Pattern discrimination and selective attention as determinants of perceptual development from birth. In *Perceptual Development in Children*, eds. A. J. Kidd and J. L. Rivoire. New York: International Universities Press.

Flavell, J. H. (1963). *The Developmental Psychology of Jean Piaget*. Princeton: Van Nostrand.

Framo, J. (1970). Symptoms from a family transactional viewpoint. *International Psychiatry Clinics* 7:125–171.

Freud, A. (1968). Remarks in panel discussion. *International Journal of Psycho-Analysis* 49:506–507.

Freud, S. (1912). Recommendations to physicians practising psychoanalysis. *Standard Edition* 12:109–120.

—— (1917). Introductory lectures on psycho-analysis: the libido theory and narcissism. *Standard Edition* 16:412–430.

—— (1923). The ego and the id. *Standard Edition* 19:1–66.

—— (1924). The dissolution of the Oedipus complex. *Standard Edition* 19:172–179.

—— (1931). Female sexuality. *Standard Edition* 21:223–243.

—— (1933). New introductory lectures on psycho-analysis: the dissection of the psychical personality. *Standard Edition* 22:57–80.

Friedman, L. (1978). Trends in the psychoanalytic theory of treatment. *Psychoanalytic Quarterly* 47:524–567.

Giovacchini, P., ed. (1972a). *Tactics and Techniques in Psychoanalytic Therapy*. New York: Jason Aronson.

——— (1972b). Technical difficulties in treating some characterological disorders: countertransference problems. *International Journal of Psychoanalytic Psychotherapy* 1:112–128.

——— (1975a). *Psychoanalysis of Character Disorders*. New York: Jason Aronson.

——— (1975b). Self projections in the narcissistic transference. *International Journal of Psychoanalytic Psychotherapy* 4:142–166.

———, ed. (1975c). *Tactics and Techniques in Psychoanalytic Therapy. Vol. II: Countertransference*. New York: Jason Aronson.

——— (1978). The analytic introject and ego development. *International Journal of Psychoanalytic Psychotherapy* 7:62–88.

——— (1979). *Treatment of Primitive Mental States*. New York: Jason Aronson.

Giovacchini, P., and Boyer, L. B. (1975). The psychoanalytic impasse. *International Journal of Psychoanalytic Psychotherapy* 4:25–47.

Greenson, R. (1967). *The Technique and Practice of Psychoanalysis*. New York: International Universities Press.

——— (1968). Disidentifying from Mother: its special importance for the boy. In *Explorations in Psychoanalysis*, pp. 305–312. New York: International Universities Press, 1978.

——— (1970). The unique patient-therapist relationship in borderline patients. Presented on a panel, The Borderline Patient, at a joint meeting of the American Psychoanalytic Association and the American Psychiatric Association, San Francisco, May 1970.

——— (1978). *Explorations in Psychoanalysis*. New York: International Universities Press.

Grigg, K. (1977). Implications of left-right cerebral specialization for psychoanalytic data collection and evaluation. *International Review of Psycho-Analysis* 4:449–458.

Guntrip, H. (1969). *Schizoid Phenomena, Object Relations and the Self*. New York: International Universities Press.

——— (1971). *Psychoanalytic Theory, Therapy, and the Self*. New York: Basic Books.

Harlow, H. (1958). The nature of love. *American Psychologist* 13:673–685.

Hartmann, N. (1939). *Ego Psychology and the Problem of Adaptation.* New York: International Universities Press, 1958.

―――― (1952). The mutual influences in the development of the ego and id. *Psychoanalytic Study of the Child* 7:9–30.

―――― (1964). *Essays on Ego Psychology.* New York: International Universities Press.

Horner, A. (1973). Ego boundaries: the last line of resistance in psychotherapy. *Psychotherapy: Theory, Research, and Practice* 10: 83–86.

―――― (1974). Early object relations and the concept of depression. *International Review of Psycho-Analysis* 1:337–340.

―――― (1975a). A characterological contraindication for group psychotherapy. *Journal of the American Academy of Psychoanalysis* 3:301–305.

―――― (1975b). Stages and processes in the development of early object relations and their associated pathologies. *International Review of Psycho-Analysis* 2:95–105.

―――― (1976). Oscillatory patterns of object relations and the borderline patient. *International Review of Psycho-Analysis* 3:479–482.

―――― (1980). The roots of anxiety, character structure, and psychoanalytic treatment. *Journal of the American Academy of Psychoanalysis* 8:565–573.

Jacobson, E. (1964). *The Self and the Object World.* New York: International Universities Press.

Joffe, W., and Sandler, J. (1965). Notes on pain, depression, and individuation. *Psychoanalytic Study of the Child* 20:394–424.

Jung, C. G. (1928). *Contributions to Analytical Psychology.* New York: Harcourt.

Kaufman, B. (1976). *Son Rise.* New York: Harper and Row.

Kernberg, O. (1975). *Borderline Conditions and Pathological Narcissism.* New York: Jason Aronson.

―――― (1976). *Object Relations Theory and Clinical Psychoanalysis.* New York: Jason Aronson.

Khan, M. M. R. (1963). The concept of cumulative trauma. *Psychoanalytic Study of the Child* 18:286–306.

―――― (1974). *The Privacy of the Self.* New York: International Universities Press.

Klein, M. (1975). *Envy and Gratitude and Other Works: 1946-1963*. New York: Delacorte.

Klein, M., Heimann, P., Isaacs, S., and Riviere, J. (1952). *Development in Psycho-Analysis*. London: Hogarth.

Klopfer, B. (1954). *Developments in the Rorschach Technique, Vol. II*. Yonkers-on-Hudson: World Book Company.

Kohut, H. (1971). *The Analysis of the Self*. New York: International Universities Press.

—— (1972). Thoughts on narcissism and narcissistic rage. *Psychoanalytic Study of the Child* 72:360-400.

—— (1977). *The Restoration of the Self*. New York: International Universities Press.

Krystal, H. (1978). Trauma and affect. *Psychoanalytic Study of the Child* 33:81-116.

Langs, R. (1974). *The Technique of Psychoanalytic Psychotherapy*. Vol. 2. New York: Jason Aronson.

—— (1975a). Therapeutic misalliances. *International Journal of Psychoanalytic Psychotherapy* 4:77-105.

—— (1975b). The therapeutic relationship and deviations in technique. *International Journal of Psychoanalytic Psychotherapy* 4:106-141.

—— (1976). *The Bipersonal Field*. New York: Jason Aronson.

—— (1978). Some communicative properties of the bipersonal field. *International Journal of Psychoanalytic Psychotherapy* 7:89-136.

Lichtenberg, J. D. (1975). The development of the sense of self. *Journal of the American Psychoanalytic Association* 23:453-484.

Lichtenstein, N. (1961). Identity and sexuality: a study of their interrelationship in man. *Journal of the American Psychoanalytic Association* 9:179-260. Reprinted in H. Lichtenstein, *The Dilemma of Human Identity*. New York: Jason Aronson, 1977.

Loewald, H. W. (1971). On maturation and instinct theory. *Psychoanalytic Study of the Child* 26:9-128.

—— (1979). The waning of the Oedipus complex. *Journal of the American Psychoanalytic Association* 27:751-775.

Loewenstein, R. (1957). Some thoughts on interpretations in the theory and practice of psychoanalysis. *Psychoanalytic Study of the Child* 12:127-150.

Lorenz, K. (1935). Der Kumpan in der Umwelt des Vogels. Berlin: *Journal fur Ornithologie* 83.

Lozoff, B., Brittenham, M. D., Trause, M. A., Kennell, J. H., and Klaus, M. H. (1977). The mother-newborn relationship: limits of adaptability. *Journal of Pediatrics* 91:1–12.

Mahler, M. S. (1952). On child psychosis and schizophrenia. *Psychoanalytic Study of the Child* 7:286–305.

———— (1968). *On Human Symbiosis and the Vicissitudes of Individuation.* New York: International Universities Press.

Mahler, M. S., Pine, F., and Bergman, A. (1975). *The Psychological Birth of the Human Infant.* New York: Basic Books.

Masterson, J. (1976). *Psychotherapy of the Borderline Adult.* New York: Brunner/Mazel.

Meissner, W. W. (1975). Psychoanalysis as a theory of therapy. *International Journal of Psychoanalytic Psychotherapy* 4:181–218.

———— (1978). Theoretical assumptions of concepts of the borderline personality. *Journal of the American Psychoanalytic Association* 26:559–598.

———— (1981). *Internalization in Psychoanalysis.* New York: International Universities Press.

Modell, A. H. (1961). Denial and the sense of separateness. *Journal of the American Psychoanalytic Association* 9:533–547.

Mullahy, P. (1949). *A Study of Interpersonal Relations.* New York: Basic Books.

Murphy, L. (1962). *The Widening World of Childhood.* New York: Basic Books.

Murphy, L., and Moriarty A. (1976). *Vulnerability, Coping, and Growth.* New Haven: Yale University Press.

Ornitz, E., and Ritvo, E. (1977). The syndrome of autism: a critical review. In *Annual Progress in Child Psychiatry and Child Development,* eds. S. Chess and A. Thomas, pp. 501–530. New York: Brunner/Mazel.

Ornstein, A., and Ornstein, P. (1975). On the interpretive process in psychoanalysis. *International Journal of Psychoanalytic Psychotherapy* 4:219–271.

Panken, S. (1973). *The Joy of Suffering.* New York: Jason Aronson.

Phillipson, H. (1955). *The Object Relations Technique.* London: Tavistock.

Piaget, J. (1936). *The Origins of Intelligence in Children.* New York: International Universities Press, 1952.

Pine, F. (1979). On the pathology of the separation-individuation process as manifested in later clinical work: an attempt at delineation. *International Journal of Psycho-Analysis* 60:225-242.

Pringle, M., and Bossio, V. (1960). Early prolonged separations and emotional adjustment. *Journal of Child Psychology and Psychiatry* 1:37-48.

Rogers, C. (1967). *Person to Person: The Problem of Being Human.* Moab: Real People Press.

Rutter, M. (1973). Maternal deprivation reconsidered. In *Annual Progress in Child Psychiatry and Child Development*, eds. S. Chess and A. Thomas, pp. 205-216. New York:Brunner/Mazel.

—— (1974). *The Qualities of Mothering: Maternal Deprivation Reassessed.* New York: Jason Aronson.

—— (1975). The development of infantile autism. In *Annual Progress in Child Psychiatry and Child Development*, eds. S. Chess and A. Thomas, pp. 327-356. New York: Brunner/Mazel.

Sandler, A. M. (1975). Comments on the significance of Piaget's work for psychoanalysis. *International Review of Psycho-Analysis* 2:365-378.

—— (1977). Beyond eight-month anxiety. *International Journal of Psycho-Analysis* 58:195-208.

Sandler, J., Holder, A., and Meers, D. (1963). The ego ideal and the ideal self. *Psychoanalytic Study of the Child* 18:139-158.

Schafer, R. (1960). The loving and beloved superego in Freud's structural theory. *Psychoanalytic Study of the Child* 15:163-199.

—— (1968). *Aspects of Internalization.* New York: International Universities Press.

—— (1976). *A New Language for Psychoanalysis.* New Haven: Yale University Press.

Schaffer, H., and Emerson, P. (1964). The development of social attachments in infancy. Monograph. *Social Research Child Development* 29(3):1-77.

Schecter, D. (1968). Identification and individuation. *Journal of the American Psychoanalytic Association* 16:48-80.

—— (1978). Attachment, detachment, and psychoanalytic therapy:

the impact of early development on the psychoanalytic treatment of adults. In *Interpersonal Psychoanalysis: New Directions*, ed. E. Witenberg. New York: Gardner Press.

———— (1979). The loving and persecuting superego. Presidential address, The William Alanson White Psychoanalytic Society, New York, May 23; *Contemporary Psychoanalysis* 15:361–379.

———— (1980). Early developmental roots of anxiety. *Journal of the American Academy of Psychoanalysis* 8:539–554.

Shapiro, T. (1977). Oedipal distortions in severe character pathologies: developmental and theoretical considerations. *Psychoanalytic Quarterly* 46:559–579.

Slipp, S. (1973). The symbiotic survival pattern: a relational theory of schizophrenia. *Family Process* 12:377–398.

———— (1976). An intrapsychic-interpersonal theory of depression. *Journal of the American Academy of Psychoanalysis* 4:389–410.

Spitz, R. (1959). *A Genetic Field Theory of Ego Formation*. New York: International Universities Press.

———— (1965). *The First Year of Life*. New York: International Universities Press.

Spitz, R., and Wolf, K. (1946). The smiling responses: a contribution to the ontogenesis of social relations. *Genetic Psychology Monograph* 34:57–125.

Stierlin, H. (1977). *Psychoanalysis and Family Therapy*. New York: Jason Aronson.

Stolorow, R. D. (1975). Toward a functional definition of narcissism. *International Journal of Psycho-Analysis* 56:179–185.

Stone, L. J., Smith, H. T., and Murphy, L. B. (1973). *The Competent Infant*. New York: Basic Books.

Sullivan, H. S. (1953). *The Interpersonal Theory of Psychiatry*. New York: Norton.

Szurek, S. (1973). Attachment and psychotic detachment. In *Clinical Studies in Childhood Psychosis*, ed. S. Szurek and I. Berlin, pp. 191–277. New York: Brunner/Mazel.

Teicholz, J. G. (1978). A selective review of the psychoanalytic literature on theoretical conceptualizations of narcissism. *Journal of the American Psychoanalytic Association* 26:831–862.

Tolpin, M. (1971). On the beginnings of a cohesive self: an application of the concept of transmuting internalization to the study of the transitional object and signal anxiety. *Psychoanalytic Study of the Child* 26:316–352.

—— (1978). Self-objects and oedipal objects: a crucial developmental distinction. *Psychoanalytic Study of the Child* 33:167–186.

Winnicott, D. W. (1951). Transitional objects and transitional phenomena. In *Through Paediatrics to Psychoanalysis*, pp. 229–242. New York: Basic Books, 1975.

—— (1965). *The Maturational Processes and the Facilitating Environment.* New York: International Universities Press.

—— (1974). Fear of breakdown. *International Review of Psycho-Analysis* 1:103–107.

Wyatt, G. L. (1969). *Language Learning and Communication Disorders.* New York: Free Press.

Zetzel, E. R. (1971). A developmental approach to the borderline patient. *American Journal of Psychiatry* 127:867–871.

Index

About the Author

Althea J. Horner, Ph.D., is Clinical Professor of Psychology, University of California at Los Angeles, a Scientific Associate of the American Academy of Psychoanalysis, and an Honorary Member of the Southern California Psychoanalytic Institute and Society. Dr. Horner is the author of *The Primacy of Structure: Psychotherapy of Underlying Character Pathology, Psychoana-lytic Object Relations Therapy, Being and Loving*, and *The Wish for Power and the Fear of Having It*. She is also editor and co-author of *Treating the Neurotic Patient in Brief Psychotherapy*. Dr. Horner is in private practice in Arcadia,